In Memory of

Ruth Wehage
Schroer

REBEL

Douglas Carswell grew up in Uganda. He worked in television and the City before standing against Tony Blair at the 2001 General Election. The MP for Clacton in Essex since 2005, he is the author of *The Plan: Twelve Months to Renew Britain* (with Daniel Hannan) and *The End of Politics and the Birth of iDemocracy.*

REBEL

How to overthrow the
emerging oligarchy

DOUGLAS CARSWELL

HEAD
of ZEUS

First published in the UK in 2017 by Head of Zeus Ltd

9 7 5 3 1 2 4 6 8

A catalogue record for this book is available from
the British Library.

ISBN (HB) 9781786691552
ISBN (E) 9781786691545

Typeset by Adrian McLaughlin

Printed and bound in Great Britain by
CPI Group (UK) Ltd, Croydon CR0 4YY

Head of Zeus Ltd
First Floor East
5–8 Hardwick Street
London EC1R 4RG
WWW.HEADOFZEUS.COM

To Clementine and Kitty

ACKNOWLEDGEMENTS

I am grateful for the comments and contributions I have had while writing this book from, in no particular order, Simon Gordon, Duncan Simpson, Daniel Hannan, Mark Reckless, Mark Littlewood, Matt Ridley and Michael Gove. My thanks.

CONTENTS

'Here's to the crazy ones. The misfits. The rebels. The troublemakers. The round pegs in the square holes. The ones who see things differently. They're not fond of rules. And they have no respect for the status quo. You can quote them, disagree with them, glorify or vilify them. About the only thing you can't do is ignore them. Because they change things. They push the human race forward. And while some may see them as the crazy ones, we see genius. Because the people who are crazy enough to think they can change the world are the ones who do.'

—Steve Jobs

PREFACE

When I first stood for election to Parliament, I believed that all we needed were the right kind of ministers, pursuing the right sort of plans. Now I believe we need a revolution.

Politics, I have come to see, is a cartel. Like the economy, it's rigged in the interests of an emerging oligarchy.

I wrote this book because I care deeply about the liberal order that has allowed us to flourish – as it has others before us. And also because I believe political pundits have failed utterly to comprehend the problem. Indeed, they are part of it.

We face a twin assault; oligarchs on the one hand, radical populists emerging in response to them on the other. Sweeping change is needed if the liberal order is to survive.

DOUGLAS CARSWELL
Clacton, 13 February 2017

PART I

POWER AND THE NEW OLIGARCHY

1

THE RISE OF THE NEW RADICALS

Something extraordinary is happening to politics. A mood of populist revolt is taking hold. Across Britain, the United States and much of Europe, a new radicalism is on the rise.

Angry, insurgent voices, which would not even have found an audience a generation ago, can be heard. Indeed, these insurgents are starting to dominate the political debate – everywhere from Slovakia to Sweden, California to Clacton. We can see the symptoms of this rising restlessness across the political spectrum, from Jeremy Corbyn's Labour Party in Britain or the uber-leftist Podemos in Spain to the rise of the right-wing Alternative für Deutschland (AfD) in Germany.

In the United States, the reality TV show host and property billionaire Donald Trump was elected president. He launched his bid to lead the party of Lincoln and Reagan by declaring that most Mexicans living in America were criminals, rapists and murderers. Less than a year later, he began his first few days in office with attacks not only Mexicans, but Hollywood actors, federal judges and anyone who seemed to question the size of his inauguration crowd.

Bernie Sanders came close to beating Trump's rival Hillary Clinton for the Democrat nomination in the US using the kind of overtly socialist language that had not been the currency of American politics since the Great Depression eighty years before. For much of the twentieth century, political debate in America took place within a narrow spectrum of political possibility. Both major parties subscribed to free-market capitalism under a modicum of state supervision, with a strong focus on individual liberty.

Yes, there were differences of tone and emphasis. Occasionally candidates for the White House took diverging views over foreign policy. But there was a recognizable set of boundaries within which the debate took place. Not anymore. Sanders implies that he wants to nationalize the banks, while Trump spoke of rounding up and deporting eleven million migrants, and imprisoning his opponents. The established consensus is starting to collapse in many Western states.

For decades, the political middle ground in Sweden was just about as far removed as it is possible to be from that in America. While US candidates vied with each other to keep taxes low and government small, in Sweden most politicians agreed on the need for cradle-to-grave welfare provision – and high taxes to pay for it all. Swedish politics was so sensible and consensual, one of their major parties was the Moderate Party – the Moderata samlings-partiet – committed to, well, moderation.

But then along came the Sweden Democrats – Sverige-demokraterna. Founded relatively recently, like many of the insurgent parties, they are fiercely anti-immigrant and in favour of economic intervention. Think of them as a Scandinavian blend of both Trump and Sanders. And like Trump and Sanders, these new insurgents have started to outpoll many of their tamer rivals. It's been a strikingly similar story across most of Europe.

Insurgents and upstarts are on the rise almost everywhere – on the far left and the radical right.

In Greece, the ultra-leftist Syriza (founded 2004) won two General Elections in 2015, with an overtly redistributionist agenda (albeit that the redistribution they most seem to favour is from Germany to Greece). Spain's neo-Marxist Podemos (founded 2014) are now the country's second largest party. Italy's Five Star Movement – Movimento 5 Stelle – (founded 2009) won over a hundred deputies and fifty senate seats just four years later, and by mid-2016 was, according to some polls, the single most popular party in Italy.

In Denmark's 2015 elections, the Danish People's Party (founded 1995) won 21 per cent of the vote. In Hungary, Jobbik (founded 2003) recently gained 20 per cent. The Swiss People's Party got 29 per cent. Geert Wilders of the radical Partij voor de Vrijheid (founded in 2005) may well be the next Dutch Prime Minister. In Britain, UKIP (a relative old-timer for an insurgent party, having been founded in 1993) won almost four million votes at the last General Election, displacing the Liberal Democrats as the third party.

People and parties outside the limits of what was once deemed to be the acceptable political order are on the rise. The old order is starting to fall apart. Why? What is going on?

NOT JUST ECONOMICS

'It's the economy,' suggest many mainstream politicians and pundits, reaching for their default explanation for almost every form of voter behaviour. 'Those who vote for the New Radicals are economic losers. They've lost out to globalization.'

It certainly is the case that for many millions in the United States, Britain and Europe incomes have stagnated over the past twenty years. The average blue-collar household in America is no better off today than they were when Bill Clinton was in the White House. In fact, it's even worse than that. The average hourly wage for non-management, private-sector workers in America, when adjusted for inflation, has not risen since Ronald Reagan first entered the White House. For millions in the US, wages in 2016 are what they were in 1981.

Globalization – or to be more specific, the addition of hundreds of millions of additional workers to the worldwide workforce (not to mention the mobility of that workforce) – has lowered the cost of labour relative to capital. But this is not to say the blue-collar workers are destitute. While incomes might have stagnated, globalization – and expansion of the Chinese manufacturing base in particular – has meant that the cost of many consumer goods has fallen at the same time. If the rise of the New Radicals was driven by economic distress, you would expect the most economically disadvantaged to be in the vanguard of support for these new movements. If anything, the opposite is true.

Those voters who propelled Donald Trump to victory were not on the breadline. On the contrary, it turns out they were the better off. The average Trump voter in the US primaries came from a household with an average annual income of $72,000, significantly above the national average of $52,000. The idea that Donald Trump arose as a response to economic collapse is a nonsense. The year before he emerged, America enjoyed the longest sustained run of private-sector job growth and the single highest annual jump in median incomes in modern US history.

UKIP voters, the election experts keep telling us, are those who have been economically 'left behind'. As someone who has previously owed their place in Parliament to actual UKIP voters, I am not convinced. Far from being left behind, I have been struck by the fact that the years have been generous to many of UKIP's most fervent supporters. Many own their own homes. The simple fact of being born in the year and place they were means that many have been the beneficiaries of an extraordinary, sustained increase in house prices. Modernity has been materially munificent to many, giving them cheap air travel, foreign holidays and homes packed with every kind of affordable modern convenience. Most enjoy a living standard far higher than their grandparents could have ever aspired to. Most have more leisure time, and more things to do with it, than ever before.

If the economy accounts for the rise of the New Radicals, it's not the economics of destitution but of perceived injustice. In 1980, the top FTSE 100 executives in Britain earned on average 25 times more than their average employee. By 1997, average FTSE 100 executive pay was 47 times greater than that of their average employee. By 2007, it was 120 times. The gap is not just growing. The rate at which it is growing is increasing too. Since 2007, the year that the financial crisis began, the salary of the average FTSE 100 executive has soared relative to everyone else. By 2016 it was 130 times average employee pay. In 2018, it is expected to be 150 times.

The super-rich are, as Boris Johnson puts it, building basement swimming pools in their London houses, yet many of their employees cannot afford to get on the housing ladder. They pay for private jets as their staff make do with ever longer commutes just to get to work. As wages have been held down and corporate salaries have soared, unease about the inequality spawned by the new digital economy is growing. Indeed, at times it seems that the digital economy is winner-takes-all, with a few successful ventures – Uber, Airbnb, Google – cornering the market. Thus, whereas the income of the bottom 90 per cent rose during the mid- to late-twentieth century, since the mid-1990s it is the richest 1 per cent whose incomes have really rocketed.

OLIGARCHY AND THE NEW ELITE

Thomas Piketty, author of *Capital in the Twenty-First Century*, is right. A new economic oligarchy is emerging, able to accumulate capital faster than the economy grows. The term 'oligarch' used to refer to something remote and distant. Oligarchs were something we previously associated with Putin's Russia or late-nineteenth-century America. It somehow seemed alien to our democratic way of doing things.

But a new oligarchy is emerging right now throughout the Western world. The super-rich are no longer millionaires, but billionaires – often many times over. This new elite is not only doing rather well economically. They increasingly call the shots politically. Indeed, they are doing well economically precisely because they are accumulating power politically.

Every year in Davos, Switzerland, thousands of officials, supranational executives and corporate bigwigs get together at the World Economic Forum, a week-long schmooze fest. They listen to each other give talks. They recycle one another's clichés as easily as they swap business cards, and generally pat each other on the back for being so well connected and clever. Public policy in many Western states is increasingly made for, by and on behalf of the kind of people who go to Davos.

The delegates and lobbyists who congregate at the alpine resort, said the late American political scientist Samuel Huntington, 'view national boundaries as obstacles that thankfully are vanishing, and see national governments as residues from the past whose only useful function is to facilitate the elite's global operations'. Davos Man prefers centralized, supranational decision-making – and for decades he has been getting his way.

Interest rates are set by the sort of central bankers who go to Davos. Energy prices are determined by quotas. Environment policy, and the subsidy schemes that go with it, are the preserve of officials. This new elite has no loyalty to or understanding of the ordinary citizen. They despise their concerns as parochial and the views of the *demos* as petty prejudice.

'But hold on!' I hear you say. 'Why all this railing against elites? Aren't elites supposed to be good?' You have a point. We rightly admire elite artists or footballers. If you fell ill, you would want to be treated by an elite doctor. Being part of an elite means being part of a select group of people who possess superior abilities or qualities – no bad thing, of course.

But when New Radicals rage against 'the elite' they do not mean those that get to the top by being the best, like a musician or sports star. Or even entrepreneurs who grow rich by providing willing customers with things that they want. The term elite is increasingly used in a pejorative sense. It refers not to those who are the best at something, but to those with unearned privileges. Those who are perceived to occupy positions of power, influence and economic fortune not through merit or open competition, but by rigging the system to their advantage.

'The elite' has become a shorthand to describe not only the oligarchs who have accumulated capital, but the sort of people – CEOs, central bankers, civil servants – that assemble in Davos each year. It's not just a question of unearned economic or political privilege either. The term 'liberal elite' is used to describe an all-too-real clique of commentators, pundits, academics – especially those with social science backgrounds – and others who shape and influence public policy.

Almost by definition, a member of the liberal elite will bridle at use of the term, sensing perhaps the contemptuous connotations. As well they might. Far from being the best of anything, such people often hold privileged positions that allow them to pontificate about public policy – with little understanding of or accountability to the public. Worse, as we shall see, the liberal elite turn out not to be very liberal, either.

Strictly speaking, perhaps *clique* or *coterie* would be better words to use when referring to people who hold privileged positions through rigged systems denoting, as such terms do, the closed, exclusive nature of those we are referring to. The author Ferdinand Mount used the term 'the new few'. But I will stick with the shorthand term 'the elite', which if imperfect, semantically speaking, nonetheless refers to something all too real.

As we shall see, there has been a concentration of both economic and political power in the hands of a few in most Western states over the past few decades. Call them an elite or clique or oligarchy, we are witnessing the rise of this new few – and the New Radical phenomenon is in part a reaction to it.

A DIGITAL VOICE

The sort of angry voices that rage against 'the elite' are being heard today for one obvious reason: they can be. Digital makes them audible. A generation ago, such voices simply did not get the airtime. For a start, there were many fewer TV stations, and far less competition between them for audience share.

Who got airtime was decided by a cosy consensus between one or two established networks. Digital has created an array of TV networks and platforms, and increased the competition between them. Twenty-four-hour news channels and the creation of a news stream, rather than a news cycle, means airtime for these new voices. And if it is seen to boost ratings, they get lots of it.

Donald Trump's bid for the Republican nomination was propelled by blanket TV coverage of his campaign. They did not just give him millions of dollars of free advertising. It almost felt, at times, as if the networks defined him as the anti-Democrat candidate, ahead of the primary elections. In Britain, Nigel Farage has had airtime on all the main TV outlets out of all proportion to his own electoral performance. He might have run for Parliament – and lost – seven times, but he has still appeared on the BBC's

Today programme and *Question Time* more times than any other party leader.

It's not just digital broadcasting that gives the New Radicals a voice. Thirty years ago, there were no blog sites like Breitbart or Guido Fawkes. Before 2004, there wasn't even any Twitter or Facebook.

When I first stood for Parliament in 2001, I ran against the then Prime Minister, Tony Blair, in his Sedgefield constituency. It was a difficult gig. Blair at the time was one of the most widely recognized politicians in the Western world. He was on every news channel and in every newspaper. I, on the other hand, considered myself lucky when halfway through the campaign I was allowed a two-minute interview on the regional news channel. Nervously, I managed to recite one or two carefully rehearsed sound bites before the interviewer cut me off. Those two minutes of airtime were pretty much it; the start and the finish of my campaign. My chance to reach out to thousands of voters in the constituency, other than by laboriously going from door to door, ended the moment that interview ended.

Not anymore.

By the 2010 election campaign in my Essex constituency, I no longer felt the need to drop everything and rush to a TV studio in distant Norwich or Cambridge. Instead of lobbying the TV producers to give me airtime, I was getting calls from them asking me to come on air. The terms of trade had changed: previously I had always been expected to make my own way to the TV studio. In the 2010 campaign, the TV studios offered to send a car. It was not that I was any more important in the contest. TV had become less central to my campaign. Of course, an interview with any television station is still important. But the point is that it is no longer paramount. Why?

Because my laptop gives me the means to communicate with tens of thousands of constituents myself. Through email, blogs and social media, I can now speak directly – and in much more personalized terms – to the voter. Instead of being background noise on millions of televisions in countless kitchens and sitting rooms across the whole region, I can be a highly personal voice on the handsets of the several thousand voters that really count electorally.

Digital technology has opened up the business of communication. Whereas a tiny handful of TV producers and newspaper editors once determined who could communicate a message to millions, today lots of candidates are able to communicate lots of different messages to many different audiences.

What I have managed to do on a relatively small scale in my corner of Essex, the New Radical leaders have done nationwide. Italy's Beppe Grillo has over two million followers on Twitter. Donald Trump has more than twenty-two million. Hundreds of thousands of people in Germany have 'liked' the leader of the AfD, Frauke Petry.

The barriers to new entrants in the political marketplace have come down. The New Radicals are those entrants. Digital communication allows the insurgents to make a noise. But why does the sound they make resonate with voters?

SIMMERING RAGE

'I'm more honest and my women are more beautiful,' Donald Trump boasted to his American audience. His own attractiveness, he proceeded to explain, was down to being 'very rich'.

Can you imagine Ronald Reagan, a former Hollywood film star, making such a claim? Would Bill Clinton, who perfected the art of empathy on television, have survived such naked narcissism? New Radical leaders do not simply have the ability to communicate in this digital age. They use it to be outspoken, sometimes saying things designed to outrage.

Trump accused an opponent's father of being involved in the assassination of President Kennedy. He appeared to encourage his supporters to 'beat the crap' out of opponents. In the run-up to the 2015 General Election campaign, Nigel Farage announced that too many immigrants clogging up a motorway were the reason he arrived late for a meeting. Italy's Beppe Grillo takes this 'shock and awful' approach to a whole new level, making foul-mouthed outbursts his hallmark.

Trump's obscene 'locker room' comments, made in 2005 and released a month before election day, might have harmed him. But not enough to keep him out of the White House. Instead of instant electoral oblivion, Trump's earlier examples of outrageous comments seemed to draw support from a growing segment of the electorate. It was his very brashness that propelled him forward – and at times it seemed as if that was his intention. Just a few weeks after Farage's deliberately 'shock and awful' comments, almost four million people still voted UKIP. Grillo's party gains from each of his utterances.

Why are voters attracted to this, rather than repelled? Because of an intense, simmering feeling of frustration – which few have yet properly understood. The insurgent anger is aimed at what they perceive to be the political clique – that cosy knot of professional politicians and pundits who get to decide where the boundaries of the politically possible lie. Voters seem fed up of being patronized by full-time politicos who they feel treat them with such disdain.

And they have a point, surely?

Rather than offering voters choice, many of the established political parties in Britain, Europe and America seem to be in the business of denying choice. They offer the electorate the same bland, off-the-peg candidates, who seem to wear the same opinions while feigning the same kind of confected concern.

All the established parties favoured bailouts for the banks

and cosy deals for big corporations. They all seemed to go along with the idea of mass immigration and multiculturalism – with little consideration of the consequences. They all adopt the same condescending tone, pretending to be on the side of ordinary people but behaving like a caste apart.

Many voters are fed up with being told that politics sits within a set of boundaries as defined by a class of professional politicians in Washington, Westminster or Brussels. So, they cheer when candidates like Trump or Farage come along and say things beyond those boundaries. They do so, not necessarily because they want to shift the boundaries, or, indeed, because they agree with what is being said, but because they so deeply resent the way that the political cliques – elites – have patronized them and treated them with such disdain.

When Donald Trump told America he would build a wall between the United States and Mexico to keep illegal migrants out, Washington insiders scoffed. But Trump's poll ratings rose. Trump's wall might be implausible – and his suggestion that Mexico be made to pay for it easily refuted. But for many voters that was not the point. It's not the (im)plausibility of Trump, but the patronizing arrogance of those already in Washington, that they are reacting to.

Why should the voters trust the political cliques? In Britain and most of Europe, the voters were told by elite opinion that the creation of a single currency, the Euro, would generate prosperity. Instead it has produced a decade of economic stagnation and a massive debt crisis, from which there is no end in sight.

The economy, we were told, was being managed by expert central bankers. The cycles of boom and bust, they said, had been abolished. The banks, they implied, would help make us all rich, the additional tax revenues generated a permanent addition to the tax base.

Then came the worst financial crisis the Western world has

seen. Banks on both sides of the Atlantic required billion-dollar bailouts. We went into a recession from which many are still recovering – while a few have amassed ever greater fortunes.

Western elites have spent a great deal of time and effort discussing how they might control CO_2 emissions and sea levels. But where are the high-level international summits urging action to control borders? Images of the mass movement of people across unguarded frontiers in New Mexico and the Mediterranean have been beamed into kitchens and living rooms around the world.

For many voters, the arrogance of policy makers is matched only by their incompetence.

MODERN EXPECTATIONS

'Everyone knows that they're bigots,' you might still insist. 'Those who vote for the New Radicals like Trump are backward-looking, uneducated rednecks, out of touch with the modern world.'

What do you mean by 'everyone'? Perhaps that small clique of political-insiders, paid to provide the rest of us with analysis, might see things that way. But the fact that they think of themselves as 'everyone' is part of the problem. Established politicians and pundits have proved clueless as to how to respond to the rise of the New Radicals because their analysis tells us more about their own preconceptions than it does about the insurgents.

Sadly, there are some bigots. Since every adult has the right to vote, whether they are a nice person or not, that means that some bigots go the ballot box. But are we really to believe that the rise of the New Radicals is due to an increase in the number of bigots? Are there more bad people today than, say, when Clement Attlee won a landslide majority in 1945 to create the Welfare State? Or when Kennedy was elected to the White House?

Actually, the opposite is true. By almost every measure, there is less bigotry and intolerance today than there was back then.

Social attitudes are more liberal and accepting than ever before. It cannot be the case that there are more people voting for the New Radicals because there are more bigots. Nor are those who won Trump the Republican party nomination poorly educated hicks. In fact, 44 per cent of Trump voters in the primary elections had college degrees, a much higher proportion than the 29 per cent average for US adults[1]. The New Radical revolt on either side of the Atlantic is partly a revolt against the 'everyone' who kept telling us otherwise.

As UK columnist and writer Janet Daley has suggested, what we are witnessing is a rebellion of electorates within two continent-wide federations – the United States and the European Union – against the growth of powerful federal administration. You only have to consider how hostile many of the New Radicals are to Brussels or Washington to sense that there is some truth in that.

But the rise of New Radicalism in countries like Norway or Switzerland – neither of whom are in the EU, and where decision-making is no more distant from the people than it was before – indicates that there is more to it than that.

It is not just those governing that have changed, but the governed. Modernity has changed public expectations. Whether or not public administration has become more distant, the public is less willing to tolerate a process of administration that increasingly feels remote and distant. A generation ago, we watched what was on television whenever a TV programmer decided to schedule it. Distant DJs selected what music we listened to. Today, Netflix and Spotify allow us to programme what we want at a time that suits us.

In *The Long Tail*, American author Chris Anderson foresaw

---

1   See Nate Silver's blog http://fivethirtyeight.com/features/the-mythology-of-trumps-working-class-support/

how the digital marketplace would mean more choice. Instead of having to put up with what is on offer, digital allows you to find the niche products and tastes that fit you. Instead of buying the whole album, you can download the track that you like. Rather than taking the generic brand on offer, you can find what suits you. In other words, self-selection has become a cultural norm. Choice and competition are things that we just take for granted.

As consumers, we think it is normal to get what we want, more or less when we want it. So why can we not have the same thing when it comes to political representation? You do not have to put up with shoddy service where the customer is not king. So why tolerate local representatives who do not actually sound as if they represent your area? Why should you elect someone who speaks for Washington or Westminster in your neighbourhood, rather than your neighbourhood in the capital?

The rage of the New Radicals is directed at distant officials and structures that decide public policy with little reference to the public. Corporate chiefs who collude to write the trade rules to their advantage. Central bankers who always have enough easy credit to pass on to corporate bankers. Large faceless bureaucracies. Remote elites that answer only to each other in a world of transnational decision-making.

Accountability is increasingly a cultural norm, not a bonus. And this is precisely why folk feel so enraged by elites that are not accountable. Modernity means hyper-accountability, so that those making decisions answer to those on whose behalf they are made. New Radicalism is on the rise because modernity has transformed people's expectations of how things could be. It is the political process, not the people, we need to change.

Instead of generic parties, digital has made room in the marketplace for brands that are niche, distinctive, particular and local. (Think of the Scottish National Party; SNP.) Digital gives these smaller players the means to communicate with, and aggregate enough votes from, those niches – and win. (Think of the SNP's phenomenal social media presence.)

What some see as populist fragmentation is really a process of realignment in the political marketplace to accommodate more tastes. They are 'populist' in the sense that there is a demand for them. The Green Party in Britain is polling better than before not because the electorate has become radically more populist. It's simply a case of having someone to vote for if the environment happens to be your overriding priority.

In every marketplace, whenever the digital disruption happens, there are vested interests that try to prevent it happening. When MP3 players started to change the way we listened to music, established record producers and retailers told us the pirates would kill the industry. When online retailers started to sell contact lenses, the established opticians called them cowboys. Wikipedia, according to those that used to produce the old kind of encyclopaedias, was full of errors.

But the digital disruption did not go away. More music is sold to more people now than ever before. Cheaper contact lenses are available to more customers than before. Wikipedia might contain subjective analysis masquerading as objective truth, but don't all encyclopaedias?

So, too, in politics. Various vested interests might disapprove of the digital disruption but that will not stop it. This realignment of the political marketplace has more of a claim on the future than the priesthood of pundits who recoil from its uncomfortable consequences.

Political insiders like to think of themselves as forward-looking, progressive types, who embrace change. Indeed, many media types have a self-image of themselves as hipsters not only embracing modernity, but defining it. Those who reject them and their way of thinking must therefore be reactionary, right? Wrong.

On the day that I left the Conservative Party and joined UKIP, I said in front of a packed press conference in Westminster that 'what we once dismissed as "political correctness gone mad", we increasingly recognize as good manners'. Political correctness is often simple decency. It's right that we are more careful in our use of language to avoid causing unnecessary offence. But if what is 'PC' is a question of politeness, it is often a middle-class, college-graduate notion of what constitutes politeness.

All cliques have manners and mannerisms that act as badges of acceptance. At times, the highly moralized linguistics of the politically correct can become a badge indicating membership of an in-group – an in-group of the self-righteous. Those inside the club of the righteous-minded know the precise nuances (people of colour or coloured people?) to use to signal their virtue and membership of the club. Far from being a generous gesture to all of humankind, PC language can be used by some to indicate their own superiority.

Thus, when college-educated TV producers and pundits react with outrage at the latest non-PC pronouncement by Nigel Farage or Geert Wilders or Donald Trump, they presume that they are discrediting them. But what many blue-collar voters hear instead is a supercilious clique preaching at them. This further reinforces the suspicion some voters have that politics is a cartel from which they have been shut out. Political insiders, meanwhile, baffled that not everyone is willing to join in the round of virtue-signalling, leap to the conclusion that they must be bigoted.

If bigotry is defined as an intolerance of those with different opinions, it's not always clear-cut to see who the bigots are. If modernity means passing power away from small elites and greater accountability, perhaps it's the New Radicals, not their critics in Westminster or Washington, who are more modern? It is not the people that are out of date and going to have to change, but our politics.

NEW CHARLATANS

A growing number of voters might be tempted by the New Radical parties springing up in many Western democracies. But have the New Radical movements got it right?

Tragically, many are led by charlatans. There is indeed a self-referential elite that presides over many Western states. This elite has lurched from one policy blunder to the next. Public policy is increasingly made in the interests of a new oligarchy, which is enriching itself at the expense of everyone else. And the public is entirely justified in resenting the way their views are treated with such disdain. Yet far from addressing people's sense of rage, those who lead the New Radical parties play on it, stoking it up. Rather than resolve popular frustrations, they almost seem to want to make things worse.

People vote for the New Radicals as an alternative, but what alternative do they offer? 'New' Radicals? Dig a little bit beneath the surface, and many of these movements have a rather old-hat habit of blaming things on some sense of the 'other'. New Radical leaders on the right – Trump, Petry, Le Pen – blame migrants. On the left, leaders like Corbyn point the finger at 'the 1 per cent'. They are opportunistic, quick to get a cheap cheer on talk shows. The more cross the electorate, they wager, the more crosses on the ballot paper.

Many of the New Radical parties are little more than personality cults. In America, the Grand Old Party feels like it has been subject to a hostile takeover by the Trumpists. Syriza's front man, Alexis Tsipras, defined them as different. UKIP, for whom I've stood for election twice, was seen by many as a platform for its then leader, Nigel Farage. For many Italians, Beppe Grillo is Five Star.

If our democracy has been subverted by small elites, how can parties run by small cliques be the answer? The New Radicals' biggest failing is not their shallow opportunism but their unrelenting pessimism. Implicit in Donald Trump's slogan, 'Make

America great again', is that America is failing. Eco-pessimism is an article of faith for every Green Party in every Western state. We are, they insist, on the verge of environmental catastrophe. UKIP fought the 2015 General Election suggesting that Britain was heading for the rocks.

The world is not getting worse. For most people, in most places, the world has got much, much better. This is not just my opinion. It's a fact. Or rather a long list of remarkable facts. Most humans alive today can expect to live longer, healthier lives than ever before. Global life expectancy is up nineteen years since 1960. That is a third more life per person on the planet on average. The average Brit today can expect to exist for an extra decade. Infant mortality has declined dramatically, down 85 per cent in Britain since 1960, and by 74 per cent worldwide. While there are still wars in Syria and elsewhere, overall the world is less violent now than it used to be. US homicide rates today are half of what they were in 1980. They have fallen even more dramatically in Africa, declining 63 per cent between 1995 and 2015.

Society is not in decline. Far from it. Divorce rates are down, and are lower in Britain today than at any point over the past forty years. There are a fifth fewer divorces per 10,000 people in America today than there were in 2000. Rates of teenage pregnancies are falling, down 85 per cent in the UK, 72 per cent in the US, 39 per cent in Africa and 50 per cent worldwide. 'In 2005, compared to 1955,' writes Matt Ridley in *The Rational Optimist*, 'the average human being on Planet Earth earned nearly three times as much money, ate one third more calories of food... and could expect to live one third longer.'

More folk in most Western states now own their own homes, and enjoy all the security that that brings. The typical British or American home is full of gadgets, entertainment systems and labour-saving devices that had not even been invented a couple of decades ago. In 1900, the average American worker would have had to work for two hours and forty minutes to earn enough money to pay for a three-pound chicken. Indeed, a chicken was such a big deal that when Herbert Hoover ran for the presidency in 1928, he promised Americans he would put one 'in every pot'. Not anymore. By 2000, the average American would have had to work a mere fourteen minutes to pay for a three-pound chicken. A pair of Levi jeans – that emblem of mid-twentieth century American prosperity – cost almost twelve hours' work in 1920. Today, they would cost two hours – and probably come in a better variety of cuts, too.

We are not on the brink of environmental disaster. As Bjørn Lomborg has pointed out, the world is less polluted now than it was a generation ago. Biodiversity is rising and the rate at which habitats are being destroyed has fallen sharply. In short, conservation is working. When they wallow in faux pessimism, the New Radical leaders on both left and right are not simply wrong. Their pessimism precludes the possibility of them being able to offer us anything better.

On the right, New Radicals seem to deny that there has been progress. On the left, many self-styled 'progressives' have little appreciation of what it is that has driven the progress there has undoubtedly been. Together they lack a credible notion of what propels progress. And if you do not recognize that things have got better, you will not be able to see how things could be made better still.

Standing for election in the 2005 General Election, I won my seat narrowly. Like many of my electorate, I was unimpressed with what my (then Conservative) party had to offer. Our pitch to the punter consisted of five promises that we repeated endlessly. A vote for the Conservatives, we insisted, meant cleaner hospitals, more police, less immigration, better schools and double helpings of apple pie, or something.

Having worked for the party policy team, I had a good idea of why we said what we said – and it was not on the basis of any sort of fundamental rethink about how we might run all those public services. Far from it. We had first used focus groups to identify the key concerns of the key voters. Then we simply played back to the voter what they had told us they most wanted to see change. We were literally telling them what they wanted to hear.

Telling voters what they want to hear is what established parties have been doing for decades – and, sensing that, it's one of the reasons why folk feel so fed up with politics. The New Radical movements – in a less scientific, more outlandish way – are doing precisely the same. They, too, are telling people what they want to hear. They, too, are saying what it is they want to change, but without thinking through the detail of how to make it happen.

If telling the voters what they want to hear about cleaner hospitals and more police induces the current level of disenchantment, just imagine the great wave of disillusionment that will wash over democracy itself when the New Radicals change nothing. It will not just be political parties that are held in contempt. It will be the process of democracy itself.

MAKING THINGS WORSE

'Tyranny', warns Socrates in Plato's *Republic*, 'is probably established out of no other regime than democracy'. Might we see something similar happen today?

After Donald Trump won the US presidential election, a flurry of fashionable pundits on both sides of the Atlantic were quick to warn that it meant the end of American democracy. It's not just that these New Radicals, as historian Robert Kagan put it, might show a 'boastful disrespect for the niceties of democratic culture'. Democracy is itself at risk, apparently.

A few days after Trump was elected, *Newsweek* went so far as to recommend a list of nine books to help readers survive the era of autocracy that Trump's election is supposed to herald. These included George Orwell's *1984*, a book called *American Fascists*, and, for good measure, the *Diary of Anne Frank*.

But hold on. The idea that tyranny is established out of democracy simply is not true. It was not even true of Plato's Athens. Democracy was snuffed out not thanks to any surfeit of people power but because of the Macedonian strongman Alexander. Nor was it the case that tyranny arose out of democracy in the Roman republic either. The tyrants, Sulla and then the Caesars, came from the patricians above, not from the plebeian faction below. And nor was it the case in those northern Italian city-states of the middle ages, where it was *signori* strongmen who overturned the republican practices of the communes.

However much you may or may not like him, Trump's election is proof of American democracy, not a subversion of it. No, the danger with the New Radicals is not that they become the oligarchy but that they justify its emergence. The anti-oligarchs – and the chaos, confusion and redistribution of resources that they bring – will make the case for rule by a few.

Democracy is already getting a bad name. In May 2016, IPSOS/ Mori asked Hillary Clinton's supporters in America why they were attracted to her. Was it her policy positions? Did they like her personally? Might it be that she stood to be the first woman president in US history? No. For almost half – 46 per cent – of her supporters, the primary motive for backing Hillary was that she would keep Donald Trump out.

Two weeks before the 2016 US presidential elections, ABC News commissioned a poll to find out what motivated supporters of Donald Trump. They discovered that for over half of his supporters, opposing Hillary was the primary motivation[2].

Already many see the anti-oligarchs – rather than the oligarchy – as the problem. For many British voters, Nigel Farage was a

2   Reported by ABC News, 24 October 2016.

good reason to vote to remain in the EU and to stay subservient to an unelected European Commission. In Greece, the mathematical madness of Alexis Tsipras was a good reason to allow the unelected Troika, a committee formed by officials from the European Commission, European Central Bank and IMF, impose a budget.

There is a powerful critique to be made in America about the behaviour of Wall Street and central bankers, Washington insiders and the political cartel. But if the person making those points is seen as a buffoon or a braggart, Wall Street and the lobbyists will win. When oligarchies began to emerge in the republics of Rome, Venice and the Dutch, each time there came an anti-oligarch reaction. Yet, as we shall see, all too often these insurgents of the past simply played into the hands of those they were meant to oppose.

So, too, today. With their incoherent, illiberal agenda, the New Radicals offer little that might actually arrest the emergence of oligarchy. Instead they legitimize the use of political power to intervene in the economy. They make redistribution – off which oligarchy ultimately feeds, as we will see – more mainstream.

Worst of all, their pessimism – that bogus sense that the world has got worse, when it hasn't – will serve as a pretext for all sorts of grand plans and interventions. So often anti-oligarch insurgencies simply pave the way for something worse. The New Radicals do not represent an embryonic oligarchy. The danger is that we leave the job of insurgency to them – and they discredit the alternative to the authoritarianism of the elite they are supposed to oppose.

That's why I decided to join them.

2

REBELLION

I know all about the anti-politics insurgency. I left the British Conservative Party to join it.

One late August day in 2014, I walked across St James's Park in central London and into a packed press conference to announce that I was switching parties and joining UKIP. In doing so, I was saying goodbye to a safe 12,000 majority seat in Parliament to join a party that had yet to win any parliamentary election ever. Not the first MP to change parties, I was however the first in a generation to insist on triggering a by-election as I did so. In the ensuing contest, I went on to win 'the largest swing to any political party in any British parliamentary election ever'.[3]

Nine months later, I had to clear an even higher hurdle when I successfully defended my seat in the General Election that followed. I was the only UKIP candidate in that election to win. In doing so, I became the first MP since 1926 to jump voluntarily

---

3   Prof. John Curtice in a BBC interview, quoted in the *Independent* on 10 October 2014.

from one party to another, trigger a by-election while making the move, win it – and then hold the seat in the subsequent General Election.[4]

Why did I do all that?

I wanted to force a referendum on Britain's membership of the EU – and at the same time make certain that the right people ran the campaign to ensure that we won it.

THE MAKING OF A SUCCESSFUL INSURGENCY

Twenty-one months after I had walked out of the Conservative Party, I strolled across London's Lambeth Bridge at 5 a.m. on a glorious summer morning. It was Friday, 24 June 2016, the day after the Brexit referendum. The orange glow of the newly risen sun silhouetted the Shard and the London Eye against an empty blue sky.

I had just come from the Vote Leave campaign headquarters, where we had sat through the night watching the referendum results roll in. First, the mood in the campaign office had been apprehensive. By 2 a.m. there was a sense of supressed elation. Finally, at around 4 a.m., when it became clear we had won, the atmosphere switched to whooping jubilation. Daniel Hannan, one of the leading figures behind Vote Leave, then Dominic Cummings, campaign director, gave impromptu speeches standing atop a desk.

Alone for the first time, I paused on the bridge to reflect. Looking to my right, I saw Lambeth Palace, the home of the Archbishop of Canterbury. To my left, the BBC studios in Millbank. Ahead of me was the Palace of Westminster, the seat of MPs and Lords. Beyond that lay Whitehall and the law courts, workplace of

---

4   Joseph Kenworthy in Central Hull, 1926, after he left the Liberals to join the Labour Party.

judges and officials. Further downstream was the City, home to FTSE 100 firms. Almost all of them had been against us. From bishops to broadcasters, mandarins to ministers, one way or another they had sided with Remain.

And we had just beaten the whole damn lot. For the first time the magnitude of what we had achieved hit me, almost as a physical force. How was it possible?

If you believe the sort of people we had just beaten, we insurgents are against the modern world. We are supposed to be a throwback, a nostalgic revolt against the way things are. But they are as wrong about that as they are about so much else. Far from rejecting modernity, it is modernity that makes our insurgency possible. Modernity has given us the attitudes and the tools to take on the sort of people who work in gleaming offices and palaces beside the Thames.

Long before any EU referendum campaign, I began to get a sense of how new technology was starting to change politics. Back in 1980-something, you needed a party to do politics. Local party associations brought together the activists, money and know-how needed to win a seat. The party also, of course, provided the big brand – Labour or Conservative, Republican or Democrat – that most voters were voting for. You had to be an appendage of a party, with the party machine behind you, to be in the race.

The reality by the early Noughties, I discovered, was that many local political parties are just not very good at campaigning. Local committees devote much of their energy to petty feuds and squabbles. Candidates wanting to get on with campaigning find there is an expectation on them to help organize stuffy black-tie events for the party faithful.

To win my seat as a Conservative candidate in 2005, I had to bypass much of the local party. When it came to organizing the delivery of a leaflet, for example, I found it more productive to send an email to possible helpers myself, rather than rely on the party locally. New technology – email and social media – combined with old-fashioned fish-and-chip-supper evenings in the community centre or town hall, allowed me to build up a genuinely grass-roots activist base of the kind that parties were supposed to provide – but seldom seemed to.

My local party branches sold raffle tickets and complained about each other. Those that came to my fish-and-chip-supper events delivered a leaflet in their neighbourhood for me each month. Party 'activists' in my experience are not always very active. By the time of the 2010 election, I had mobilized several hundred people in my constituency outside of any party. By the time of the Clacton by-election I had about a thousand such helpers, and despite having lots of party members bussed in from outside, the bulk of my leafleting and door-to-door campaigning was done by local folk helping out in the street where they lived.

With the arrival of broadband, many local voters set up email addresses and I started to harvest them. Once I had tens of thousands of addresses, synced to the electoral roll on my laptop, I could communicate directly with thousands of voters on topics that mattered to them personally. For me, a big moment came when, out of frustration with the Conservative Party data system, I opened an Excel spreadsheet and began a crude attempt at building my own. I soon went a bit better than Excel, creating my own data management and voter ID capability, and even started my own predictive modelling.

Previously, voter ID systems, databases and the enormously important direct mailing that they make possible required big computing power and deep pockets – and that meant being part of a big party. Not anymore. I discovered I could do it on my laptop – and do it better.

I was no longer doing things outside party structures through necessity, but increasingly through choice. I felt I could bring people together, work out which voters to target and then mobilize them with the right messages better than the big corporate parties, with their generic approach to everything. With the Clacton by-election result, I feel I proved my point.

The internet has started to disrupt the political marketplace. It is stripping away the barriers to entry and the in-built advantages that many of the big-brand parties possess. Vote Leave won the referendum campaign because it was run by people who understood all this.

Overwhelmingly the ground campaign on the Leave side came not from any political party, but what was in effect a 'pop-up party'. Not unlike what I had done in microcosm in Clacton, Vote Leave built up at a national level a campaign organization using the internet, without a cumbersome party attached. It allowed anyone to get involved in the practicalities of campaigning where they lived, building a national movement in almost every corner of the country. In the last ten weeks of the campaign, Vote Leave had an army of over 12,000 regularly active volunteers on the ground.

When Boris Johnson, Gisela Stuart, Michael Gove, Theresa Villiers and other 'Big Beasts' publicly joined Vote Leave four months before the referendum, we were ecstatic. The cavalry had arrived – but it was thanks to the pop-up party Vote Leave had created that there were legions for these MPs to lead.

Together, Vote Leave's army of 'pop-up' activists delivered over 70 million leaflets. While I had fiddled about with data in my constituency, creating a predictive model that helped me win two subsequent parliamentary elections, Vote Leave created a new software system and data to identify likely Leave voters on a vast scale. They did it all with an unrelentingly empirical approach.

In the old days, the 'air war' in politics was fought through the press and broadcast media, with a narrow clique of producers, editors and spin doctors battling it out to set the narrative. Conventional campaign managers think in terms of broadcast media and the press, with social media as some sort of added extra. Not Vote Leave.

It's not just that the narrative – the way that the press and broadcasters present things – is no longer determined by quite such a small clique. Increasingly it's possible to communicate directly with the voters, and bypass the pundits entirely. In Clacton, I had long used email and blogs to get my version of events over to the few thousand voters that mattered most to me. More recently, I made a video on Facebook watched by over 1.4 million people.

But Vote Leave took things to an entirely different level. Vote Leave's Dominic Cummings and Matthew Elliott understood that many of the key people we needed to reach were no longer really influenced by the press or broadcasters as they once were. Instead, they could be reached through Facebook. With newspaper readership plummeting and pundits deeply distrusted, it is the micro-conversations online that are becoming big.

Vote Leave delivered one billion targeted adverts through Facebook during the last few weeks of the campaign. And Vote Leave had tested what ads were offered and to whom. It's not that Vote Leave turned the orthodoxy of political advertising on its head. Digital turned it on its head. We recognized how things needed to be done.

On the night that the referendum polls closed, I was being interviewed by the BBC when I saw the result come in for Sunderland. I knew then that Vote Leave's campaign had found its mark. Vote Leave won because it was run by people who understood the sort of anti-politics insurgency we needed in order to win. Yet we were continually plagued by those who, despite lacking any of these insights, insisted that they knew how things should be done.

As the campaign progressed, it became obvious that many of the wannabe political insurgents seeking to speak for the Leave side had precious little idea about how to use the new tools to fight a successful insurgency. Fortunately, it was a problem we had foreseen some time before.

THE FARAGE PARADOX

'Nigel Farage is going to lose us this referendum!' MPs constantly complained to me in the run-up to polling day. 'His outbursts are off-putting to the people we need to win over,' I kept being told – and that was before he appeared in front of his notorious 'Breaking Point' posters.

I did not disagree. Indeed, a small group of us had been pondering precisely this conundrum long before. As far back as 2010, a few of us reflected on the two fundamental problems that we faced. First of all, we had to get David Cameron – himself in a coalition with the Liberal Democrats – to agree to a referendum. Second, we had to win it.

Getting Cameron to agree to a referendum was a slow, frustrating process of attrition. Mark Reckless and a small group of backbenchers sought out opportunities to force votes in the Commons to keep making our point. One such moment came in October 2011 when David Nuttall, MP for Bury North, brought forward a bill demanding an In/Out EU referendum – 111 MPs voted in favour of it.

Yet however successful we might be in pressing the case for a referendum, the Downing Street clique seemed immune to persuasion. More or less the moment they walked into Number 10 in 2010, they had stopped listening.

Special advisers in Downing Street smirked each time we tried to make our case. They seemed to have forgotten that it was thanks to us, elected MPs who had won their seats, often after campaigning in them for years, that Cameron and co. had been able to form an administration in the first place. Perhaps they needed reminding.

Some of us started to contemplate more drastic action.

In 2012, Daniel Hannan and I started to meet at the Tate Gallery, a discrete distance from the House of Commons, to consider the options. Dan suggested it as the perfect place to meet on the grounds that few in politics would have the aesthetic taste to pop into an art gallery in the afternoon. We would be undisturbed. And so it proved. Not once did we run into anyone from Parliament or the press lobby.

One of the ideas we toyed with at the Tate was that some of us should switch to UKIP. Perhaps one after the other. We considered the idea of triggering by-elections as we did so to focus the Cameron clique's mind. We talked about the practicalities of fighting a by-election. Should we run as UKIP or as independents – or, in effect, as both? What impact would all this have in terms of getting us the referendum?

But then, in January 2013, David Cameron gave his Bloomberg speech, proclaiming his commitment to a referendum – provided he was prime minister after the next election. Maybe his special advisers had started to see some sense. Or, despite our discretion, perhaps they had got wind of what was afoot. Or perhaps it was a consequence of our success in defeating the government at the end of October 2012 over the EU budget. After Bloomberg, it looked as if we were close to getting what we wanted. But as so often with Cameron, the up-front promise was somehow not matched by follow-through.

The backsliding began right away. Despite his promise of 'fundamental change' in our relations with the EU, it became increasingly apparent he was not even seeking this in his negotiations. One of Cameron's advisers made it clear to me that his 'new deal' was not about changing UK–EU relations, but about getting just enough to win the referendum to keep us in. Far from fundamental change, I had begun to fear that Cameron was seeking to outmanoeuvre the Eurosceptics on his own backbenches.

As well as pressing for a referendum, we were also giving a great deal of thought as to how we might win it when it came. We had started to reach out to potential donors and to think about the mechanics of an 'Out' campaign. We held exploratory conversations with senior centre-right strategists as early as 2012 about setting up a nascent organization that was to become the campaign team.

As part of all that, we had pored over any polling data we could find, looking for trends. We spotted, for example, how every time the Eurozone crisis flared up – a bank bailout, or riots in Athens – support for Leave rose. Yet we also saw another rather disturbing trend at work too; one that became known as 'the Farage paradox'.[5]

However high support for leaving the EU might be, the more that Nigel Farage's profile and UKIP's poll ratings grew, the more that support for Leave seemed to shrink. The numbers were clear: disapproval of Britain's EU membership, once running at about 60 per cent, fell to below 50 per cent as UKIP's poll ratings took off. This dominated much of our discussion – all the more so once we started to suspect that Cameron's plan was not to fundamentally change our relationship with the EU, but to win a referendum to rout his own Eurosceptic MPs. Farage, it seemed to us, was going to help him do it.

Talking it through in the Tate Gallery months before, we could foresee the emergence of a symbiotic alliance between the Cameronian Remainers on the one hand, and the Faragistas on the other. It suited both to present Nigel as the chief voice of Euroscepticism. Nigel would get the attention, the Cameronians would get the support of middle England.

---

5 To my knowledge, it was Sunder Katwala who first coined the term 'the Farage paradox' in an article for the *New Statesman*. A former Fabian, he was not, I should point out, party to any of our meetings in the Tate Gallery. He seems to have come to a similar conclusion to us entirely separately.

Then in 2014, UKIP topped the polls in the Euro elections. The Farage paradox showed up in the polls as powerfully as ever. Far from being on the march, Euroscepticism now had as its highest-profile spokesman a man that was inadvertently pushing the swing voters over towards Cameron. It was crystal-clear to us that if the referendum became a Cameron v. Farage contest, we would lose. And Downing Street knew it and was manoeuvring to make it happen.

It very nearly turned out that way. Throughout the referendum campaign, both Downing Street and Nigel Farage pushed to try to make Nigel the voice of Leave in the television debates. Indeed, ITV set up its debate as a contest between the two. Farage's focus on immigration, it seemed to us, animated an already Eurosceptic base of support. However, in a referendum where we needed to get 50 per cent plus one to win, it was not going to be enough. Worse, Farage's focus on immigration would allow the Cameronians to frame the referendum choice as one between tighter immigration controls or the economy.

Indeed, polling evidence consistently confirmed our view; immigration was not the primary reason why Leave voters voted leave. Nor was it the primary focus of Vote Leave's upbeat, optimistic campaign. If we had allowed Farage and co. to become the official voice of the Leave campaign and focus primarily on immigration, we would have lost.

Early in 2014, before I had decided to join UKIP, I wrote of how some Outers believe that 'immigration is our strongest card' since it 'links one of the public's number-one concerns with the question of our EU membership'. But I went on to warn, 'the Out campaign must not descend into any kind of angry nativism'. I said that to win any future referendum 'we must change our tune to sing something that chimes with the whole country'. The Outers, I argued, must offer an optimistic vision of the future.

Before fighting any referendum campaign to take back control from Brussels, we first needed to take control of Euroscepticism. What, we wondered, if some of us were to join UKIP? What if we were to speak up for a softer, more sensible sort of Euroscepticism?

WHAT DO YOU CALL AN UN-CONSERVATIVE?

It was easy to leave the Conservative Party once I realized I was not a conservative. Like every new MP, when elected for the first time, I was elated. Entering the Commons after a career in the City, I assumed that all we needed were the right sort of people running things, with the right kinds of plans in place, and all would be well.

Elation soon gave way to a sense of disappointment. And then disillusionment. Why? I started to sense that Westminster is a cartel. Parliament has become pointless. Things have been rigged so that no matter who you vote for, public policy is not made by anyone properly accountable to the public. Those you elect to Parliament rubber stamp decisions made elsewhere.

Parliament has become perfunctory. Power has seeped away from those we elect, downward to officials, sideways to central bankers and the judiciary, and upwards to supranational institutions.

As an MP, constituents might contact me with various sorts of concern. All too often, the only thing I could do was lobby various arms of officialdom; the health quangos that decided who got what treatment, the local education bureaucracy that decided who went to what school, the planning quangos that decided what got built and where.

It became clear to me that public policy is decided by executive agencies and officials, who tick the boxes but never answer properly to the public. Rather than deciding things, too many MPs sit in their offices drafting press releases that make it appear that they are taking action – yet the power to act rests elsewhere and they are not honest enough to say so. You might elect new MPs or a new government, but all you are doing is electing a new cast of characters to read the same old script, written in the interests of the same vested interests.

I started to think that we needed a revolution. If there was any point in being in politics, it should be to make government properly answerable to Parliament, and Parliament accountable to the people. In the early days, I held out high hopes that David Cameron, the fresh-faced leader of the Opposition, understood all this. It's one of the reasons I backed him to be party leader.

In the wake of the MPs' expenses scandal, he seemed to be a champion for change. He even took up many of the ideas Daniel Hannan and I had outlined in our 2008 book, *The Plan*: directly elected police chiefs, open primaries and right of recall. He wrote about a 'new politics', which would pass power outward and downward, away from Whitehall to the people.

But in office after the 2010 General Election, his government turned out to be just another managerialist administration. Meretricious, he flitted from one faddish idea – the Big Society, localism – to the next – a 'nudge unit'. I did not just lose faith in Cameron. I was also questioning what it was to be a conservative at all.

For many folk enjoying a twenty-first-century Western lifestyle, modernity is something they take for granted. Enjoying a standard of living their great-grandparents could scarcely comprehend, many simply do not see the progress happening all around them. I see it everywhere.

Brought up in 1970s Uganda, I grew up in a world without telephones or television. So, a little bit of me still marvels each time I use my iPhone. I grew up in a world of sugar shortages and flour rations. Petrol was precious and people queued for it for days. Smugglers risked life and limb to import foodstuffs inside the inner tubing of tyres. So, I find myself smiling at the simple thought that I can order a pizza and have it delivered to my front door. In the Kampala I grew up in, shooting happened almost every night. England today seems a pretty safe place to me. Actually, so, too, was Kampala the last time I was there.

You see, I know that the world has got better – for Britons, Africans and almost everyone – with a few terrible exceptions, such as for those poor folk living in Syria, Iraq or North Korea. I know, too, that the modern way of life – with its mobile phones and medicine, its gentler systems of justice and greater equality – is vastly better than what went before.

Yet so much about conservatism is built on the idea that the world is getting worse. There's a pervading sense of pessimism about it all. Conservatives, it seems to me, want to conserve things because they fear change. I don't. Deep down I came to realize that I am actually an un-conservative. I'm less certain if there is an obvious party for people who see the world this way.

COUNTER-INSURGENCY

Once the Tanzanian army had advanced to within range of Kampala, they started shelling us. My parents and I took to sleeping in our cellar.

Idi Amin, Uganda's self-proclaimed president-for-life, had finally overstepped the mark the previous year when he launched an entirely unprovoked invasion of northern Tanzania. Driven to respond, the Tanzanians counter-invaded us, one might say, and were now slowly closing in on Kampala. Like most of the city's inhabitants, we were willing them to arrive as fast as possible – without wanting to be on the wrong end of their Soviet-supplied shells.

In our cramped, musty cellar, the orange glow of a hurricane-lamp illuminating geckos on the wall, my parents and I listened to the whistle and thud of incoming artillery. Aged eight, I knew the difference between the short staccato sound of a real gun-fight and the rhythmic burst of drunken soldiers fooling around. In the early hours, one pattern would blend into the other.

At last victorious, the Tanzanian army brought with them order – of sorts. And, although we did not know it at the time, a deadly new disease: AIDS. It was a few years after the last Tanzanian soldiers had returned home that my father, who along with my mother was one of the few practising doctors in the country, noticed an increase in a virulent form of the rare skin disease, Kaposi's sarcoma. His interest aroused, my father sent nine samples from Kaposi's sarcoma sufferers off to the British government research facility at Porton Down to be tested for HIV antibodies (or HTLV III, as the virus was still called in those very early days). The results came back showing that seven of the samples had tested positive.

At the same time, my father had become aware of a mysterious wasting disease – 'Slim' – which had started to strike down hundreds of previously healthy young Ugandans. Suspecting a link, he sent samples from Slim sufferers to Porton Down, too. They came back positive as well. He realized he had an epidemic on his hands.

My father understood the implications way ahead of almost anyone else – and he was vilified for it. His warnings were not believed. Even when he published papers in respected medical journals showing beyond doubt the rate of infection, he was regarded as the problem. Who was this irksome Scottish doctor, claiming lots of Ugandans had some sort of venereal disease?

I learned early on that there are not always prizes for being right ahead of everyone else. My father was ordered to stop banging on about the AIDS epidemic. When he refused, he – and by extension my whole family – were ordered to leave the country we had lived in for almost twenty years. We were given three weeks to get out of the country I called home. The military authorities did not politely ask us to depart. A cook and a gardener, who had worked blamelessly for my family for years, were bludgeoned to death in our home to make certain that we got the message.

As my father feared, in the years that followed, AIDS killed tens, perhaps hundreds, of thousands of Ugandans – including friends I had grown up and gone to school with. Clacton on the morning of 10 October 2014 might have been a long way away from late-1980s Kampala. But twenty-something years on, even if flush with success from a landslide by-election win the day before, HIV was still a sensitive subject with me.

And yet HIV, for some reason, seemed to be the only thing that the wild press pack that thronged Clacton High Street wanted to ask me about. Why? I was baffled. I ought to have listened to the *Today* programme that morning. Given a prime-time slot in light of our win, Nigel Farage had talked about HIV.

The point he wanted to make, apparently, was that people with HIV were travelling to the UK for treatment and thereby obtaining costly medical care they were not entitled to. It was not something that had come up during the by-election. Or indeed on any doorstep or conversation with voters I had ever had in any of the dozen elections I had been involved with in the past twenty years.

It is my opinion that Nigel said what he said to put himself back in the spotlight. Not content with being the leader of a party that had just won its first seat in Parliament, he had in my view to make himself the absolute centre of attention, even if it meant negative attention.

It was a pattern of behaviour that I felt I saw repeatedly. As UKIP's candidate in Thanet South, he grandly declared that if local people did not elect him, he would quit politics. Big headline. Bad move. He handed, in my view, every sceptical voter an incentive to go and vote against him – which they duly did. In the run-up to the referendum, he repeatedly and publicly suggested that Remain would lose because their supporters could not be bothered to vote – thereby driving up turnout on the other side.

And then the week before the referendum, Nigel unveiled his deliberately provocative 'Breaking Point' poster featuring Syrian refugees. Like his HIV comments, I do not see how there can have been any electoral logic in doing what he did. In my view it was all about trying to be the centre of attention.

Can you imagine what the referendum result in 2016 might have been if that lot had run it? A small group of us had done precisely that some years before, and were so concerned about the possible consequences we decided to do something about it.

Before I had joined UKIP, I was under absolutely no illusion as to what I was dealing with. I joined because I recognized how electorally toxic UKIP's leader was in the eyes of many. The political capital I had with my new party following my by-election win, I started to spend.

Making my acceptance speech in Clacton town hall on the night of the by-election, I spoke of UKIP as 'a party for all Britain and all Britons – first and second generation as much as any other'. It was a theme I kept returning to. Writing for the *Mail on Sunday* and *The Times*, I criticized 'angry nativism' and argued that UKIP should be an upbeat, optimistic and inclusive party for change. Not every Kipper entirely agreed with me, but my audience was the 99.9 per cent of voters who weren't UKIP members. I was determined that they should not be repelled by UKIP in the coming referendum.

I contacted Sunder Katwala, of British Future, asking if I could give a talk on 'Why Enoch Powell was wrong'. Why be subtle? I wanted to challenge people's assumptions about UKIP while I had their attention – and to work with British Future to do it. I accepted every TV or radio interview – facing endless questions from presenters that began with 'But the leader of your party says…' I took every opportunity to sound reasonable. Not everyone in my new party appreciated it.

Mark Reckless, who had boldly followed me in joining UKIP, was in the middle of his by-election in Rochester. Under considerable pressure to make immigration and Nigel the focus of his campaign, I urged him to keep the focus local. Mark won. I was thrilled not just for him – but for our bigger agenda. During the Rochester by-election David Cameron promised to legislate for the EU referendum within the first few weeks of forming a government. It was, he said, to be a condition for any future coalition.

A week or so after Mark was re-elected, a poll showed UKIP on around 20 per cent in the polls – and there did not seem to be any discernible decline in support for the 'Out' side either. The Tate plan seemed to be going to plan.

To get elected in a parliamentary constituency, you needed to have concentrated appeal amongst the 70–80,000 electors that live there. And to have that kind of appeal in one area, you needed to focus on the issues that were specific to that area. Focus too much on the macro issues, and you might get support – but it would be dissipated across many different seats.

And so it proved with UKIP. With Nigel focusing on macro issues, like the EU and immigration, we polled almost 4 million votes. But we only won where we had been obsessively local. On the night of the General Election I was initially alarmed to discover that I was to be the only UKIP MP. I was especially sad to see my friend and fellow UKIP MP, Mark Reckless, lose his seat. He had taken an even bigger risk than me when he crossed the floor. And he paid a far higher price.

Nigel's 'shock and awful' antics had, in my view, done immense damage, not least to his own standing. A year before the 2015 General Election, his approval rating had been +4, with the number of voters saying they approved of his record as UKIP leader marginally ahead of those who said they disapproved. A year later, on the eve of the General Election, his rating was -26, with nearly six out of ten voters saying they disapproved of him.[6]

Worse, as Nigel and his team descended into parody, the risk they posed to the Leave side in the referendum campaign loomed ever larger. When Nigel announced he was staying on as party leader, I realized that there was no chance of detoxifying UKIP. Instead, I threw everything I had into trying to keep the toxic parts of the party out of the referendum campaign.

Politicians, being human, like to imagine that they are central to events. They often assume they play a more important role than they really do. Throughout the referendum campaign, I saw my job as to give support and space to those that could make the difference. Ensuring that the right people ran the referendum campaign – rather than have a front-line role myself – had been at the forefront of my mind even before I had walked into that press conference and UKIP all those months before. Supporting Vote Leave wasn't just about helping the embryonic group I had been involved with even before I had joined UKIP. Had the Leave. EU/Grassroots Out organizations vying to get designation been allowed to run the campaign, it is my view that the Leave side would have lost – and badly.

The Farage paradox would have become unmanageable. Even with Vote Leave gaining official designation, it was hard enough trying to stop Nigel taking part in the televised referendum debates, making ill-judged interventions and, in my opinion, costing the Leave campaign votes.

Along with Suzanne Evans and Patrick O'Flynn, I formally joined the Vote Leave campaign. Our little trio proved important

---

6   Compare Ipsos MORI party leadership net approval ratings for 5–7 April 2014 with Nigel Farage's approval ratings for 12–15 April 2015.

in ensuring that Vote Leave won the competition to be put in charge of the official Leave campaign by the Electoral Commission. We backed Vote Leave's bid in the face of angry, at times unpleasant, protests from others within the party. But it meant that we wrested back control of Euroscepticism. Just. And in doing so made Euroscepticism's wider win possible.

Oddly, some UKIP MEPs seemed to me to have understood the counterproductive consequences of a Farage-led campaign all too clearly. Yet many were happy to fall into line behind him – even if that cost us the very thing our party had come into existence to secure.

The struggle to ensure that the right people ran the campaign cemented in my mind the fact that many would-be political insurgents are rather hopeless at insurgency. Indeed, their muppetry often plays straight into the hands of the established order.

3

WHO STOLE DEMOCRACY?

The New Radicals have a point, don't they? There is something wrong with mainstream politics.

Of course, elections still happen. Votes are still counted, winners declared and victors assume office. Democracy on either side of the Atlantic has retained its outward form. But it has been hollowed out from within. It has, as the political scientist Francis Fukuyama puts it, 'decayed'.

In a democracy, the *kratos* – or state – is supposed to answer to the *demos* – the people. But, increasingly, our *kratos* answers to vested interests. The *demos* are an afterthought.

POINTLESS POLITICS

How many elections between different parties allow the electorate much of a choice? What major policy differences do elections between parties really decide?

A growing number of people think that elections between

parties make little difference. Which is why fewer and fewer people bother to take part in election contests between parties – and why a growing share of the electorate are willing to vote for people and parties outside the mainstream.

Voter turnout in elections between parties has been steadily falling almost everywhere. In French assembly elections, turnout declined from 58 per cent in 1988 to 43 per cent in 2007. In Britain, voter turnout has declined over the past fifty years from over 80 per cent in the 1950s to around 60 per cent over the past decade. In the most recent mid-term United States congressional election of 2014, turnout was a mere 37 per cent – the lowest since 1942.

You are interested enough in the world around you to be reading this book, so the chances are that you did vote in the last General Election. What were you thinking as you dropped your ballot paper into the ballot box? What did you think you were voting for when you opted for party candidate X, rather than Y?

Perhaps you were voting out of habit, or a sense of civic duty? But did you really imagine that how you voted that day would change the sort of education your child received at the local school? Would your vote for one party rather than another put more police on the streets or ensure that there are enough local doctors? Would it halt a proposed development or stop the bank bailouts? Would it reduce the rate at which the government accumulates more debt? Would it change your government's energy policy or foreign policy? No? Then what were you voting for?

Be honest. Perhaps you voted for one party not because you harboured any real enthusiasm for it, or because you believe it could change much, but because you cannot stand some of the other lot? Increasingly people will vote for Boodle's party because they cannot stand Doodle.

Of course, that is when politics is a choice between political parties. Look at what happens when elections happen without the political parties getting in the way, and the electorate is asked to make a direct, binary choice.

During both the Scottish and then the Brexit referendums, turnout was extraordinarily high: 72 per cent voted in the referendum on Britain's membership of the European Union; an amazing 85 per cent voted in the referendum on Scotland's independence from the United Kingdom.

The electorate was enthused because they could make a real choice, not the sort of Hobson's choice they normally face on polling day. Touring the country in the big red Vote Leave battle bus with Boris Johnson and Gisela Stuart, I was struck by how animated and excited the crowds were. Despite having campaigned in, and contested, quite a number of party political elections, I had not experienced anything quite like it. I suddenly got a sight of what real democratic choice feels like.

But when choosing between parties in elections, there is nothing like that sense of making a choice. Why? Because the mainstream political parties in most Western states have formed a cartel to diminish choice.

CARTEL PARTIES

What are political parties for? Why do we have them?

If everyone is going to have a vote, it's helpful if they know what it is that they are voting for, according to the apologists for political parties. At the most elementary level, they tell us, parties exist to allow voters to exercise choice.

It's not a very convincing argument. Firstly, it presumes that without party labels, folk would be incapable of making up their own mind about who to vote for. Secondly, political parties today seem to be in the business of restricting voters' choice.

Typically, Western states have a two-party system. American Democrats battle it out with Republicans. French Gaullists go up against Socialists. In Britain, politics for most of the past century has been a contest between Labour and the Conservatives.

Different parties used to represent different sectional interests. In Britain, the Conservative Party stood for the business interest. The Labour Party, as the name implies, represented the interest of organized labour. In the US, the Democrats had close ties with unions. The Populist Party, at the turn of the nineteenth century, stood for farmers.

As well as championing different interests, parties used to champion opposing points of view; the free market v. statism, federalism v. states' rights, foreign policy interventionism v. isolationism. But in many Western states, the established parties no longer articulate opposing philosophies. Bipartisan clashes over issues of fundamental consequence have been replaced more often than not by a soggy, managerialist consensus.

Until very recently, both main parties in Britain supported EU membership. Both back a statutory minimum wage. Both subscribe to the idea of the welfare state. Both believe in raising energy prices in a shared desire to curb carbon emissions. Both advocate an expansive monetary policy and state subsidies for the banks.

In the United States, the gap between Democrats and Republicans is often said to be wider than ever. But is it? Despite controlling both Houses of Congress, the GOP failed to mount effective opposition to President Obama. Instead, on key issues – from immigration reform to the debt ceiling – Republican leaders made their peace with him. As Washington insiders, the centralization of power in an expanding federal government comes as naturally to many of them as it does to him.

The politicians all seem to have agreed to agree on many of the big macro questions. The focus of legislative debate has narrowed to questions of which barely differing technocratic means are best suited to achieving the same uncritically accepted ends. Many voters do not share the consensus – and feel resentful that they are being ignored.

It's not merely that the parties have similar outlooks. They look and sound the same. In Britain, both main parties field remarkably similar candidates, with similar backgrounds and seemingly interchangeable opinions. A generation ago, many Labour MPs had manual occupations before entering the Commons. Today, that applies to only two Labour MPs. At the 2015 General Election, six out of ten Labour candidates standing in their most winnable seats were already working in Westminster. It's a similar story on the Tory benches.

For much of the past thirty years, those on the front benches in the House of Commons got there following a similar path: Oxbridge, followed by a stint as a researcher/special adviser, followed by selection for a safe seat – then rapid elevation to front row in the Commons.

Today, the sectional interest that the two major British political parties best represent is that of career politicians. Even in the United States, where the selection process in the parties is famously decentralized, there is a feeling that politics is dominated by 'beltway' insiders. Too many in Congress are seen as acting on behalf of vested interests and lobbyists.

Special interest groups fund incredibly expensive campaigns, which has made candidates increasingly dependent on special interest groups – and ever less distinguishable in terms of the political positions they espouse. Politics is seen to be run by those beholden less to Main Street than to K Street.

It was partly in reaction to this that during the 2015–16 presidential primary contests, perceived outsiders – like Donald Trump, Ted Cruz and (initially) Bernie Sanders – did so well against those candidates who were seen as politically established, such as Jeb Bush, Marco Rubio and Hillary Clinton.

It's rather similar in France and Germany, where the party-list systems mean that party bosses have enormous patronage. With a much weaker constituency link than exists in either Britain or the United States, voters often can't choose between individual candidates on the ballot paper but only between parties. Consequently, candidates are invariably favourites and placemen chosen not by voters or even by local party members, but by party headquarters. The fastest way to the top of politics is to work for an insider already at the top.

How did political parties end up so similar? Because, as in any cartel, the main players have agreed to limit the competition. The rules of the political game have been gamed by the parties.

HOW PARTIES RIGGED THE RULES

Cartels, be they in banking or drugs, always have one thing in common: agreements to limit competition between members of the cartel. And so, too, in politics.

The established political parties have, over the years, put in place arrangements and come to understandings with one another in order to accommodate their mutual interests. Arrangements that suit them as the purveyors of politics, not voters as the buyers.

I once went to stay as a guest of a US congressman in California. While teaching me to surf, my host drove me around his district in search of the perfect surf spot. I soon discovered that his district formed a remarkably long coastal strip. It joined together the predominantly white and Asian neighbourhoods on the sea front, while excluding Hispanic communities just a few blocks inland. It is almost as if someone had done it deliberately, I thought.

And indeed, some would say that they had. In the United States, Congressional districts in the different states are drawn up – or gerrymandered – in order to favour political parties. Gerrymandering is perhaps the most brazen example of parties colluding to rig the system. Locally, Democrats and Republicans will agree to draw the district boundaries to create 'safe seats' – effectively disenfranchising people in the process. In a properly functioning democracy, voters get to choose their representatives. Thanks to gerrymandering, representatives choose their voters.

It's not much better in Europe or the UK, either. The party list system in many continental European states means that sitting members of the legislature get to choose who sits in the legislature. Party favourites are placed high up the list. Only a minority of candidates lower down the list on each side are, in effect, chosen by the electorate, when they vote for a party. Competition is limited.

Of course, in the UK almost all parliamentary seats have been 'safe seats', never shifting party allegiance at a General Election for as long as anyone can remember. Between 1987 and 2005, there were five General Elections in the UK. Yet in four of those five elections, only one in ten seats was won by a different party. Even in the great Labour landslide of 1997, fewer than three in ten seats changed hands.

In most seats, most MPs can assume that they are more or less immune from the views of the voters. Party insiders can be parachuted in as candidates for safe seats almost regardless of what the locals think. Which is precisely why in counties like Suffolk in England, although almost six in ten people voted to leave the EU, each of the county's seven members of Parliament (all of whom are Conservatives) backed Remain.

'But it was ever thus,' I hear you say. 'There have always been "safe seats" and that's just the way it is.'

It hasn't always been this way. Until 1885 in Britain, most constituency seats were represented by two or more MPs. In other words, there was choice and competition locally – even in areas where one party traditionally prevailed. The year after the Reform Bill of 1884 gave the working man in Britain the vote, however, the parties colluded to create a monopolistic seat system. Previously 459 out of the 652 MPs had come from multi-member constituencies (representing 70 per cent of the total). After the 1885 Redistribution of Seats Act, 93 per cent of MPs came from single-member constituencies (622 out of 670).

The 1885 act might have equalized constituencies, but it also created a monopolistic system, with hundreds of fiefdom constituencies, devoid of much choice or competition. Soon after that, in the late 1880s and 1890s, both the Liberal and Tory parties started to create London-based committees to oversee the process of selecting candidates. Presumably, now that the working man had the vote, there was a need to control whom he might elect.

A number of seats continued to have two MPs right up to the 1950s. It is rather ironic that what was eventually phased out as an anachronism had once helped ensure that, even in solidly Tory or Liberal voting areas, voters had a choice.

Choice and competition in constituencies is not the only thing that got phased out for supposedly being an anachronism. For 225 years in Britain, there was a remarkable – if long forgotten – rule. Whenever a sitting member of Parliament was invited to join the government, they did not – as they do today – stride off towards their new department in Whitehall. First, they had to resign from Parliament. Then they had to return to their constituency, stand and win in the by-election that followed. Only then were they permitted to be a minister.

In other words, it was not just the patronage of the prime minister that decided who became a minister. There was, if you like, a giant confirmation hearing, involving every local voter. This convention, which dated to the Act of Settlement, was to guarantee a separation of powers between the executive and the legislative branches of government. Never quite as deliberate as the arrangements outlined in the US Constitution, the arrangement was nevertheless a check and a balance against an overbearing executive. The people had the final say over ministerial appointments.

But then in 1926, the Re-Election of Ministers Act (1919) Amendment Act abolished the convention on the grounds that it was an outdated inconvenience. I rather suspect the act owed more to the fact that, in the decades preceding it, there had had to be rather a lot of ministerial by-elections. Between 1885 and 1926, there were a total of 127 ministerial by-elections alone – or three ministers-designate facing a by-election each year.

This proved to be a career-ending inconvenience for some. And just an inconvenience for others. One of the most famous casualties was Winston Churchill, who, appointed President of the Board of Trade, came a cropper in Manchester North West in 1908. That not only put an end to his appointment as a minister. He was out of Parliament, too.

He was not the only one. In 1912, Sir Arthur Haworth, a Treasury minister, was vetoed by Manchester South. Charles Masterman got a thumbs-down in 1914 not just once, in a by-election in his Bethnal Green seat, but again in Ipswich, when he tried to get back into Parliament there.

Tellingly, some of the highest-profile ministerial by-election defeats – Arthur Griffith-Boscawen in Dudley in 1921, and Thomas Lewis in Pontypridd the following year – saw the incumbent defeated by the new insurgent party, Labour. The 1926 act was not just a deliberate attempt by a Liberal–Tory establishment to remove the risk of ministerial by-elections. Fear of organized labour as a force in politics, which somehow made the risks seem all the greater, no doubt played a part, too.

'Hang on a moment!' I hear you think. 'Britain today is a far more democratic place than she was back then – even if the rules on when to hold by-elections were different.'

'Women only got the vote in 1918,' you continue. 'There were property qualifications to be on the electoral roll. Things can hardly have been more democratic, if so few people had the vote.'

You make a good point. The franchise was restricted back then. Fewer people had the vote. In terms of who has the vote, we are more democratic today than we were before 1918. But those who did have the vote had meaningful power then in a way that today they do not. Those with the vote could veto the appointment of a minister. They had a choice, even in parts of the country where only candidates from one party stood much chance of getting elected.

The franchise might have been widened, but there are restrictions on what those with the vote can do with it. Cartels not only agree to limit competition, they often collude to ensure that whatever it is that they do – financial transactions, drugs, politics – must be done through them. The party cartels that dominate our democracy have made sure that they are centre stage.

At election time, voters are given a choice of candidates. For many years in Britain, the party affiliation of the candidates was incidental. Strictly speaking, it still is. Anyone on the electoral roll – more or less – could stand as a candidate for Parliament. A candidate standing with an affiliation to a particular political party is no more nor no less a candidate than any other. As a candidate in various elections, I have – quite rightly – had to take my place alongside all manner of independent candidates.

Until 1969, it was illegal to print the name of the party on the ballot paper. The law expected you to vote for a person, not a party. But, as has happened so often, the political small print was rewritten by the established parties for their convenience. Parliament passed the Representation of the People Act (1969), which allowed candidates to add a few words about themselves on the ballot paper. Party names and logos started to appear.

There was, at a stroke, less incentive for the candidates to make their own names known. In an era of broadcast television, they would operate as subsidiaries of their party brand. Election campaigns began to be transformed from localized, varied choices between individual candidates to uniform, national contests between labels.

At around the same time, rules came into force to regulate election spending. Introduced in the name of fairness, and to ensure that big money could not swing elections, they capped the amount that could be spent by both local candidates and national parties.

Yet there is something rather curious about these caps. The spending limit for each local candidate – approximately £15,000 at the last election – without question limits what candidates might otherwise do in terms of campaigning. We know this because almost all candidates spend close to the legal limit. Yet each party's spending limit for national campaigning seems to have been set so high that it is hard to see what, if anything, it curtails.

At the last General Election, the Conservative Party was not allowed to spend more than £19.4 million and Labour £18.9 million. Yet neither party spent anything like that upper limit. The Tories spent £15.5 million and Labour just over £12 million. In other words, the legal spending limits do not so much restrict what parties spend. They limit what individual candidates can spend.

These rules help ensure that political campaigning more or less has to be done through the national party machine. How convenient for those who run the national party machine – and who work with counterparts running other party machines to help agree the limits.

In Britain, political advertising on radio and television has been banned. This is, we are told, to protect us from the vulgarity of American-style political advertisements. Far better, they say, to have the system of party election broadcasts that we have. At about the same time that the rules on election spending were introduced, rules governing party election broadcasts were created. They ensured, firstly, that the existing big political parties got the airtime. Secondly, these arrangements made certain that any upstart candidates or campaign groups with a bee in their bonnet simply could not get the airtime.

It's a democracy, you see. But you only get to choose between the parties that are on offer. To me, the most egregious example of political cartelism is the recent Lobbying Act. Introduced by the Coalition Government in 2014, it claimed to be about limiting the influence of lobbyists. In fact, what the Act does is restrict non-parties from doing politics. The law specifically limits the amount of political advocacy that any organization that is not a registered party can do. When I confronted the minister at the time of the bill, he explained that 'politics is what political parties are there to do'.

Parties have not only rigged the rules to ensure political campaigning must be done through them. They have continually changed the rules inside Parliament to make them – and their whips – central to proceedings. Until the 1930s, when a budget was presented to Parliament, any MP was free to try to table an amendment – as with pretty much any other piece of legislation. Muster enough support for the measure and, if the Speaker called a division, you could meaningfully change what ministers proposed to do with taxpayers' money.

But then the parties colluded to ensure that individual MPs could only agree or disagree with what their front bench proposed. There was no longer a mechanism to try to change things – or indeed to even understand what tax and spending decisions were being proposed.

Parties have colluded to ensure that almost everything in Parliament is done along party lines. Room allocation for MPs? Each party is given a quota, allowing the party whips to reward favourites and send troublesome backbenchers to the basement. (I know; I was in a windowless broom cupboard for years.) Select committee chairmen? They are divvied up by party.

Individual members of each committee are elected – but only by members of their own party.

When did we give parties permission to write themselves into the small print of our constitution? We never did. But the parties colluded to write a role for themselves into Standing Orders of the House. Surely an elected MP is first and foremost the representative of the town or county that sent them?

I find myself rather resenting any reference to my party affiliation when taking part in parliamentary proceedings. I am the MP for Clacton, first and foremost. That I happen to be a member of the Conservative Party or of UKIP should, in terms of parliamentary proceedings, be incidental.

POLITICS FOR POLITICIANS

Once a week in Westminster, a group of Tory MPs get together for breakfast in the tea rooms. Since several of those in this regular little gathering have been in Parliament for over twenty years, I assume they have probably been meeting like this for at least that long.

Watching this little gossip-fest from the other side of the room, I suspect that, for a number of them, it is one of the highlights of their day. They are never more animated or excited than when speculating as to which of their colleagues might be given what reward. There might be a new office in Portcullis House for Boodle. Or ministerial promotion for Doodle. Or – *such schadenfreude at the thought* – demotion for McOodle! The excitement.

In every workplace in Britain, people gossip about co-workers. They speculate about the boss and complain about conditions. It's part of what makes us human. Yet for many MPs, particularly the longer serving ones, this kind of tittle-tattle is not merely of passing interest over breakfast. It has become the essence of the job. Politics to them is not about the things that matter to us, but that game of pettiness played out in SW1. It is what happens when politicians only answer to other politicians. It's all about them.

Party whips often script the questions for MPs to ask. Sometimes they even hand out sheets of the key points that they want MPs to make in debates. Sucking up to the whips becomes more important to the ambitious MP from a safe seat than representing the views of constituents.

Rather than debating issues of substance, MPs talk about the trivial. The Commons chamber is a forum for virtue-signalling, with MPs expressing viewpoints that other MPs like them value, in order to make themselves look good. Because politics has become a cartel, those in Westminster and Washington arrange things for their convenience – not democracy's.

In Britain, party whips on both sides of the chamber colluded to create the notorious system of MP expenses, which caused so much scandal and outrage in 2009. When details of what had been going on were leaked, there was uproar. Yet for years, party bosses had not only been fully aware of what was going on, they had helped put the rotten system in place as an alternative to raising MPs' pay.

The expenses scandal in Britain saw politicians behave as if the expense regime was some sort of off-balance-sheet remuneration. Seventeen years earlier, in Washington, the House banking scandal saw representatives act as if Congress was their private bank account, ready to give them salary advances.

That's not the only way that parties have worked together to help themselves to taxpayers' money. Parties have colluded to ensure that opposition parties are given a state subsidy to run their Westminster operation. This Short Money, as it is known, is now worth about £7 million a year.

Details of how the money is spent are sketchy. Labour's £6 million a year grant, for example, goes straight into party coffers. There is little accountability but some evidence that, as well as paying for party staffers, some of the money pays for things like hotel bills during party conferences. As with MPs' expenses under the infamous old system, we just do not know the detail.

The established parties worked together to draw up the rules on the assumption that they would be the only parties getting the money. To ensure that this was so, the funding formula they devised linked the amount of Short Money each party got to the number of votes each party won at the last election.

Then along came UKIP in 2015, with almost 4 million votes. This meant that I, as the only UKIP MP, was suddenly entitled to about £670,000 per year. The absurdity. Naturally, I turned down most of it. Despite those in my then party insisting otherwise, I knew that I could not justify spending that sort of money on my parliamentary office. Yet instead of returning the hundreds of thousands of pounds to the taxpayer, the mainstream parties got together to rig the rules again. UKIP's share of Short Money was, in effect, reassigned to Labour.

'What is it like being the only MP for your party in Parliament?' I often used to get asked. It was a lot of fun. I got invited to an audience with the Queen to wish her a happy ninetieth birthday in Buckingham Palace. On a different occasion, I got invited to tea with President Xi of China.

But – week in, week out – it also meant I had to think carefully for myself ahead of every Commons vote to decide which way I might vote. Previously, I was sent a text message each day by my party whips instructing me how to vote. I did not even need to know the motion I was voting on.

Having to find everything out might be a lot of extra work, but it has made me wonder: what on earth I was doing before? Most MPs in most parties for most votes simply follow the whips' instructions. Even rebellious MPs only rebel on a tiny minority of overall votes. A very large number of MPs have never voted against their party line. On anything. In what sense are they representing their constituents? Looking at the huddle of middle-aged MPs gossiping about one another in the tea room, I wondered what their constituents would make of it all.

Stop one of their constituents in the street and ask them what they want politicians to focus on, and they might say the economy or immigration. I doubt they would really care about who is to be the new Parliamentary Under Secretary at the Department for Widgets. In order to become the junior minister in the Department of Widgets, an MP only has to stick to the party's line on widgets. Indeed, it would almost certainly be a disadvantage to your promotion prospects to have thought anything original about widgets. A willingness to subscribe to an unreflective groupthink is what counts. The whips call it 'loyalty'.

Loyalty to the groupthink makes politicians look and sound bogus. To maintain the fiction that they are as one on every issue, ministers and MPs contort themselves into painful positions during interviews. They resort to carefully phrased sound bites. Occasionally, it leaves them looking plain ridiculous.

The massed ranks of government ministers who had been advocating Remain in May 2016 became a phalanx of ministers pushing the merits of Leave by July 2016. Despite being on the wrong side of one of the most important macro questions of the day, few ministers who had campaigned for Remain – with the exception of the prime minister, David Cameron – saw fit to stand down from office. They simply switched sound bite. For most ministers, the volte-face happened as if nothing had changed. I struggle to buy it. Why should the voter?

Nick Clegg and the Liberal Democrats earnestly explained why they opposed tuition fees before the 2010 General Election. Until they equally earnestly explained why they were in favour after the election. It is as if politics is simply about saying the right lines. Politicians all recite from the same script. Until they switch to another. They all espouse one set of deeply held principles. Until they change to another.

The voter notices this sort of thing – and resents being taken for a fool.

CRAP PUNDITS

Thank goodness we have a free press to take our politicians to task, eh?

With politics run by a cosy cartel, and the rules rigged to suit the insiders, journalists – you might imagine – have lots to expose. The media, especially in Britain and the United States, have an image of themselves as fearless. In the spirit of Watergate's Woodward and Bernstein, they like to believe that they are on hand to scrutinize the powerful. On several occasions, I have even heard journalists explain rather grandly how they 'speak truth to power'.

Really? In my experience, they are more likely to be buying the powerful lunch in a top London restaurant. 'Fearless' is not the first word that springs to mind when trying to describe the attitude of many members of the parliamentary press lobby to those at the top. 'Toadying' might be nearer the mark. On that amphibian theme, I am reminded of a remark made by one of the characters in Leo Tolstoy's *Anna Karenina*: 'All the papers say the same thing... they are like frogs before a storm! They prevent our hearing anything else'.

Far from holding the powerful to account, the media collude with them, as they trade identikit opinions. Journalists exchange favours for access, and have an unhealthy dependence on those they are supposed to scrutinize. The Westminster press lobby is literally a closed shop. Passes to join it are restricted and existing members get to decide who joins the club (Bloggers?! No, thanks!).

Like all cartels, it has its own code of conduct, with briefings given on 'lobby terms'. Lobby-term lunches allow politicians to brief: the journalist gets something to write about, the politician gets his or her version of events into print. The voter gets spin masquerading as news. The latest set of immigration statistics, or GDP figures, are often not reported in terms of what they might mean for the country. Political correspondents will write them up in terms of what it might mean for the career of Boodle, or his arch-rival Doodle.

Rather than encouraging MPs to focus on matters of substance, pundits seem to revel in tea-room trivia as much as any MP. Indeed, there have been times when matters of national import-ance *only* get mentioned by the press lobby in the context of what it means for the careers of politicians, not the country.

In the run-up to the 2015 General Election, and then the Brexit vote, most national newspapers – unsurprisingly – took a side. For several weeks before polling day, almost every political story each paper wrote had a slant. Often what a paper chose to write about in the first place was selected to fit that agenda.

And that, in a free country, is how it works – and how it should work. Those who buy their daily newspaper know that they are buying a subjective view of the world. Editors, I suspect, more often reflect the views and outlook of their readers than shape them. The trouble is that many broadcasters tend to behave in much the same way but without the honesty about who or what it is that they are backing. The *Daily Mail* might have blatantly backed Vote Leave, and the *Mail on Sunday* Remain in the recent referendum, but Sky News, the BBC and other broadcasters all claimed to be balanced.

Yet what the broadcasters present to us as analysis is often little more than opinion. Reporters tell us what they think, not what is really going on – and call it the news. Consider for a moment how certain broadcasters and journalists reacted when, on 23 June 2016, a majority of British voters voted to leave the EU. A quick examination of their Twitter feeds reveals a great deal about what they were thinking.

Many were keen to present the result as a disaster. Britain, according to their timelines, had just decided to walk off a precipice. ITV's chief political correspondent, Chris Ship, tweeted that the UK economy would shrink dramatically. His colleague, Robert Peston, who had reported on the banking crisis of 2007–08, tweeted that we should 'brace for tumult like little we have ever witnessed'.

'Britain teeters on the brink of Ozymandian collapse,' wrote David Rennie, while the *Economist*, for which he writes, ran a front-page headline about how Britain had gone 'off the rails'. We were, said this venerable publication, adrift. But the prize for the greatest hyperbole should, perhaps, go to Channel 4's Jon Snow. Young people, he wrote, would lose the 'right to study, live, love and work' abroad.

It's not just that many pundits were keen to big-up any downsides. Many seemed keen to belittle the result. Leave voters regretted voting Leave, some seemed to imply. BBC editor Louise Compton wrote about how 'most' Leave voters had woken up thinking, 'What have I done?' Not in my experience. They were joyous and celebrating that summer morning.

The BBC gave prominent coverage to an online petition set up to demand a second referendum. Much was made of the million-plus signatures it got in the space of a few days. What was less widely reported is that over 40,000 'signatures' were apparently from people living inside the Vatican. The petition might have been bogus in many ways but it suited the pundits' narrative, so they reported it as fact.

ITV's Libby Weiner tweeted about a taxi driver she had spoken to who was appalled at how the vote had 'fuelled racist sentiment'. It's not just that many people regretted voting to leave the EU, according to some broadcasters. Those that had voted to leave did so because they were beastly bigots and racists.

Several days after the results, a couple of US journalists at a press conference put a series of questions to Boris Johnson – a leading light in the Vote Leave side – that seemed to imply that he disliked foreigners. What 'great questions' they were, tweeted Chris Ship. The referendum result should be set aside, ventured the journalist and broadcaster David Aaronovitch. 'There is no democratic reason why there cannot be another referendum,' he declared. 'The margin of victory was small, and many Brexiters are suffering terrible buyer's remorse.'

Not everyone at the BBC perhaps shared its journalist Hugh Sykes's view that 'the referendum was an act of stupidity by Cameron. Worse than war.' But it is fair to say that many of his colleagues seemed to disapprove of the outcome. Yet these are the people who had been providing us with supposedly balanced and neutral coverage and analysis ahead of the referendum.

Mercifully, during the formal referendum campaign, there was a legal requirement on broadcasters to provide some degree of balance. The Hugh Sykes tendency was reined in. Up to a point. Often the BBC would go through the motions of balance – equal airtime for each side, an opportunity to rebut what the other side had said. But on several occasions they seemed to frame the debate in a way that favoured Remain – and the 'experts' that backed Remain.

In my part of England, BBC East wanted to host a televised public debate. 'Would you take part?' I was asked. 'Yes!' I said, with the relish of someone who had spent twenty years pushing for this moment. But my initial enthusiasm evaporated when I discovered that the debate would not just feature two Leavers against two Remainers, but a panel of four 'experts'. When I made a few enquiries, I discovered that at least three of the four 'experts' had views that were, in my view, deeply antithetical to Vote Leave's case. Others eventually agreed, and the idea of having a panel of 'experts' was quietly dropped. But why on earth did BBC East not simply contact each of the designated campaigns and ask them to provide spokespeople?

Halfway into the campaign, ITV announced that in their main Brexit debate, they were going to have Nigel Farage speaking for Leave against David Cameron for Remain. It was news to the Leave campaign. By behaving in this way, ITV was effectively colluding with the Remain side – read Downing Street – to pick the Leave spokesman. Downing Street was delighted to have Nigel speak for Leave precisely because they understood how it would help the Remain campaign.

Can you imagine if during a General Election the leader of one party was able to decide with the broadcasters whom they should debate against from the other party? ITV's behaviour made a mockery of having a designation process to decide who ran the referendum campaign in the first place. Why bother bidding for designation if the broadcasters put who they want on the platform?

Vote Leave reacted angrily. Many pundits reported the row with great glee – yet knew full well why Vote Leave felt so strongly about it. We had every right to be furious. It was as if Eddie Izzard – the flamboyant comedian – had somehow been invited on air as the official spokesman for the Remain side. Giving Nigel Farage media coverage out of all proportion to his electoral significance never seemed to strike them as undemocratic. It struck me as the essence of anti-democratic.

During the referendum campaign and the aftermath, I found myself constantly asking why the broadcast coverage was so bad. Despite all the broadcasters' claims that Brexit would take us off an economic cliff, a Bank of England report a few weeks after Vote Leave's win confirmed that there was 'no clear evidence of a sharp general slowdown in activity'. Got that? No evidence, just a lot of tweets. The report went on to say that there was 'little sign of any impact on consumer spending'. So much for the massive Brexit-imposed shock.

When Jon Snow tweeted about young people in Brexit Britain no longer being able to study, live, love or work in other countries, was he unaware of how young people around the world are free to do those things in dozens of different countries outside the EU?

When Reuters journalist Jamie McGeever suggested that the Brexit crisis was so great it was like 'Black Wednesday times two', he may have been more accurate than he knew. The original Black Wednesday, when Sterling left the European Exchange Rate mechanism (ERM) on 16 September 1992, was also greeted as a catastrophe by many expert pundits. However, as we now know, escaping from the ERM actually allowed the UK economy to begin the longest period of sustained economic growth since records began.

I suspect the problem runs a little deeper than one or two injudicious tweets. The problem is that for years many pundits have reported about the fraught issue of Britain's relations with the EU almost entirely through the prism of Tory Party soap opera. It did not seem to occur to them that there might be wider issues at stake.

Three months after the referendum, the BBC's Head of News, James Harding, penned an absurdly self-defensive piece in the *Guardian* (where else?). 'In the months ahead,' he wrote, 'our job [at the BBC] is to understand what Brexit actually means.' Did it not occur to him to maybe do that before the vote?

David Cameron might have trounced Ed Miliband, suggested ITV's Libby Weiner right after the poll, but his misjudgement was to believe he could defeat a far more dangerous foe, Boris Johnson. Somehow, she seemed to imply, we should view the verdict of some 30 million-plus adult voters as an extension of the Boris v. Dave show. Shortly after the referendum result, Robert Peston tweeted a link to an article by Boris Johnson in the *Telegraph* with barely concealed incredulity. He seemed to scoff at what Boris was writing.

Yet when I read the article, it simply set out what Vote Leave had been advocating for months. Change, argued Boris, would be gradual. There would continue to be unrestricted movement of goods and services. We would be outside the single market but able to access it. I felt incredulous that Peston was incredulous. Had he not taken seriously the points we Leavers have been making about the economy, trade policy and democracy for months – if not years? Or did he, too, see it all as part of some Westminster tea-room game, and only begin to listen once we had won?

'Do we', asked Peston on his Facebook page the day after the referendum, 'have any idea what we have chosen?' He would have had a pretty good idea of what a vote to leave would mean if he had read a thousand-page report, *Change, or Go?*, published by *Business for Britain* – one of Vote Leave's affiliate organizations. It would be a pity if he had never bothered to read it, while reporting on what Vote Leave wanted.

'I and all relevant broadcasters and journalists', wrote Peston, 'told you day after grinding campaign day that Leave would be a journey into the unknown.' Indeed, many did. But Brexit might have seemed a little less of an unknown if those reporting about it had studied what the Leavers were really after – and given them a fairer hearing. Having only ever talked about Euroscepticism as some sort of Tory disease, rather than as something central to our democracy, it must have come as quite a shock to realize that those beastly Eurosceptic backbenchers spoke for the majority of the country.

Perhaps the pundits are as bad at reading the political runes as they are at the economic ones? That would seem to be the view of a rising number of their listeners and viewers. The anti-politics revolt of the New Radicals is as much a reaction against an out-of-touch *commentariat* as it is a rebellion against career politicos.

Immediately after Vote Leave's victory, BBC Radio 4 commissioned the ardent Remain supporter, David Aaronovitch – he who had already insisted the referendum result be set aside – to make a programme to explain why people had voted to leave. It might be a bit like asking a Hanoverian princeling to explain the American Revolution. I am still waiting for them to commission those who supported the Vote Leave campaign, such as the best-selling historians Andrew Roberts or David Starkey, to explain why we won.

Not surprisingly, Aaronovitch's half-hour was full of suggestions that Leave voters were nostalgic, old-fashioned types, out of touch with contemporary Britain. It does not seem to occur to many commentators that it might be they who are out of touch with the country. Far from siding with the people against the politicians, the *commentariat* colludes with the political class to condescend. Far from holding the powerful to account, journalists cosy up to them.

Political journalists, once observed the great Australian election guru Lynton Crosby, come across ordinary members of the public when picking up their laundry at the dry cleaners. Or in the case of some, when taking a cab.

THE RULING CLIQUE

Shortly before the Brexit referendum, I was invited by the directors of a very august British institution to a rather grand gathering. Held in one of London's most magnificent landmark buildings, the guest list read like an extract from *Who's Who*.

The urbane peer who greeted me as I walked in was a former civil-servant-turned-minister, who had also run a major bank. Over drinks before dinner, I chatted in a crowded atrium to a man with a knighthood who chaired one of the largest (publicly funded) arts organizations in the country. He explained to me how hideous it had once been to have to appear before a Commons select committee to explain what he did with all that public money. Out of the corner of my eye I spotted various TV presenters and household names. Over dinner, I was seated next to a former UK ambassador to the United Nations, and opposite one of the richest hedge-fund managers in the world.

These are the kinds of people who really run the country. If you think I exaggerate, then let's just pluck one person out from that gathering who I had spied over drinks – Catherine Ashton – and examine her CV a little more closely.

Catherine – or Baroness Ashton of Upholland GCMG, PC – once worked for the Campaign for Nuclear Disarmament, before moving on to the Central Council for Education and Training in Social Work, a statutory body for social workers. From there, she went on to chair Hertfordshire Health Authority.

In 1999, she was made a Labour peer, before being appointed Parliamentary Under Secretary of State for Education. Then Parliamentary Under Secretary of State at the Department of Constitutional Affairs. Then Parliamentary Under Secretary of State at the Ministry of Justice.

In 2007, she was appointed a Cabinet minister and Leader of the House of Lords. Then an EU commissioner responsible for EU trade negotiations. She was eventually made the EU's first High Representative for Foreign and Security Policy: the Foreign Minister for some 500 million people.

But here's the thing. Catherine was never once elected to any of these offices. Despite having a major say on public policy throughout her career, from healthcare in Hertfordshire to the EU's global role, she has not once been voted to office by the actual public. Very many of those assembled at that gathering had had a great say over public policy – from funding of the arts to UK policy at the UN. And yet they were almost all entirely divorced from the public and what the public thought.

Of course, those at this dinner event represented only a tiny sample of the gilded clique that run the country. Not every quangocrat in Britain was there, but almost everyone there was representative of the sort of people who now run our country in the absence of effective democratic oversight.

All over the Western world, a new elite, or clique, has emerged, and it has detached itself from the rest of the *demos*. This new elite has little loyalty towards and even less interest in the life of ordinary people. It does not just not understand the concerns of ordinary voters – it treats such people with disdain, on everything from their attitudes to immigration to their coping with the cost of living.

Not surprisingly, those not on the guest list feel abandoned by this self-regarding clique and their virtue-signalling. As government has grown in most Western states, power has been centralized. Yet, paradoxically, far from putting more power in the hands of the politicians we elect, power has shifted from the formal executive branch of government into the hands of an 'extra-executive' branch.

In each of the five Parliamentary elections I have contested – as well as the one referendum campaign – the NHS featured a great deal. Voters in Britain care deeply about their system of publicly funded healthcare, and they vote accordingly.

But it is not those that we elect in Britain that run the NHS at all. The Care Quality Commission (CQC) decides if local doctors and hospitals are up to standard. The Clinical Commissioning Groups (CCGs), together with the National Institute of Clinical Excellence (NICE) determines what treatments might be available to local patients. Write to the health minister to complain about the (lack of) treatment a local voter is getting, and they will pass it on to the local NHS Trust.

As government has grown, more areas of public policy are run by an alphabet soup of government agencies – the FSA (Food Standards Agency), FCA (the Financial Conduct Authority), the Health and Safety Executive (HSE), to name but a few – all presided over by the kind of people I encountered at my dinner in London.

A panel of experts on the Bank of England's Monetary Policy Committee sets interest rates. Human rights lawyers decide migration rules. Regional quangos tell us where to build our houses. As an MP, I am only able to lobby, bully or cajole this hodgepodge of officialdom to give people the treatment they want. No wonder people lose faith in democracy if elections are fought about outcomes that no one elected can deliver.

Having spent much of that day campaigning for Vote Leave in Aston, Birmingham, I had hardly come across a single Remain supporter all day. Yet here over dinner in London, I was confronted by several fellow guests who expressed ill-concealed horror at the prospect of a Leave win. 'It would be unthinkable!' scoffed one particularly forthright fellow – a retired senior civil servant.

GROUPTHINK

To the kinds of people who run the country, leaving the European Union may indeed have seemed unthinkable. But that is not so much because it is a bad idea. Rather it reflects the solipsistic nature of those that govern us. They only ever mix with like-minded people.

A cliquey coterie decides public policy, yet they do not understand the concerns and aspirations of ordinary people. Because politics is a cartel, on everything from arts policy to foreign policy, MPs and ministers all too often end up accommodating themselves to the groupthink they find at the top – rather than challenging it and changing it. They often seem relieved to be able to cede decisions to unelected branches of government entirely.

Media scrutiny, instead of challenging assumptions, more often reinforces them. Many of the governing coterie think alike. They read the same books, discuss the same fashionable theories and ideas. They mix with people who think like them. Groupthink is a bad way to run anything. When combined with wishful thinking, it leads to disaster.

Wouldn't it be nice, thought officials, politicians and experts in America, if everybody could own their own home? So, they set about removing what they regarded as barriers preventing every American from buying. Even when the 'barrier' preventing people from taking out large loans was the fact that they plainly could not afford to do so.

HUD – the federal housing agency – together with Fannie Mae and Freddie Mac – the government-backed lending agencies – promoted changes to the law. They made it illegal to refuse a home loan to someone on the grounds that they might be considered by the lender to be a bad bet. The media was supine. There was no effective democratic oversight. The groupthink was never questioned.

And for a while, it seemed to work. More folk borrowed in order to buy their own home. Cheap loans pushed up the housing market. For two decades, both Republican and Democrat administrations presided over a gargantuan housing bubble. But no amount of wishful thinking can rewrite the laws of maths. Eventually reality reasserted itself. The bubble burst spectacularly, taking down not only home-owners but major banks around the world.

In Britain, the new elite had a certain image of the country's financial service sector. The City, they wanted to believe, was a golden goose that could pay our way. It would not just provide jobs and bonuses for those that worked there. Banks, they convinced themselves, would generate the tax revenue needed to pay for all expanded public services. Opposition parties that ought to have known better bought into the myth about 'sharing the proceeds of growth'. Financial journalists described as prudent one of the most imprudent chancellors Britain has ever had.

But no amount of wishful thinking could make that temporary surge in tax revenue a permanent addition to the tax base. So when the bubble burst, the country was left with a massive budget deficit, which a decade on we are still struggling to close.

Nowhere has there been more wishful thinking than in foreign policy. For the past decade, Western powers have waged a series of disastrous wars in the Middle East. We won them, thanks to the prowess of the military. But they have ended in strategic failure. Wishful thinking prevented us from seeing our enemies, like Iran, for what they were. Iran's strategic position has been immeasurably strengthened because of, not despite, the wars we have fought.

Worse, wishful think meant we did not see our 'frenemies' – enemies masquerading as friends, like Saudi Arabia and Turkey – for the anti-Western influences that they have proved to be. Last summer, over a million migrants predominantly from Syria, north Africa, Pakistan, Eritrea and Ethiopia crossed the Mediterranean into Europe. Some were refugees fleeing war. Most were migrants moving in search of a better life. Any sensible assessment of the situation would suggest that having a million-plus migrants from areas outside the West move, in the space of a few months, to settle in the West was going to present challenges.

Before welcoming them, as Angela Merkel did, as a useful addition to the workforce, it might have been prudent to ask how many were really going to join Germany's car-production lines. Would they welcome the opportunity to adopt a Western lifestyle, and all the freedoms that came with it? Or might they demand that the West conform to their cultural norms?

Rather than address any of that, policy-makers and pundits indulged in another fairy-tale fantasy. Media reporting ducked the big questions. Migrants, we were told, were welcome here – and anyone who said otherwise was morally suspect. Several British politicians told us they would house migrants in their own homes.

A year on, a series of bloody terror attacks – often perpetuated by those that crossed into Europe – have left almost 300 dead in Paris, Nice, Brussels and Berlin. Only now are the kind of questions that should have been posed from the outset being asked – and not just about open border immigration, but about two decades of Western intervention in the Middle East.

Only now has the glib analysis of the public policy implications of having hundreds of thousands of people flock into Europe begun to give way to a more grown-up conversation about questions of cultural compatibility. And no, there is nothing morally wrong in refusing to indulge in the new elites' fantasies about the merits of multiculturalism. Tens, or even hundreds, of millions across Europe do not either.

In the United States, under both Democrats and Republicans, twelve million illegal, unskilled migrants have been allowed to enter. It might not seem a problem if those migrants provide you with cheap home-help and gardening. But for many Americans, the welfare, justice and education systems have been clogged up as a consequence.

Even to make this kind of point on the broadcast news would be to invite the opprobrium of the presenters. But tens of millions of Americans are angry about it. And increasingly furious that they are not allowed to even mention it.

The new elite are so self-absorbed that they have failed to get to grips with some of the fundamental challenges facing many Western states. And they did not even notice how alarmed and angry voters have become.

4

THE CORRUPTION
OF CAPITALISM

You do not need to be an academic like Thomas Piketty or
an anti-capitalism activist like Paul Mason to be concerned
about rising inequality. It is something that should bother
us all.

In the UK, the richest 10 per cent of households in 2007–08
were over a hundred times wealthier than the poorest 10 per
cent. The top 10 per cent of households had wealth (including
personal possessions, financial assets, housing and private pension
rights) in excess of £853,000. For the poorest 10 per cent, the
figure was below £8,000.[7] In America, the top 10 per cent of
earners accounted for 45 per cent of all income by 2010, as
against 33 per cent forty years before. And everybody knows
that this rising inequality explains the rise of the New Radicals.
Right?

7   Hills, J. et al, *An Anatomy of Economic Inequality in the UK: Report of the National Equality Panel* (2010).

It's not quite so straightforward. The idea that the rise of the New Radicals is a consequence of increased inequality is part of what you might call the 'spirit-level' theory of happiness. In their highly influential book, *The Spirit Level*, Kate Pickett and Richard Wilkinson argued that a more equal society is a happier one. The less equal, the more malcontent.

Having accepted this assumption uncritically, many pundits plunge straight into discussing the causes of inequality – and globalization tends to be their number-one suspect. There certainly has been a lot more globalization. That worldwide network of economic interdependence, specialization and exchange has expanded enormously over the past few decades. Since the late 1980s and early 1990s, hundreds of millions of additional workers have been added to the productive base of the world economy. As China and India opened up economically, and the Cold War brought down the Iron Curtain, the labour supply in the global trading system approximately trebled in size.

In China alone, over seventy million manufacturing jobs have been created since 2000 – vastly more than the combined total of forty-two million manufacturing jobs recorded in the whole of Europe and the United States in 2012.[8] All that additional cheap labour meant lower median wage growth for Western workers. In America, the real median income of working-age males has only increased by 6 per cent since 1971.[9] It's why, they say, only 66 per cent of working-age American men today hold full-time jobs, a record low.

The rise of the New Radicals around the Western world is happening as foreign workers compete to do the same kinds of jobs for less pay, they tell us. Or to put it the way Donald Trump did, China and Mexico are 'stealing our jobs'. While he

8   King, M., *The End of Alchemy* (2016), p. 27.
9   Gilder, G., *The Scandal of Money: Why Wall Street Recovers But the Economy Never Does* (2016), p. 4.

rails against Mexicans, those on the New Radical left target 'neo-liberalism'. Neither side might like to admit it but by rejecting the free market they have more in common with one another than they imagine. They just cannot agree who is to blame.

To be fair to those a little queasy about sharing Donald Trump's language, they do sometimes point the finger at a second suspect for increasing inequality: technology. Wealth is becoming increasingly concentrated, they say, because of the new digital economy. How so?

Because in the digital world, marginal costs are low. The cost of producing one app once, or producing it a million times, are not that different. The leading product in the digital marketplace does not just hold a large share of the market. It often ends up monopolizing the market.

Think of the top-selling family cars. General Motors has 17 per cent of the American market. Ford has 16 per cent. There is even space in the market for Volkswagen and Mazda with a tiddly 3 and 2 per cent respectively. But compare that to digital products. Who uses any search engine besides Google? What was the name of that thing you used to talk to friends online before Facebook? For many, Facebook *is* social media. Uber started out as one of a number of taxi-summoning apps. It has become ubiquitous – not only in New York or London, but Delhi and Nairobi, too.

The winner takes all. There is not much reward for being second best. While digital concentrates enormous wealth in the hands of a few superstar successes, the new technology, we are told, is starting to automate jobs that Joe Average might have once done. Mark Zuckerberg and co. might be able to amass vast fortunes, but millions of low-skilled workers lose their jobs. Or so the theory goes.

But is this really the case? Have digital technology and globalization really impoverished blue-collar America or working-class

Brits? It's a fact that in 1964, 97 per cent of working-age men in America with just a high-school education were in the labour market. Today, it is just 83 per cent.[10] And to be sure, many of the jobs that working-age blue-collar workers would have done in 1964 have disappeared.

But it simply does not follow that globalization and technology have driven down living standards. Hundreds of millions of extra Chinese, Indian and Eastern European workers might have joined the global workforce. But at the same time tens of millions of new jobs have been generated in the West, too.

In 1990, there were 109 million Americans in employment. Today there are 144 million. In Britain, the workforce has increased from 27 million to 31 million. Far from mass unemployment, there are more jobs in Britain and America today than ever before[11] – and this great growth spurt in job-creation has coincided with greater global economic interdependence.

Many of the new jobs might be low paid, but globalization also means lots of cheap, more affordable consumer goods. If globalization has dragged down median wages for blue-collar America and Britain, it has also slashed the cost of living for millions.

Since 1996, the real cost of household appliances has fallen by over 40 per cent. The cost of footwear and clothes by 60 per cent. Previous generations of mums and dads struggling to make ends meet complained about not being able to afford shoes for their kids. Today's parents can buy them from Tesco for five quid. With the real price of TVs and music players down by 90 per cent, their kids don't just have more shoes. They probably have a TV in their bedroom, too.

10 Heath, A., 'Yes, some people really struggle, but inequality isn't the problem' (*Daily Telegraph*, 27 July 2016).
11 And just in case you think that population growth in America or Britain accounts for the rise in the workforce, bear in mind that the rise in the number of jobs has grown faster than the increase in population.

Right-wing Republicans might not mention it, but if Joe Six-pack now earns less due to globalization, he is also able to afford an awful lot more from Walmart or Wilko because of it. Hardly a driver of inequality, global trade now means that average income earners can have the kind of consumer goods we once considered luxuries.

In the late nineteenth century, America went through an industrial revolution. Rather like today, a fortuitous few amassed great wealth. Cornelius Vanderbilt, the Mark Zuckerberg of his day, made his first fortune from steam boats, before moving into railways. Many of the 'robber barons' of late-nineteenth-century America – Andrew Carnegie, John Rockefeller – were, if not directly involved in railways, instrumental in supplying the steel and the coal that powered them. Perhaps today's technological revolution, rather like the previous railway revolution, is creating a new class of 'digital barons'?

Of course, some digital entrepreneurs – Peter Thiel, co-founder of PayPal, Amazon's Jeff Bezos, Google's Larry Page or Sergey Brin – have made fortunes. However tempting it might be to write them up as 'digital barons', these new tech fortunes cannot account for the rise of the new rich since the 1960s. For a start, the big spurts in income inequality happened in the 1970s and 1980s, long before businesses like Amazon, Facebook or PayPal were even conceivable.

Last year, the top six highest-paid CEOs in Britain worked for WPP (an advertising group), Shell (the oil conglomerate), Reed Elsevier (a publishing house), TUI Group (a tourist firm), Prudential (the financial service group) and Lloyds Bank. Even in America, where there are many more digital giants, many of the best-paid CEOs worked for companies in long-established sectors, such as entertainment and television.

The emergence of a new super-rich might be happening. It's just not got as much to do with the digital economy as many suppose.

ASSET WEALTH V. WAGE WEALTH

There is an even more fundamental problem with the 'Globalization + Digital = Inequality' equation: there has just not been enough inequality. Over the past two decades, we have seen much greater globalization and the take-off of the digital economy. *But if anything, income inequality has actually declined.*

You read that right. The big increases in inequality in almost every Western nation happened before 1990, and ahead of globalization and the digital revolution. Inconveniently for many, facts about inequality just do not fit their theories.

In Britain, the Gini coefficient – that benchmark measure of income inequality – rose sharply in the decades before 1990. It has stopped rising and, if anything, has shown a slight decrease since. In 1977, the richest 10 per cent in Britain accounted for 22 per cent of total household income. Today, they collect 26 per cent of total income. But all of that increase took place between 1977 and 1987. Since the end of the 1980s, the top 10 per cent's share of total income has hardly changed.

In fact, since 2007–08 it is the bottom 10 per cent who have enjoyed a 7.7 per cent growth in incomes, against 2.2 per cent for median earners, and roughly zero change for the top tenth of earners.

In America, the top 1 per cent of income-earners still make 13 per cent less than they did in 2007 before the recession, according to Emmanuel Saez, a professor at Berkeley. The bottom 90 per cent make around 8 per cent less. The gap between rich and poor has therefore narrowed. The Congressional Budget Office's latest calculations suggest that inequality was almost 5 per cent lower in 2013, the latest year for which figures are available, than it was in 2007.

By focusing on income inequality, the 'spirit-levellers' have missed the point about inequality. There are two kinds of inequality: inequality of income – what you earn, or receive in payments of one kind or another – and inequality in terms of overall wealth – the value of things you own, like a house or shares. With everyone debating income inequality, few seem to have noticed that since the early 1990s there has been the growth of a different kind of inequality. It is not the one between income groups but between those who own assets and those who don't.

Asset prices have risen very steeply since the early 1990s, far faster than average earnings. This means that those with assets are wealthier, and those with only earnings much poorer relative to the value of assets.

In Britain in 1985, for example, the average house price was approximately 2.5 times average annual income. By 2005, it was approximately 5 times average annual income. In large swathes of London and the South East of England, average house prices are 7 or 8 times average regional incomes.

Since a lot of (older) wage-earners own their own homes in Britain and America, they have been to some extent insulated from the worst effects of asset price increases relative to wages. But of course, the younger generation – who do not generally own their own homes – have not been. This helps explain why, in 2014, an extraordinary one-third of all Americans between the ages of eighteen and thirty-one had not yet moved out of their parents' home.[12]

Blue-collar Britain and America are not unhappy because they are not keeping up with the Joneses – or even the Zuckerbergs. The problem is that their wage wealth has fallen far behind the rising value of those assets – like houses – that they aspire to buy.

The problem is not that incomes are too unequal. They are simply too low. According to the McKinsey Global Institute, 81 per cent of Americans in 2016 were in an income bracket that

12 Gilder, G., *The Scandal of Money: Why Wall Street Recovers But the Economy Never Does* (2016), p. 4.

had either flatlined or fallen over the previous decade. In Italy, the figure was 97 per cent, in the UK 70 per cent and in France 63 per cent.

Since 1990, it is only the very, very rich – the 1 per cent, or perhaps the 0.1 per cent, not the top 10 per cent – who have seen their relative income share grow significantly. According to Thomas Piketty, the rise of the super-rich is an inevitable consequence of free-market capitalism. Why? Because capitalism, he suggests, has reached a stage where the returns on capital – profits, rents, dividends – will inevitably grow faster than the economy overall. Oligarchy is emerging from capitalism's unavoidable concentration of wealth.

Piketty is right to identify the emergence of a class of super-remunerated corporate 'fat cats'. But he is wrong to suppose that this is a natural consequence of capitalism. It's the story of capitalism's corruption.

THE RISE OF A CORPORATE KLEPTOCRACY

The average Chief Executive Officer of a FTSE 100 firm in Britain in 2015 earned £3.8 million, or 138 times the median annual salary of £27,600[13]. This was a 49 per cent increase on what the average FTSE 100 CEO had been paid the year before. The six highest-paid UK CEOs took home a combined total of over £100 million. Six average Brits would have earned £166,000 between them over the same period. That was small change, compared to the $363 million that the six highest-paid CEOs in America received – an average of over $60 million each.

While generous final-salary pension schemes have been rolled up for most workers in the West, dozens of executives have continued

13 See Office of National Statistics data https://www.ons.gov.uk/employment andlabourmarket/peopleinwork/earningsandworkinghours/bulletins/annual surveyofhoursandearnings/2015provisionalresults

to get the most extraordinary pension privileges, paid for by the business over which they preside, even after tax incentives for this were withdrawn.

GlaxoSmithKline's Sir Andrew Witty received a payment of £735,000 into his pension pot. Lloyd's bank boss Antonio Horta-Osorio was paid a cash sum of £568,000, about half his annual salary, in lieu of pension contributions. The average employee, however, now receives pension payments worth just 2.5 per cent of their salary.[14]

'But that's just what CEOs get paid,' I hear you say. 'It's the market rate.' Really? It might be the going rate, but does that make it the market rate? If high pay was a reflection of market value, you would expect poor performance to be punished with lower pay. On the contrary, recent corporate history shows that inflated pay packets and corporate incompetence more often go together.

In a free market, reward is associated with risk. But the FTSE 100 chiefs who get the largest rewards are not taking any risks with their own money. They are corporate administrators, not entrepreneurs. So why the big rewards? Corporate pay is not rising because of 'the market' but because conventional corporate governance no longer works. The rules that underpin capitalism, and which ought to make those that run businesses accountable to those that own them, have been subverted – allowing executives to pay themselves ever more.

In a capitalist system, capital resides in private hands. And in private hands, it mobilizes labour and other resources to produce things. This is typically done through a company, a legal vehicle that allows the owners of private capital – the shareholders – to club together as joint owners of an enterprise, uniting not only capital, but labour, ideas and innovation. The shareholders might run the business themselves or appoint directors to run it on their behalf.

14 The *Sunday Times*, 'Business' section, 6 November 2016.

That is the theory. In practice, those appointed to run the company on behalf of the owners might seek to help themselves to company resources at the shareholders' expense. This is hardly a new problem. It's as old as capitalism itself.

On 31 December 1600, Queen Elizabeth I granted a charter to a new venture, the East India Company. The charter gave the Company a monopoly to trade between England and India, and, for the next couple of centuries, the Company set about taking full advantage of such rights to enrich itself at the expense of just about everyone.

In India, the Company obtained local monopolies on everything from indigo to cotton. It became a military machine, issuing its own currency and collecting taxes. In China, the East India Company smuggled in drugs, when it could not find anything else to sell the locals. And it was, of course, tea from East India Company ships that was thrown into Boston Harbor in 1773 by irate Americans, upset not so much about the tax on the tea as the fact that only East India Company ships were permitted to carry it.

Nor did those that ran the East India Company only extort distant colonials. They exploited their customers and shareholders, too. Far from aiming to provide cotton and tea to the masses at affordable prices, the Company ran a racket, lobbying to outlaw any competition in order to hike up its prices.

Shareholders were consistently cheated by the Company Men that ran the business when they set aside space on the Company ships for goods they were trading privately, alongside trade being done on the Company books. This was so rewarding for a few Company Men that it created a new class of super-rich in England, known by the Indian term *nabobs*, or nobs.[15]

---

15 The term 'nob' is still in use today as a slang term to denote a person of great wealth or high social status.

The Company itself constantly needed to be bailed out by the government.[16] Writing in the late eighteenth century, Adam Smith was highly critical of the charter-company model generally, and the East India Company specifically. He particularly objected to the behaviour of the Company in Bengal. But he saw how the charter-company model had allowed those that ran the business to prioritize their interests over those of the shareholders.

In the early stages of the Industrial Revolution, most businesses in England and America simply were not big enough – or far-flung enough – to experience this kind of conflict between shareholder and manager. Before the mid-nineteenth century, and the 1844 Joint Stock Companies Act, most businesses would not have been incorporated at all.[17] Most in Britain, America and much of Europe were in fact individually- or family-owned outfits, or unincorporated associations and partnerships. The question of how those who owned these businesses might oversee those that ran them seldom arose.

It was only in the last two decades of the nineteenth century that business really started to get big. Industrial giants emerged both in America – Standard Oil, Edison, J. P. Morgan, General Electric, Carnegie Steel, AT&T Bell, Sears, Woolworths – and in Germany – Krupps and IG Farben. Initially, the 'robber barons' who built up these big industrial businesses maintained owner-control. Often notoriously so.

Yet eventually the buccaneers who created these behemoths

16 During its 275-year history, the East India Company frequently benefited from state support of one kind or another. Perhaps the biggest direct bailout came in 1772, when the government rescued it from failure following famine in Bengal. To help the Company pay back its debt to government, it was granted mercantile privileges to export tea to the American colonies, provoking a little difficulty in Boston Harbor in 1773.

17 There were a number of Charter companies created in the seventeenth and eighteenth centuries – the French called them *sociétés anonymes* and the Dutch had their *Vereenigde Oost-Indische Compagnie* or *VOC*. Yet these kind of state-sponsored businesses were the exception rather than the norm.

ceded control to a new cadre of managerial executives. The problem that Smith foresaw in the eighteenth century, which occurred when ownership and control were separated, suddenly became widespread. It was recognized as a major problem in the early 1930s by Adolf Berle and Gardiner Means, whose masterful *The Modern Corporation and Private Property* showed the extent to which those who legally own companies no longer had effective control over them.

Corporate law in America had evolved, they suggested, in such a way that those with day-to-day responsibility for the management of the company were able to manage the resources of companies to their own advantage without effective shareholder scrutiny. Courts, Berle and Means found, had gradually diluted shareholder rights. 'The property owner who invests in a modern corporation', they noted, 'so far surrenders his wealth to those in control of the corporation that he has exchanged the position of independent owner for one in which he may become merely recipient of the wages of capital.'

It was to strengthen shareholder rights that, in the early part of the twentieth century, governments passed new legislation. Statutory audits were introduced in the UK in 1900, and in 1907 public firms were required to file balance sheets. The 1928 Companies Act allowed shareholders to insist that they see a copy of audited accounts. Similar changes were introduced in America.

Tighter corporate governance reined in the new breed of corporate executives that managed corporate America and Britain. Executive largesse in the form of big salaries and expenses-paid packages, such a feature of American capitalism in the 1920s, receded. Income inequality had declined by the middle of the century.

So, what has changed since then? Why are shareholders who own the business suddenly no longer able to exercise control over those that run the business? Why is this problem of shareholder control, recognized by Adam Smith in the eighteenth century, once again such a pressing problem in the twenty-first century?

RENTIER INVESTORS

Between 2000 and 2008, the FTSE All-Share Index fell 30 per cent. In other words, shareholders who had invested in FTSE All-Share companies had lost, on average, close to one third of what they had put in.

Yet while those that owned those firms lost a third of the value of their investment, what did those who managed those businesses do? Did they tighten their belts? Did they take a pay cut? Not at all. Executive pay of those running FTSE All-Share firms rose a staggering 80 per cent.

A 2016 report by Weijia Li and Steven Young of Lancaster University Management School found a negligible link between CEO pay and investor value among the top 350 publicly listed UK firms. Between 2003–2014, CEO pay rose on average 82%, but returns for investors in those firms increased only marginally.

Those that run big FTSE firms today might not trade much in the way of tea, indigo or cotton. And they might treat their overseas suppliers with a little more respect. But like the East India Company of old they are in the business of enriching themselves at the expense of both their customers and their shareholders. This helps account for the emergence of the new class of corporate nabobs since the 1960s – and the problem is getting worse.

Corporate boardrooms are stuffed full of those adept at helping themselves to other people's wealth. Rather than do it via derring-do on the high seas, they prefer to do it through remuneration committees. 'The salary of the chief executive of the large corporations is not market reward for achievement,' explained the economist J.K. Galbraith. 'It is frequently in the nature of a warm personal gesture by the individual to himself.'

Or rather from the non-executives on the remuneration committee that he recruited.

J.K. Galbraith also once remarked that for a career in finance 'a nicely conformist nature, a good tailor and the ability to articulate the currently fashionable cliché have usually been better for personal success than an excessively inquiring mind'.[18] He could have said much the same about those found in City boardrooms today. Boardrooms are supposed to hold the CEO and senior management to account. In reality, they very rarely oust a mediocre boss. Underperformance is more often excused than exposed.

So why don't shareholders do something about it? Very occasionally, they try. In 2016, for example, BP shareholders revolted against a £14 million-a-year pay packet that the board of BP had approved for CEO Bob Dudley. There have been other similar rebellions against the pay packets of senior executives. Yet what happened at BP rather neatly illustrates the problem. The shareholder vote was simply ignored by the management. Bob Dudley got his money regardless of what those that owned BP thought about it.

Those who control the boardroom – the CEO, chairman and finance director – are able to fend off such shareholder revolts with relative ease. Rather like the small print of our representative democracy, the small print of corporate governance has been watered down to ensure that those at the helm do not have to answer to those to whom they are supposed to be accountable. The BP shareholder vote was deemed to be non-binding in law. The small print said that it was only advisory.

But even so, why don't shareholders revolt more often? Because the nature of shareholding has changed over the past three or four decades to such an extent that there often isn't a body of shareholders to revolt.

18 Galbraith, J. K., *Money: Whence It Came, Where It Went* (1975), p. 315.

Until a generation or so ago, millions of individual shareholders – large or small – tended to own shares directly. As late as the 1980s, when British Gas or British Telecom were privatized, tens of thousands of people bought a slice of them. Today, instead of owning shares directly, an increasing number of investors hold shares indirectly. They might do so via a pension fund. Or perhaps they will buy unit trusts, or save in some sort of individual savings account.

Instead of being shareholders in the traditional sense, investors own a stake in an investment fund instead. This fund might consist of a mixture of shares in, say, UK small cap firms, or businesses that trade with emerging markets. Sometimes an investor might not just own a stake in a fund, but in a fund that itself comprises a mixture of funds – a so-called fund of funds. There are even funds of funds of funds you can invest in.

And managing all these funds will often be a fund manager – paid a large fee for doing so. There has been an explosive growth in the fund management industry over the past thirty or forty years. What was once seen as just an off-shoot of the banking industry is today a multi-billion-pound business. Fund management has become the mainstay of the City of London and Wall Street, eclipsing investment banking in terms of the bonuses it pays.

By investing through fund managers, investors are not simply contracting out responsibility for selecting stocks. They are also delegating oversight of the executives who manage the businesses in which their money is invested. It doesn't work.

Many of the conventional safeguards given to conventional shareholders to enable them to protect their interests – pre-emptive rights when new capital is required, votes at the AGM – are simply not tools that most fund managers would want to wield. Corporate law allows shareholders to appoint directors to the board, committed to acting in their interest. But as often as not, when a boardroom vacancy occurs, it is filled by word of mouth. Or a head hunter, paid to find someone who would fit in.

A mini-industry has grown up to fill such vacancies with the kind of people whose careers, as Ayn Rand might have put it, 'depend on keeping faces bland, remarks inconclusive and clothes immaculate'. In practice, the board recommends who should join the board – with shareholders left to rubber-stamp their decision. Presiding over almost every big publicly listed company is the very definition of a self-perpetuating clique.

Between 2000 and 2008, HBOS's exposure to commercial property rose 600 per cent. The board nodded along with it. Far from recognizing the danger, fund managers seemed to think it was a good thing, increasing their investors' exposure to HBOS. RBS's exposure to commercial property likewise soared by 21 per cent a year. In 2007, RBS compounded that existential risk with the ill-judged acquisition of ABN Amro. No one on the board seems to have asked the obvious questions about the wisdom of the deal. Few of those highly paid City analysts seem to have analysed the big black hole at the heart of the takeover.

Perhaps they were influenced more by the PR hype about RBS boss Fred Goodwin than they were by the numbers? Which, if you think about it, is odd for a profession that is supposed to be all about numbers. In 2003, HSBC spent $14 billion buying the US subprime lender Household International. The firm turned out to be worse than worthless. Did any of the great institutional investors that held shares in HSBC spot any of these elementary flaws?

Things have been exacerbated since the 2007 financial crisis, with a massive shift in investor funds out of so-called active management funds – where at least the fund managers were supposed to assess how the firms performed before putting in any money – into so-called passive funds. In a passive fund, capital is allocated by indexes and algorithms. No one even pretends to assess how the businesses the fund invests in are being run.

PUBLIC-SECTOR FAT CATS

'You see! Private-sector fat cats are the problem,' you intervene. 'Owen Jones and those other anti-capitalist campaigners are right. The private sector is full of people and organizations enriching themselves at everyone else's expense!'

Corporate fat cats are no more an expression of free-market capitalism than the East India Company was about free trade. They represent a corruption of capitalism. Free-market capitalism has morphed into a form of crony corporatism. And crony corporatism is not confined to the private sector at all. If corporate 'fat cats' are a product of the free market, why are there so many of them in the public sector, too?

Corporate avarice exists wherever there is a big organization presided over by a remote, unaccountable elite, overseen by a supine board. Such as the BBC. In 2005–06, the BBC boss Mark Thompson was paid £609,000, at a time when the BBC was making 3,000 job cuts. Mr Thompson was paid £788,000 the next year, and £834,000 the year after that. Over two years, the increase in his salary alone – £225,000 – was more than ten times the average total household income of licence-fee payers in my corner of Essex.

Did anyone in the BBC boardroom challenge this at the time? Or did they all keep their faces bland and remarks inconclusive, too? They can hardly have argued that Thompson was getting the 'market rate'. At that time, commercial television providers were cutting corporate pay in response to belt-tightening in the television sector. Tony Hall, the current Director General of the BBC, earned £450,000 this year. Over fifty BBC executives now earn more than the prime minister. The head of OFCOM, the broadcaster regulator, is on £400,000 a year.

Public-sector employees, it was once said, trade in lower salaries for more job security. Not anymore, it seems. Big-buck salaries, like those at the BBC, are increasingly commonplace across the corporate public sector. Network Rail management are paid banker-style salaries. Simon Kirby, the CEO of HS2, earned £750,000 in 2015. The head of Transport for London, £345,000. Jim O'Sullivan, head of Highways England, over £330,000. Antony Douglas, CEO, Defence Equipment and Support, more than £285,000.

NHS Trusts, like the one Catherine Ashton used to run, routinely pay over a quarter of a million a year to their top officials. Tricia Hart, chief executive of South Tees Hospitals NHS Foundation Trust, earned a package worth £1.26 million, much of it in pensions contributions, in 2014.[19] Alan Perkins, the head of something called the NHS Health and Social Care Information Centre, was reported to have received a pay packet worth £844,794.[20] There are now over 50,000 NHS employees on pay deals worth more than £100,000 a year.[21]

Cumbria County Council's Jill Stannard had a pay deal worth over £410,000.[22] Dozens of local borough council bosses now get over £300,000 a year. In Scotland, the deputy chief constable, Steven Allan, was on an eye-watering £737,500.[23]

Big government seems to be doing its best to drive up income inequality, too. In 2011, Britain's Ministry of Defence handed out £45 million in bonuses to its top bureaucrats. Last year, the US Department for Veteran Affairs gave out $142 million in bonuses – to its top officials, of course, not to actual veterans. US federal officials now earn 84 per cent more than workers in the private sector.

University academics might claim they are underpaid and undervalued. Perhaps they should have a word with their

19 *Daily Mail*, 9 November 2015.
20 Ibid.
21 Ibid.
22 Ibid.
23 Ibid.

vice-chancellors. In 2014, 7,554 university staff were on over £100,000 a year, with the average annual pay packet for a university vice-chancellor over a quarter of a million pounds.[24] In 2014–15, Oxford's vice-chancellor, Professor Andrew Hamilton, was reported to be taking home £462,000. King's College London's Professor Edward Byrne, £458,000. Imperial College's Professor Alice Gast, £430,000.

Corporate avarice is not free-market capitalism at work. It is what happens when those that run big, resource-rich organizations are able to help themselves to a larger and larger slice of those organizations' revenues.

GRAFT

'Until August 1914', wrote the English historian A. J. P. Taylor, an 'Englishman could pass through life and hardly notice the existence of the state... Broadly speaking, the state acted only to help those who could not help themselves. It left the adult citizen alone.'

You could not say the same of his great-grandchildren today. From the moment he gets out of bed, a blizzard of EU rules and regulations touches everything around him. Martin Durkin's *Brexit: The Movie* shows Mr Average literally rising from his bed. There are 109 EU rules or regulations specifying how the pillow his head rests on must be made. Thirty-nine for the sheets and ten for his duvet. Assuming he has a radio-alarm clock, mobile phone and pair of glasses on it, almost 400 EU rules will prescribe what is allowed on his bedside table. When he cleans his teeth, there are 31 rules for his toothbrush and 47 for the toothpaste, 172 for the mirror, 454 for the bathroom towel. When he has breakfast, there are 1,246 rules for bread, 52 for toasters, 84 for the fridge, 99 for his bowl, 210 for his spoon, 202 for the orange juice and

24 Ibid.

625 for the coffee. He has not even made it out of the house, and the minutiae of everything around him is regulated.

Why? How come there are so many rules regulating the smallest details of our existence? Perhaps you think it's because folk today want more rules. We're less sturdy and devil-may-care, you might think. And to be sure, I suppose most mums and dads today would expect the toys they buy their children to have been checked for toxic substances. And the food they buy for their family to be deemed safe for our consumption. But regulation in Britain, Europe and America often goes far beyond that.

But if all this regulation was by popular demand, why is it being introduced by unelected officials? Increasingly European Union rules do not just specify what can be produced, but how. The question we should ask instead is *cui bono*? Who gains from all this rule-making?

It's pretty obvious who gained from the rules that were introduced across the EU in the 1990s and early Noughties to promote the use of diesel cars, rather than those that ran on petrol. As a direct result of EU rules, there was a massive switch in the European car market from the late 1990s towards diesel engines. In the mid-1990s, less than one in ten cars sold in the UK was diesel. By 2012, it was over half.

Why did EU officials encourage this drive for diesel? It was to help the environment, apparently. Diesel emits marginally less CO_2 than petrol. Forcing EU consumers to make the switch would cut carbon dioxide. Yet for those pushing for this change, perhaps this was only the pretext. The real reason why European car-makers had lobbied the EU institutions to rig the rules in favour of diesel was because it suited their commercial self-interest. German car-makers in particular had a technical advantage over their rivals when it came to diesel engines. If they could make Europeans buy more diesel, they would do better against their non-European competitors.

Far from being better for the environment, diesel is actually much, much dirtier. Thanks to the new rules, European cities, like London, now have dangerous levels of nitrogen dioxide (NO_2). Europeans have died as a direct consequence of the change in policy to favour diesel.

But to conceal the consequences of their dirty diesel, guess what the corporate car manufacturers did next? Having rigged the EU's rules to favour diesel, some car companies appear to have rigged the engine emissions tests to make it seem as if their toxic engines were only producing a fraction of the pollutants that they were generating. And, of course, hundreds of lobbyists engaged by EU car companies earned a very good living working in Brussels by promoting this anti-competitive agenda.

In a normal competitive market, businesses would spend their marketing budgets seeking to persuade customers to buy their product at a price they are willing to pay. Instead many big businesses and corporations spend much of their marketing budget paying an army of lobbyists to rig the rules so that the customer has to buy what it is selling – and to keep out the competition.

It's not just the car industry. Just as the EU claimed to be promoting diesel to enhance the environment, they banned the use of something called hexavalent chromium. As a direct consequence, a small business in my part of Essex had to stop producing some of its most successful products.

To be fair, hexavalent chromium, unless used in carefully controlled conditions, can do dreadful damage. But many in the industry suspect that the real reason for the clamp down was that various vested interests, which operated a rival coating process, wanted to close out the competition. So, the small business that used to manufacture using the newly banned process, and sell what it made around the world, now imports alternative components from China.

It's a similar story with a small steel fabrication business in my constituency, which suddenly found it could no longer sell what it had produced for generations. From July 2014, it became a serious criminal offence to sell steel products that did not comply with the European Construction Products directive. Of course, the big steel fabricators, who had helped lobby for the new rules, could meet the cost easily. A village-based business in rural Essex could not.

Who gained, eh? EU rule-making is often supported and encouraged by big business interests – pharmaceutical corporations, banks, multinationals – who know that they can absorb the costs of compliance but that their smaller rivals cannot. Thousands of lawyers and lobbyists, representing all manner of corporate interests, fill the bars, restaurants and corridors of Brussels, seeking to ensure they get the outcomes that suit their clients. A tax break here. A new regulation to shut out the competition there.

Big corporates co-opt political insiders to influence policy-making. It's hardly surprising. With so much hanging on good relations with officialdom, big business needs members of the new elite to help get the public policy outcomes it wants. The new elite trade their insider expertise. Public policy is made with little reference to the public.

Public or private sector, an organization's commercial success boils down to one thing: the difference between costs and revenues. If revenue exceeds cost, it turns a profit. If the reverse, it makes a loss – and in time would normally have to fold. Corporations in both the public and private sector – be they FTSE firms, universities, mega-charities or the BBC – all have one thing in common. Their revenues, costs and profit depend less on a mass of paying customers, students, donors or viewers, and more on officialdom.

That is not to say they do not have individual paying customers.

It is just that a corporation's most important relationship is with government, either as customer, benefactor or regulator.

For many big businesses, government is not merely an important source of income – it is *the* customer. In Britain, the big four corporate contractors – Atos, Capita, G4S and Serco – are routinely awarded contracts worth billions to deliver public services. According to the National Audit Office, 50 per cent of the public sector's £187 billion expenditure on goods and services is spent through contracting out.

In the United States, defence contractors are big business – and their customer is almost exclusively the Pentagon. Contracts are negotiated with officials. Prices are fixed by official fiat. In Britain and the EU, energy is generated by a handful of large producers, not according to cost considerations and the customer but in compliance with quotas. A state regulator, OFGEM, oversees what prices providers charge British customers and on what terms.

Nuclear generation alone receives a direct subsidy of £2.3 billion a year in Britain. British Telecom might have been privatized a generation ago but the firm still took a £1.2 billion subsidy to roll out rural broadband. Between 2007 and 2011, government gave the UK's five largest rail firms direct subsidies totalling £3 billion.[25] A rail regulator determines how much rail-service operators can charge passengers to travel.

Like the railways, the BBC has millions of paying customers. But they, too, are a captive market. Licence-fee payers contribute £3.7 billion a year into the Corporation's coffers. The alternative to buying a TV licence is often criminal proceedings: in 2014, 185,621 people were prosecuted for non-payment, according to Ministry of Justice figures.

25 Jones, O., *The Establishment: And How They Get Away With It* (2014), p. 172.

Universities in Britain receive 24 per cent of their income directly through government grants. It is officialdom that gives out the Tier 4 visas that allow universities to offer lucrative places to overseas students to come and study in the UK. Even the 32 per cent of funding that universities get from student tuition-fee-paying customers comes with official backing. It is thanks to a government-backed lending scheme that many students are able to borrow the fees in the first place. Meanwhile, the not-for-profit sector, despite repudiating the idea of profit, depends even more than many big businesses on official largesse to run a surplus ('surplus' meaning any money left over after paying staff salaries).

Despite the best efforts of many thousands of individual fundraisers, cake-bakers and fun-runners, big corporate charities depend more on government than private donors for their funding. Of Oxfam's £401 million revenue in 2014–15, government provided almost twice as much (£191 million) as private donors (£100 million). Save the Children depends on the UK government and the EU for £199 million of its £390 million budget – almost half. Private donations from individuals, although important, account for a mere 30 per cent of its total revenue.

It is because the success of big organizations – businesses, corporate charities, universities, the BBC – depends on what officialdom decides that lobbying has grown into a multi-billion-pound industry. Major corporate organizations including BP pay Peter (Lord) Mandelson, the former Labour cabinet minister, for the services of his 'strategic advisory firm', Global Counsel. Geoff Hoon, the former defence minister, was taken on by a big defence contractor on leaving office as the managing director of international business. Former health minister Alan Milburn was hired by Bridgepoint Capital, Lloyds Pharmacy and even PepsiCo. Patricia Hewitt, shortly after standing down as health secretary, was take on at £300 per hour by Alliance Boots, who get 40 per cent of their money from NHS contracts. A private equity group, which ran hospitals, hired her at £500 per hour. She went on to become a director of healthcare company Bupa, and even a £75,000-a-year non-executive director of BT.

Perhaps these former ministers got these jobs because they had some previously hidden entrepreneurial flair? Maybe they had a razor-sharp commercial sense? Or perhaps, for businesses that depend so much on government largesse, these ex-ministers knew their way around government?

Here's the stinking hypocrisy at the heart of contemporary politics. Sophisticated commentators endlessly assert that New Radical supporters are losers. They have, we are told, been 'left behind' by globalization and greater competition. Actually, it's the corporatist oligarchy that is endlessly lobbying to limit competition and control the market.

Like British businessmen in the late nineteenth century, who felt threatened by the advent of industrial competition from America and Germany, today's corporatist cartels in Britain, Europe and America are on the defensive. They might talk as if they are embracing global competition, but it turns out they are circling the wagons. In 1974, the output of the top 100 US industrial firms accounted for 35.6 per cent of US GDP. By 1998, that had fallen to 17.3 per cent. Big was in retreat, with giant firms like AT&T or British Leyland running into trouble. For much of the 1980s and early 1990s, boardroom talk was all about small, nimble upstarts and start-ups.

But big is back. Since the late 1990s, there has been more corporate concentration. There's been a sharp surge in mergers and acquisitions. The share of GDP generated by America's one hundred biggest companies rose from 33% in 1994 to 46% in 2013.[26] A new class of corporate titans – Google, Apple and co. – has arisen. Despite the image we might have of lots

26 *Economist*, A Giant Problem, Sept 17, 2016.

of free-wheeling, entrepreneurial hipsters on the West Coast of America or in East London, there has been a marked decline in the number of start-ups.

On Wall Street, the five largest US banks have increased their share of US banking assets dramatically in the past decade and a half, from 25 per cent in 2000 to 45 per cent today.[27] For all the talk of disruption, big corporations have consolidated their grip on those parts of the economy – such as pharmaceuticals or finance – where officialdom plays a major role. But perhaps officialdom plays a major role precisely because big corporations want it that way.

The superstar firms can entrench their position through lobbying – which is why so many hi-tech firms in the US give quite so many jobs to Washington insiders. Many of the recent regulatory changes on either side of the Atlantic – the Sarbanes-Oxley Act, EU online VAT rules, changes to the US tax code – hurt smaller firms far more than they effect the giants, with their big compliance departments.

Crony corporatism is prevalent in the protected and regulated sectors of the economy. It's there that lobbying pays – and where big business has a vested interest in ensuring that lobbying pays. Today's corporate elite might have accumulated great fortunes for themselves, but their prime business agenda is to preserve the source of that wealth. Like every oligarchy, they use political power to exclude competition and pre-empt any challenge.

Those late-nineteenth/early-twentieth-century British business-men hit upon an idea to stave off the competition: imperial preference. Setting aside a century-old commitment to free trade, businesses lobbied to turn the British empire into a giant market, surrounded by a tariff wall. TTIP – the Transatlantic Trade and Investment Partnership – is something remarkably similar. Like

27 Ibid.

imperial preference, it might use the language of open markets but it is essentially protectionist. It is an attempt by US and EU business interests to protect themselves against the advent of China.

Early-twentieth-century Brits tried to keep out the Germans with tariffs. Today's TTIP protectionists aim to do it through regulations and standards. The goal is to establish international – or at least transatlantic – trade standards before China – or anyone else – is strong enough to set them.

TTIP aims to extend to transatlantic trade the sort of system already used to regulate trade and commerce inside the European single market. Far from giving businesses more freedom to produce and sell their wares in more markets, the EU single market is a permission-based system. A firm can only produce and sell its wares if it does so in compliance with complex single market rules – often drafted by vested interests to keep out the competition.

Single-market rules no longer simply specify what can be produced in any given market. They have become highly pre-scriptive, detailing how producers must supply the market. Each week, hundreds of new regulatory requirements are generated by a bureaucratic machine in Brussels, on everything from environmental standards to flower imports. The size and colour code of every fire-safety sign is set out in law. The pricing scheme for every letter and postcard sent is defined by rules.

From food-processing to car-manufacturing to house-building, multiple agencies determine what producers can sell to customers and on what terms. Regulation means that the big providers do not have to compete on price for custom. The punter often has to take what is on offer. The irksome need to constantly innovate or to keep ahead of the competition can be dealt with by stifling change and keeping out alternative providers.

Such a regulatory system helps explain the EU's appalling underlying economic performance. However much it might harm Europe's economic prospects, it suits the sort of corporate vested interests who can afford to pay for lobbyists in Brussels. It's hardly surprising that during the Brexit referendum, the new elite and the big corporate cartels joined forces to tell us we should vote to remain in the EU. The EU was created for and by people like them.

5

NEW MONEY,
NEW OLIGARCHY

Richard Nixon has gone down in history as a bad American president. And rightly so. His name will be forever associated with the Watergate scandal, when his cronies broke into the Democratic Party headquarters in Washington. But sanctioning a burglary was not the worst decision he made in the Oval Office.

Watergate might have made Nixon a crook, but it was his decision to break the link between the dollar and gold on 15 August 1971 that led to the corruption of capitalism. Often presented as a minor tweak, ending an outdated monetary relic from the past, or as a pragmatic response to the inflationary pressures that came with fighting the Vietnam War, it was a decision of monumental import – and we have been grappling with the consequences ever since.

The new way of managing the money has given rise to the new oligarchy.

———

MANIPULATING THE MONEY

Before August 1971, the US dollar was pegged to gold at the rate of $35 per ounce under what was called the Bretton Woods System. Under this international agreement, the American government was committed to backing every dollar overseas with gold. Crucially, this meant that the quantity of US dollars that the US government could put into circulation was limited by the amount of gold that the US government had.[28]

The 'Nixon shock' meant that the US government unilaterally cancelled the convertibility of the United States dollar to gold. Nixon announced it as a temporary measure but it turned out to be permanent.

America wasn't the only country affected. Under Bretton Woods, most Western currencies were indirectly tied to gold by their peg to the dollar. Once the dollar's link to gold was broken, currencies in most Western states became fiat money. Why was all this such a big deal? Because from that moment on, each dollar bill or pound note became no more than a paper promise. And the US or UK government could make as many paper promises as it pleased. After August 1971, the only thing that constrained the amount of money in the economy was government.

Setting a currency 'free' sounds uplifting. But if it isn't bound to something external with independent worth, why should it retain its value? By the end of the 1970s, the US dollar had depreciated

---

28 To be sure, Bretton Woods was already creaking before Nixon made his announcement. Immediately beforehand, there was a run on US gold reserves, with foreign governments converting the dollars they held into gold. But this was itself a consequence of the US government increasing the money supply too fast. Under Bretton Woods the dollar was convertible to gold at a fixed rate (for foreign governments, not individuals). This meant that if the Federal Reserve increased the money supply, inflating the dollar, the real value of the dollar fell but the nominal price in gold did not. Naturally, other countries then swapped their dollars for gold, causing the gold run. Incidentally, this also explains why West Germany felt the need to leave the Bretton Woods System in April 1971.

by a third. Inflation in America surged to 12 per cent in the immediate aftermath of the Nixon shock. In Britain, it reached 24 per cent by 1975. It remained persistently high on either side of the Atlantic for a decade after the presidential announcement.

Suddenly, the primary purpose of money was no longer to serve as a store of value but merely to be a means of exchange. And officialdom had been granted a total monopoly over that means of exchange. It wasn't currency that was set free on 15 August 1971, but government. What would restrain government as it exercised its monopoly? If government was free to manage the money supply as it liked, in whose interest would it do so?

Ever since, governments have used their control of the money supply to create a bloated financial-service sector, stuffed full of overpaid executives. They have inflated asset wealth at the expense of income, creating inequality. And, all the while, they have presided over a series of ever more destructive booms and busts.

When, on 14 October 1987, stock markets around the world crashed, central banks rode to the rescue, slashing interest rates to boost spending, cut savings and make shareholding more attractive to investors than holding cash. Alan Greenspan, head of the Fed, even promised to lend to any bank or broking firm that needed it. A decade later, when the Asian financial crisis erupted in July 1997, they did much the same. As they did the following year when the collapse of LTMC, one the world's largest hedge funds, and default by Russia, overshadowed the world's financial markets. And as they did again two years later, when the dotcom bubble burst. And once more after the 9/11 attacks on the Twin Towers.

Every time over the past thirty years when the financial markets – supposedly the embodiment of free-market capitalism – have fallen significantly, those that run monetary policy have ridden to their rescue. So reliable did this kind of intervention become that investors started to believe that the US Fed was underwriting asset prices – the so-called 'Greenspan put'. It might be a good thing that our money-masters are protecting us from the fallout from financial chaos. But doesn't this kind of market intervention mean that the whizz kids of Wall Street are able to privatize the market gains, yet socialize their losses? Are central bankers, when they intervene, not saving City speculators from the consequences of their own investment folly?

Besides, weren't many of these market corrections – Black Monday in 1987, the Asian flu in 1997 – a consequence of excessive monetary expansion in the first place? No one seemed to ask. Giving the state control over the money supply has centralized power in the hands of those that hold the monetary levers. Slowly but surely, central bankers have been granted greater independence.

Monetarism – the idea that the money supply growth should be limited – has morphed into monetary Keynesianism – the idea that the money supply should be controlled to steer the economy. Interest rates and the availability of cheap credit are being used to generate employment and boost output. 'Emergency' interest rate cuts seem to remain in place long after the emergency has passed. By the late 1990s, a crisis was no longer necessary for central bankers to hose easy money at the economy. Many of them have apparently come to believe that as masters of monetary policy they can engineer benign economic conditions.

And for a while, it seemed that they had. Between the early 1990s and 2007, the US, UK and European economies experienced what former governor of the Bank of England Mervyn King calls 'the Great Stability'. Interest rates were kept low. Inflation in the UK, which had averaged 12.6 per cent in the 1970s and 7.5 per cent in 1980s, was only 3.2 per cent in the 1990s and Noughties. Output increased – but without the sort of wilder swings in GDP growth that there had been before.

But the 'Great Stability' was an illusion.

THE GREAT DELUSION

At the time of the Nixon announcement in the early 1970s, there was approximately $1 trillion in the US economy – as measured by the M3 measurement of money. By 2006, M3 money in the American economy totalled over $10 trillion.

This expansion in the money supply initially manifested itself in soaring retail price inflation. Consumer prices in America increased fivefold between 1970 and 2010. In the UK, they rose tenfold. Central bankers might have latterly managed to get a grip on rising retail prices, but they could not prevent the rise in asset prices. All that extra money had to go somewhere.

Underlying the so-called 'Great Stability' was an enormous expansion in debt and credit creation. In 1984, US economic output was $3.5 trillion, with private-sector credit about the same. By 2007, output had risen to $14 trillion, while credit had surged ahead to a staggering $25 trillion. Output had quadrupled, yet debt had increased sevenfold.[29]

More debt means higher asset prices. Why? Because if you are able to borrow more to buy assets, the price of those assets rises – on everything from houses to shares. Since the 1990s, central bankers have held interest rates too low for too long. Low interest rates make it more affordable to borrow. Being able to borrow more, folk can buy more. While this might stimulate consumer demand in the economy (which is what the central bankers tell us they were aiming for), it also boosts demand to buy assets.

Higher debt levels and higher asset prices become self-reinforcing. As asset prices rise, lenders become more willing to lend – boosting prices yet further. The bubbles that built up were not caused by the free market. They were a consequence of central bank interventions trying to buck the free market.

29 Coggan, P., *Paper Promises: Money, Debt and the New World Order* (2012). p. 146.

Interest rates are a price: the price borrowers pay savers to borrow their savings. By setting interest rates so low, central bankers ensured that savers had much less incentive to lend on their savings. So they stopped saving. At the heart of the capitalist system, capital came to be allocated by central-bank fiat, not the pricing mechanism.

In 1990, the average American household saved 7 per cent of its income. By 2005, that had fallen to just 0.4 per cent. In the UK, the savings rate by then was actually negative, with the average household spending more each month than it earned.[30] Low interest rates work as a form of stimulus precisely because they encourage folk to spend, rather than save. Years of low interest rates and easy money encouraged some serious overconsumption. Both the US and the UK have run consistent current account deficits since 1971 – getting progressively worse with each new round of monetary stimulus.

In any free market, the price of something serves as a signal. So, too, the price of credit. But when central banks distort the price of credit, the signals no longer send clear messages. Before any entrepreneur undertakes a business venture, they will look at the amount they need to borrow, calculate the rate of interest they need to pay on any loan – and (if they are sensible) only proceed if the return they expect exceeds the interest they will have to pay. The interest rate should serve as a useful reality check and put paid to any daft business venture before anyone takes on any debt.

But if interest rates are at rock bottom, suddenly an awful lot of daft business ideas seem a lot more plausible. In Spain, Ireland and America vast numbers of properties were built by developers during the 1990s and early Noughties because, with interest rates so low, that smart new housing development in Barcelona,

---

30 See Coggan, P., *Paper Promises: Money, Debt and the New World Order* (2012).

Cork or Dallas looked sensible. No one seemed to ask who might actually want to live in it.

This is known as 'malinvestment' – as in bad investment; bad since the capital invested has been put into a business or a project that it ought not to have been invested in, such as a condominium complex that no one wants to live in or a business venture that won't make much money. This pouring of immense amounts of capital into bad investments happened on an epic scale. Every time an intervention prevented a market correction from happening, another layer of malinvestment formed.

'Preventing recessions', notes the economist and journalist Philip Coggan, 'may be a little like the old practice of preventing even small fires in national forests; the effect is to allow a lot of brushwood to build up so that when a fire does happen, it is catastrophically big'.[31] All the layers of brushwood that had been building up in the global financial system since 1971 almost caused a cataclysmic conflagration in 2008.

On 9 August 2007, BNP Paribas announced that investors would no longer be able to withdraw their money from one of its funds that invested in asset-backed securities. Shortly afterwards, it became clear that entire banks were in trouble. In mid-September 2008, Lehman Brothers, a long-established investment bank, failed.

There was panic. So many banks held so many financial assets comprised of financial froth, no one for a while knew who might be next to fold. Private investors started to flee. In Britain, Northern Rock triggered the first bank run in Britain since 1866. So, once again, central banks rode to the rescue. They did what they have done each time a market correction has responded to the excess credit that they put into the system to start with. Only more so.

31 Coggan, P., *Paper Promises: Money, Debt and the New World Order* (2012). p. 166.

Except, unlike in 1987, it was not just the stock market in freefall but the viability of the Western banking system. It was not individual funds or brokers that needed to be bailed out, like when LTCM failed, but banks that had been seen as pillars of the financial universe itself. Banks were given direct, taxpayer-funded bailouts worth hundreds of billions. Fannie Mae and Freddie Mac, two state-backed lenders that had helped inflate the housing bubble, were rescued with $187.5 billion. In Britain, RBS and HBOS were bailed out to the tune of £66 billion. In Europe, it was soon entire countries – Ireland, Greece and Spain – that needed bailing out.

Interest rates were slashed again. But of course, after a couple of decades of pushing down interest rates, you eventually get to zero. Go beyond zero, as central bankers in Japan have done, and you end up in the topsy-turvy world of negative interest rates, where you end up paying people to borrow money. Our monetary masters have given themselves an even more interventionist tool in order to keep hosing cheap credit to try to reflate the financial bubble. They have resorted to conjuring it out of thin air.

Using QE – or Quantitative Easing – central banks have given corporate banks new money that they have made out of nothing, and traded it with corporate banks for assets. In doing so, they are subsidizing asset prices directly, with over £400 billion of new QE money in the UK alone.

As so often when central bankers ride to the rescue, many of the emergency measures have become permanent. UK lending rates have been at their lowest level in recorded history for almost a decade. They have been lower for longer than even during the 1930s. Banks that were bailed out 'temporarily' have since announced that they have made profits – and paid out bonuses. The costs of rescuing them are still being borne by the rest of us. A new round of QE in Britain was announced in the summer of 2016, almost a decade after the crisis first erupted.

QE is about supporting the state's fiscal needs. New Radicals on the left have criticized QE, suggesting that instead of conjuring money from nowhere to allow bond purchases and borrowing, new money should simply be spent instead. There is even talk of 'helicopter money' – producing new cash and giving it to people. At least that might ensure that the benefits of this monetary bonanza are more widely shared.

Like all those other central bank interventions, QE amounts to a massive transfer of wealth to those with assets from those without. Between 2009 and 2016, cuts in interest rates in the UK have reduced the average mortgage rate by 31 per cent. But look at what has happened to house prices over that period. They have increased by 32 per cent. The stock market has risen by 87 per cent.

Monetary policy, not the free market, has given a massive subsidy to the 1 per cent. Those with assets haven't even needed to go to work in the morning to get rich rather quickly. Yet at the same time, consumer price inflation has pushed up prices by 16 per cent, eroding the wages of those who do.[32] Despite the myth that central bankers have brought inflation under control, when you consider its cumulative effect, it has eroded real incomes significantly in recent years.

Young people in their twenties in Britain today earn 7 per cent less than their predecessors did before the financial crash of 2007. But they struggle to get by not because someone else used to earn more than they do, but because the cost of some of the things they might aspire to buy has rocketed.

Many young people will grow into middle age unable to own a house – unless they inherit one. As Britain's prime minister Theresa May once put it, easy-money policies 'helped those on the property ladder at the expense of those who can't afford to own their own home'.

32 Nelson, F., 'Forget QE. Theresa May should cut taxes if she wants to drive growth' (*Daily Telegraph*, 12 August 2016).

Between 1997 and 2015, the average Londoner working full time earned £550,000 gross. Yet the average house price in Islington rose by £532,000. In Camden, by £673,000. Even in low-income Hackney, house prices rose by £477,000. Monetary policy, not the free market, has created a world where it pays more to own a house than to work. Investing in bricks and mortar does not improve productivity. Or foster a culture of enterprise and innovation.

The asset boom has disfigured the economy of the UK – and indeed those of the US and EU – making it less competitive, less innovative, and less able to grow.

BONDS AND BANKSTERS

So why do central bankers keep doing it? Why do they endlessly ride to the rescue of investors when the markets deflate? Why do they persist in hosing easy money at the economy, even as it becomes apparent that it enriches a few, without strengthening the wider economy?

Because it suits those at the heart of our crony-capitalist financial system – the central bankers, the corporate bankers and the Treasury officials – to keep believing in the magic money tree. To carry on conjuring cheap credit out of nothing. Nowhere is the nexus between big business and political power stronger than in finance and banking.

It's not simply a case of inviting a few former finance ministers to join the bank's board.[33] Or paying failed politicians, like Nick Clegg or David Miliband, tens of thousands of pounds in speaker

---

33 There are plenty of examples. Mervyn King, former governor of the Bank of England, sat on the board of Citigroup. Axel Weber, ex-chair of the Bundesbank, heads the board at UBS. Ben Benanke, formerly of the Fed, is with PIMCO. Jean-Claude Trichet, former president of the European Central Bank, and José Manuel Barroso, former president of the European Commission and prime minister of Portugal, joined Goldman Sachs.

fees to share their unique insights into world affairs. There is a systemic interdependence between banking and big government. At the heart of the emerging new oligarchy is a nexus where the vested interests of the two meet.

The bond market is often viewed as the embodiment of raw capitalism. In fact, underpinning the bond-market booms of the 1980s, 1990s and even the Noughties, were the actions of government agencies and authorities. Re-reading Michael Lewis's *Liar's Poker*, an insider's account of working for Salomon Brothers in the 1980s, I was reminded of how it was the actions of US regulatory agencies that had allowed mortgage debt to be repackaged as a viable investment, years before the US subprime crisis in 2007.

Far from being the undiluted expression of the free market, so much of what happens in the bond market is influenced by officialdom – not least officialdom's own appetite for debt. Governments, you see, love to overspend. If they can, they will nearly always spend more each year than they take in taxes. In only eight of the past forty years, has the UK government not spent more each year than it has raised in tax. France last balanced the books in 1974. The US government last ran a surplus in 2001, when US public debt stood at under $6 trillion. So great has overspending been since then that US public debt had doubled to $12 trillion by 2009 – and then risen by the same amount again to £18 trillion by 2015.

Fiat money allows governments to grow, since officialdom is able to spend without seeking approval from the taxpayer. Able to spend without permission from taxpayers, governments cease to answer to taxpayers. Rule by taxpayer through the ballot box becomes rule by central bankers and financiers through the bond market.

To keep living beyond their means, governments need to borrow. So they issue bonds – or IOUs – and sell them at auctions, promising to pay the bondholder back the original amount, with interest. And who tends to buy up these bonds? Banks, of course. Government needs lots of credit out there to keep borrowing.

And banks like lots of credit in the economy since they are in the business of selling the stuff. Even before we moved to QE, governments were in effect handing cheap credit out to the banks, who just happen to buy up ever more of those IOUs.

Governments do not act for some higher purpose or according to an elevated notion of the public good. They act in their interests. Especially when it comes to managing the money. Inflation, we are constantly told, is low. Reducing it is, apparently, one of the central bankers' great successes. Low compared to the disastrous runaway inflation of the 1970s, inflation today is still high by historic standards. Assuming that the Bank of England met its 2 per cent inflation target every year for the next thirty-five years, the value of the pound would halve.

Central bank inflation targets are not about ensuring the currency retains its value – if they were, the target would be zero. Instead they are about systematically debasing the currency at a predictable rate. This is not done to help you or your savings. It is done in the interests of debtors – of which government is the biggest. It is a deliberate policy to transfer wealth from millions of earners and savers to officialdom.

Of course, it's not quite true to say that government has had a monopoly over money creation since 1971. You see, banks, too, create money and credit. Indeed, it was their willingness to create so much extra money and credit in the absence of credit controls in the aftermath of the Nixon shock that helped push up inflation.

Every pound or dollar that you pay into a bank ceases, under the law, to be yours. You own a claim to the money, but the bank owns the money – and because of that legal fact, is able to lend it on again. And again, and again. So-called 'fractional reserve banking' means that a bank need only hold a fraction of its balance sheet in actual deposits. Much of the rest of its balance sheet consists of credit that it has conjured out of nothing.

Except this is a pretty profitable kind of nothingness. And so the more of this nothingness that the banks are able to create, the more they gain. Much of the malinvestment poured into ghost housing estates in Cork or Massachusetts came from this sort of candy-floss credit. The banks that had generated it had a vested interest in ensuring that market corrections never wiped out their Mickey Mouse investment. So, too, by extension, did government. Time and again since 1971, officialdom has managed money in such a way as to boost asset prices in order to protect corporate banks, allowing them to keep on conjuring up credit and buying up those bonds.

It isn't free-market thinking that guides central bankers. They 'corrected' each market correction in an attempt to override the free market's verdict on decades of monetary folly driven by a desire to fund fiscal folly. The banks, meanwhile, have done very well out of easy money and asset price inflation polices. The banking sector has ballooned. In the US, the value of assets held by the banking industry has grown rapidly from around 50 per cent of GDP to over 170 per cent of economic output since 1971. In Germany, it's over 300 per cent of GDP. In the UK, between 1870 and 1970 banks assets typically were valued at about 50 per cent of GDP. By 2007, they had increased to 500 per cent of GDP.

Banking has not just got bigger, though. Like all good cartels, it has become more concentrated. In 1990, the top four US banks held about 10 per cent of total bank assets. By 2007, they had increased their asset share to 40 per cent-plus.[34]

GROWTH DESTROYED

Thomas Piketty's complaint is not just that those with capital are accumulating it too fast. The economy, he says, is growing too slowly. The world economy used to expand at 3 per cent a year

---

34 Coggan, P., *Paper Promises: Money, Debt and the New World Order* (2012). p. 158.

on average. Now it's down to 1.5 per cent. Soon, it will be down to 0.8 per cent, apparently.

Why? For Piketty, it's all about inequality. But for other pessimists, like Robert Gordon, this secular stagnation isn't just due to inequality. There are a whole series of what he calls 'headwinds' slowing down growth.

Demographic change means that there is no longer the economic additive there once was as the post-war baby-boom generation came of age in the 1960s and 1970s. Post-war improvements in education, some argue, boosted output – but further educational attainment provides only diminishing returns. Plus, there is environmental depletion acting as a drag on growth, too.

This 'secular stagnation' theory, some suggest, is a return to normality. The productivity boom of the twentieth century was an aberration. There was a unique convergence of inventions – electricity, the internal combustion engine, plastics, telecoms and TV. These generated a one-off spurt.

Maybe. Or maybe not. The secular stagnation theory still can't really explain why the massive monetary and fiscal stimulus that the US, Europe and Japan has been subjected to over the past few years should have yielded such little growth to show for it all. When economists discover that their theory does not work out the way they told us, perhaps it's a case that they invent another to explain it. Perhaps secular stagnation theory does account for slow growth but merely confirms that economists were wrong to assume that endless stimulus would work.

Now that easy money interventions are not stimulating output like they were supposed to, economists and their dismal science[35]

---

35 Economics was first described as 'the dismal science' by the nineteenth-century historian Thomas Carlyle, who believed that many economists, from Malthus onwards, were unduly pessimistic in their forecasts about the future. Carlyle might perhaps be cheered to know that many remain as doom-laden in our time as they were in his.

present us with a new theory. Not many economists seem to want to ask if monetary Keynesianism hasn't run its course. 'Monetary stimulus', Mervyn King writes, 'works by giving incentives to bring forward spending from the future to the present. After a time, tomorrow becomes today. Then you have to repeat the exercise and bring forward spending from a new tomorrow to a new today. As time passes, we will be digging a deeper and deeper hole in future demand.'

Maybe monetary stimulus doesn't just lose its potency. Perhaps the real headwind that we now face is chronic malinvestment caused by how we manage the money. An awful lot of the economic numbers started to go wrong in the early 1970s. Looking at long-term GDP growth in Britain, America, the Eurozone or Japan, it's difficult to disagree that there is less dynamism since the early 1970s.

But the idea that this is because technological innovation fizzled out in the 1970s is absurd. Many of the great innovations – microchips, PCs, semi-conductors and biotech – have had an accelerating impact since the 1970s. Between 1890 and 1971, US productivity grew fast, by on average 2.33 per cent each year. Since 1971, productivity growth has fallen by 40 per cent. Between 1971 and 1996, it only improved by 1.38 per cent a year. In 2014, it grew by 0.5 per cent.

Productivity improves when businesses invest, especially when they invest in more capital-intense production. Since 1971, long-term interest rates have no longer been stable. Yields on ten-year bonds have swung wildly. After the Fed's Paul Volcker, desperate to curb inflation, announced in 1979 that growth in the money supply would be kept constant, interest rates started to gyrate – and not only in accordance with the business cycle. Bond prices lurched around as though they were equities. This was great news for bond dealers on Wall Street, who made a killing. But it was a disaster for longer-term investment in business.

Thanks to central bank policy, more capital has been tied up in unproductive assets, like houses. This has choked off the business investment needed to boost productivity. Businesses in Britain, America and the EU have relied on cheap labour to a greater degree than they otherwise would have as a direct consequence of monetary policy. Malinvestment has even meant more migration.

With interest rates so low, many businesses that would have otherwise gone bust are able to keep going. They can service the interest on their debts but never pay it back. They can serve existing customers but not expand. They can carry on doing what they do but never innovate. An estimated one in ten British businesses is now one of these so-called 'zombie companies'. No wonder they are so slow to export. It's hardly surprising we seem to have lost our zing.

Earlier I used Coggan's metaphor to describe malinvestment as brushwood. Building up on the forest floor, each time a recession was averted by monetary intervention, the layer got thicker – until eventual conflagration. Perhaps it's better to look at malinvestment as cholesterol. Layers of it build up in the economic arteries, causing the economy to grow less fit. After forty years, we are starting to wheeze.

Cheap credit has created a kind of chancer capitalism. By borrowing vast amounts of money very, very cheaply, anyone able to invest that money in any venture with a good chance of generating even a modest return, can grow rich on the difference. From buy-to-let investors to hedge fund managers, this is what has happened. There's more money to be made in being a rentier than an entrepreneur.

In 1990, hedge funds had $39 billion of assets under management. Two decades of state subsidies for financial services and asset price inflation, and the value of those assets under management had increased to $2 trillion. The fees alone generate the hedge fund management industry $40 billion a year. In 2008, the top ten hedge fund managers earned $10 billion between them.[36]

Those hedgies are hardly masters of the universe. With all that subsidized credit, and those rising asset prices, it's actually a pretty fool proof business model. If interest rates are kept low and the value of assets rises, you would need to be an idiot not to make money. And thanks to the low-interest-rate bonanza of the past decade or so, plenty of idiots have made lots and lots of money.

Those idiots are increasingly resented by the mass of the population who have not used this monetary bonanza to accumulate great wealth at the expense of the rest of us.

SO WHERE DO WE BEGIN?

Depressing, isn't it? Democracy has been subverted. Capitalism has been corrupted and the economy rigged for the few. Perhaps most depressing of all is that none of our mainstream politicians even see it.

Leaving the money to be managed by central bankers is accepted orthodoxy. Republicans or Democrats, Labour or Conservative – they only ever seem to compete with one another over whose idea it was to let technocrats manage the money in the first place. None of them has developed a compelling critique of how the money managers have corrupted capitalism. None of them see the incompatibility of having capital allocated by fiat in a free-market capitalist system.

Mainstream politicians trip over each other to be seen as the most 'business-friendly'. They all want the endorsement of big businesses and so none of them seems to look critically at how

36 Coggan, P., *Paper Promises: Money, Debt and the New World Order* (2012), p. 154.

those big businesses are run – even when a moment's consideration would suggest that corporate governance no longer works the way it should in a capitalist system.

Only mavericks and charlatans sense that something has gone wrong. And so more of those who know that things aren't right listen to them. But, of course, we need more than pessimism and anger to put things right. Yet anger and pessimism is all that the New Radicals seem to offer.

To change things for the better, we need to offer the hope of something better. We are going to need more than the pound-shop populism of Nigel Farage or Donald Trump to do that.

So where do we begin? New Radicals might be on the rise, but not because the liberal order is over. There is nothing inevitable about its demise. If we want to see the enormous human progress that the liberal order has achieved extended for future generations, perhaps the next thing we need to do is properly understand what gave rise to progress in the first place.

PART II

PROGRESS, PARASITES AND OUR PAST

6

PROGRESS V. PARASITES

Terror attacks. War in the Middle East. Climate change. Syrian refugees. Migration crises. It's easy to think the world is getting worse.

Many New Radical parties and leaders are not just pessimists. They play on people's fears. Many on the far-left sound almost apocalyptic when warning us of the consequences of neo-liberalism or environmental collapse. We are about to destroy the planet's life support system, insists Naomi Klein. On the right, people like Katie Hopkins writing for the *Daily Mail* constantly suggest that our Western way of life is in peril.

While Ronald Reagan came into the White House declaring that it was 'morning in America again', Donald Trump entered the Oval Office by implying that the American way of life is under threat. Nigel Farage seems to me to be at his most cheery when telling the rest of us how Britain has gone to the dogs. The doomsters are wrong. We should cheer up. Britain, America and indeed most of the rest of the world are actually getting better.

THE WORLD IS GETTING BETTER

We are living longer, healthier and happier lives than ever before. Life expectancy in America in 1950 was sixty-eight years. Today, it is seventy-nine. Within the space of sixty years, the average American can expect to live for an extra twenty. In Britain since 1980, life expectancy has extended each year by an average of thirteen weeks for men and nine weeks for women. Anyone in Britain who makes it to the age of a hundred gets a birthday message from the Queen. When Elizabeth II first ascended to the throne in 1952, she sent a handful of messages. In 2015? Over 7,500.

In 1960, average life expectancy worldwide was fifty-two years. Today it's seventy-one. That means on average almost a third more life for every person on the planet. In many countries, like Mexico, where life expectancy was once way below the Western average, it has now more or less drawn level, at seventy-five years. African life expectancy is up almost eight years over the past four decades.

Infant mortality has plummeted. Infant deaths are down almost 90 per cent in the UK since 1960. They have more than halved in the United States since 1990. The most dramatic fall, however, has perhaps been in Asia, where infant mortality is now lower than it was in the UK in the 1960s. In the mid 1960s, out of every 1,000 babies born worldwide, 113 died before their first birthday. Today, that number is down to thirty-two. Infant mortality worldwide is today half what it was in 1990.

Malaria kills fewer people today than ever before. Deaths from malaria have fallen from 166,000 in 2009 to below 100,000 today. There are now almost no deaths from malaria outside of Africa. Rates of HIV infection, once frighteningly high in sub-Saharan Africa, have dropped dramatically too. And when Nigel Farage chose to complain about people being treated for HIV during the 2015 General Election in Britain, he might have hit the headlines but he missed the point; *people today can be treated for HIV*. Thanks to advances in science, retroviral treatments are available that mean that this once incurable disease is now a manageable condition. Falling rates of infection and better medicine help explain why the number of people dying of AIDS each year fell from 1.5 million in 2003 to 800,000 by 2014.

Stroke deaths in the US have halved since 1990. In South Korea, they have fallen by about two thirds. UK road traffic deaths have fallen from almost 8,000 in 1965 to less than 2,000 today – and that is with many times more cars on the roads. Heart disease in the United States fell by half between 1963 and 1990, and it has almost halved again since. Cancer survival rates are also increasing. In 1975, cancer killed 187 per 100,000 UK men. Today, that number is down to 125. In the US, deaths from cancer are down by a fifth since the 1970s. The type of skin cancer that killed my big sister, Alice, in the prime of her life a decade or so ago is no longer incurable.

We are not only living longer, but are, on average, much better off than before too. The average income in the UK today is 119 per cent[37] higher than it was in 1950, and 29 per cent[38] up on what it was in 1990. In America, average incomes have risen over that period by 130 per cent[39] and 35 per cent[40] respectively. The rise in incomes has been even more dramatic in countries like Spain, where incomes have risen four-fold since 1960, and the Netherlands, up almost three-fold since 1960. The average Japanese income today is almost five times

37 Figures derived from the *Annual Abstract of Statistics 1950*, which shows the Average Gross Weekly Earnings (AGWE) for adult male and female manual workers. Uses the same PPP exchange as USD for conversion as the OECD source.

38 OECD Average Annual Wages, using the 2015 constant prices at 2015 USD PPPs (https://stats.oecd.org/Index.aspx?DataSetCode=AV_AN_WAGE#).

39 Average Wage Indexing Series of the Social Security Administration. Figure from 1951.

40 OECD Average Annual Wages, using the 2015 constant prices at 2015 USD PPPs (https://stats.oecd.org/Index.aspx?DataSetCode=AV_AN_WAGE#).

what it was in 1960 – and that's despite two decades of lost economic growth.[41]

Worldwide, in the mid 1960s the average income per person on the planet was $6,000 a year. Today it's $16,000. Of course, not everyone is better off. As we saw in Chapter 4, blue-collar workers in the West have not done as well as others. There are still some pockets of deprivation. But even the poorest households in America and Britain today enjoy household goods and a standard of living that half a century ago would have been the preserve of the rich.

Millions of American's voted to put Donald Trump in the White House on the promise that he would 'Make America great again'. But when was America ever better than she is today? Industrial decline? Nonsense. Today America's industrial output is approximately twice what it was in 1980.[42] It's nearly three times what it was when Lyndon Johnson was in the White House.

Which period of America's past would you prefer to live in? In 1913, the average American worker worked 1,036 hours – compared to a mere 746 hours in 2003. (For Brits, it was 1,181 hours worked in 1913 and 694 in 2003). Yet here's the remarkable thing. Despite only putting in about half the hours, workers got paid far more. In 1913, average pay in the US was $5.12 per hour. By 2003, it was almost eight times that amount; $38.92 per hour (both at 1990 prices). Something similar happened in the UK, too.

Among those officially classified as 'poor' in America, 99 per cent live in homes that have electricity, water and a fridge; 95 per cent have a television; 88 per cent have a phone; 71 per cent own a car. And 70 per cent have air conditioning. In 1950, many middle-class Americans did not have many of those things.

41 See TradingEconomics.com for details.
42 See HumanProgress.org data on US manufacturing output.

In 1969, only rich people had television sets, since they cost the equivalent of a month's wages. Today, they cost less than two days' wages. In 1951, just 14 per cent of UK households had a car. Now 6 per cent of households own four. Most homes in the UK did not have central heating in 1970. Now almost all of them do.

It's not only poor people in rich countries who are better off than ever. With a handful of exceptions, like Afghanistan, Syria and Somalia, almost every country today is better off than it was in the mid-twentieth century. In 1950, the average person living in China was not simply poor. They were poorer than their ancestors would have been two thousand years before. The average income in China in 1950 was little different from what it had been in AD 50!

Yet since 1950, GDP per capita in China has increased by 8,456 per cent. The country – home to a fifth of humankind – has gone from rice paddies to iPads in two generations. In the past decade alone, Chinese GDP per capita has risen five-fold – a larger leap in ten years than China experienced at any time between the birth of Jesus and the death of Mao. In 1981, almost nine in ten Chinese were living in extreme poverty. Now it's fewer than one in ten.

It's not just China. In 1980, GDP per capita in India was US$271. Today it's over US$1,500. Worldwide, average incomes rose by 57 per cent between 1980 and 2015. Average income in Africa rose by 68 per cent. The average person living in Botswana today has a higher standard of living than the average Finn had in 1955.[43]

In 1981, just half the world had access to clean water. Today, 91 per cent do. Over the past twenty-five years, an additional quarter of a million people have gained access to safe drinking water *every day!*

Countries that we once rather condescendingly called 'the Third World' have been growing faster than many in the so-called

43 Ridley, M., *The Rational Optimist: How Prosperity Evolves* (2010), p. 15.

'First World'. More importantly, in development terms, economies are expanding faster than their populations grow. Worldwide, almost everyone eats better today than they did in the mid-1960s. Average calorie intake is up from 2,300 per person to 2,800. That's almost a fifth more food, making overconsumption, rather than hunger, a bigger public policy problem in many countries.

Since 1990, the proportion of human beings suffering from malnutrition has fallen from 19 per cent to 11 per cent. Thanks to new strains of wheat, produce is up seven times what it was in 1965 in India and Pakistan. In that same year, 43 per cent of people in developing countries lived in extreme poverty, defined as an income of $1 or less in 1990 prices. Today, that proportion has fallen to 21 per cent. For the first time in human history, the share of the world's population living in extreme poverty – defined as less than $1.90 per day – is now less than 10 per cent, and falling rapidly. The global price of food has fallen by 22 per cent since 1960. Workers worldwide have 17 per cent more free time than they did in 1950. Child labour has halved since 1990.

Each year, tens of millions of new middle-class Indians, Chinese, Turks and South Americans join the global economy. They live middle-class lifestyles, reflected by a surge in demand for everything from cars to fridges, air conditioning to air travel – and university places. As the world has got more prosperous, more children have been sent to school for longer. In 1950, the average African had one year of education, compared to six today. Britons had an average of six years of schooling in 1950. That has since doubled to twelve. Globally, the average child can expect eight years of education. Critically, from a developmental perspective, in many countries girls can access education as easily as boys.

We are not only better off, but we all benefit from technology that allows us to do things that once only rich people could do.

It's not just that fewer people had a TV. There was less to watch. In England in the 1980s, there were only four channels. Today we have a wide array to choose from, plus on-demand streaming that lets you watch what you want, when you want.

In the 1970s, air travel was so expensive that people who flew regularly were referred to as the Jet Set. Today, the cost of air tickets is so cheap that tens of millions can fly. Similarly, in the 1970s, international phone calls were so expensive that Brits with relatives in Australia would save up to call them at Christmas. Calls were so difficult, you had to book ahead to make one via a telephone operator. Today, my seven-year-old is free to chat away to her cousin in Melbourne using a tablet on Sunday mornings.

Oh, and as if that was not good enough, we are – for the most part – a lot safer than before too. In the United States, the murder rate has dropped dramatically since the mid-1990s. Cumulatively, there are 600,000 more Americans alive today who would not have been had the US homicide rate in 1995 remained constant.[44]

In Britain, violent crime has fallen dramatically too, down from 4.2 million recorded violent crimes in England and Wales in 1994–95 to 1.32 million recorded in 2014–15.[45] Globally, the UN tells us that the number of people dying violently has fallen by 6 per cent since the year 2000.

Of course, there are still savage conflicts. Terror attacks in France, Iraq, Afghanistan and West Africa have killed thousands. Tens of thousands of Syrians have perished in the conflict there, with millions more displaced. UN statistics are of little consolation to someone who has had to try to live through the catastrophes

---

44 The fall in US homicide rates is partly attributable to improvements in the medical treatment of victims of shootings and stabbings. More people are surviving such attacks. But there has also been a dramatic fall in the number of shootings and stabbings in America in the first place.

45 According to the Crime Survey for England and Wales 2015, violent crime peaked in 1995. There has been a 31 per cent fall in recorded violent crimes in the past five years alone.

that have unfolded in Syria, Sudan, Iraq and Rwanda over the past few decades. But even taking all of that into account, as a person living on the planet today, you have less chance of coming to a grisly end at the hand of another human than at any point in history.

And did I mention that the world has become cleaner and greener, too? No? Well, there are 99 per cent fewer oil spills today than there were in 1970. A moving car in 2017 emits less pollution than a stationary car did in 1970. China has taken the Giant Panda off the endangered list. British rivers and waterways are cleaner now than they have been for 200 years. Global CFC emissions have been dramatically cut; so much so that the hole in the ozone is disappearing. The earth is literally getting greener thanks to a naturally-occurring process known as global greening. There has been a large, gradual increase in green vegetation on our planet since the 1970s.

Ranga Myneni, a scientist at Boston University, has used satellite photos to show that the amount of green vegetation cover on earth is up 14 per cent over the past thirty years – in almost all ecological systems. As Zaichun Zhu of Beijing University puts it, this is the equivalent to adding a new green continent twice the size of the mainland USA over the course of one lifetime. Global greening, rather than global warming, is surely the really big environmental news of our time.

But, for me, the really remarkable thing is not just that life is getting better. It's that life has got better for twice as many people. The population of the planet has doubled since 1950. Yet, despite having twice as many mouths to feed, we eat more. We have higher living standards, better clothes, houses and healthcare – and an abundance of material possessions and tools that no other age could have even imagined. It wasn't always this way. Historically, most people lived in extreme poverty and amid high levels of violence.

THE PAST WAS WORSE

Digging for potatoes in my vegetable garden one evening, I came across a pear-shaped piece of flint, little larger than an iPhone. It turned out to be a Palaeolithic hand axe. As I washed the clay off, wondering if it really was what I thought it might be, I was overcome by the thought that I could be the first person to have held that primitive stone tool since the person who made it. If the hand axe I found is as ancient as the flints discovered in a neighbouring field on the other side of the valley and made by *Homo Heidelbergensis*, a sort of early proto-human, it would be about a quarter of a million years old. That is two – possibly even three – ice ages ago.

What was the person who made it like? Were they male or female? How old were they? What kind of life did he or she lead? What was the place we now call Essex like back then? Would it have been a life of rustic idyll?

There are plenty of people who believe that life in those distant days, before we had technology, trade and farming, would have been good and simple. Ever since the eighteenth-century, when French philosopher Jean-Jacques Rousseau (1712–78) pondered what primitive life must have been like, there has been no shortage of romantics who have imagined that early man lived at one with nature. There was, wrote Rousseau, 'nothing more gentle than [man] in his primitive state'.

If Rousseau is right, the person that made my hand axe would most likely have had a happy life in what is now my vegetable patch. What a pleasing thought! Geoffrey Miller, author of *Spent*, portrays Palaeolithic life as a sort of rural camping trip. One endless summer of adventure, rather like an ancient version of *Swallows and Amazons*.

But he and Rousseau are wrong. It might be nice to think that the person who made that hand axe lived a blissful life, but it is unlikely. Things would have been more like *Lord of the Flies*.

Humans, we now know, used to often prey off other humans. Literally. Some 14,000-year-old remains found in Cheddar Gorge in England show clear signs of cannibalism. So, too, do some even older Neanderthal remains found in Spain.

When evidence of cannibalism was first found, there was – and still is – an enormous reluctance by some academics to accept it. The pull of Rousseau – and the attraction perhaps of wanting to think nice thoughts – is powerful. 'Those butchered bones', some insist, 'are evidence of ritual burial.' It's a strange sort of burial ritual that breaks bones open to get at the marrow.

Cannibalism might have been occasional, but the evidence from the fossil record implies there were numerous such occasions. But that is the whole point. Our early ancestors were constantly desperate. Life was a grim struggle. Or, as the seventeenth-century English thinker Thomas Hobbes (1588–1679) put it: '... solitary, poor, nasty, brutish and short'.

In 1991, the remains of Otzi were found high up in an Alpine glacier on the Italian–Austrian border. When news of this Neolithic corpse, preserved in the ice for around four thousand years, broke, there was lots of speculation about the kind of Arcadian existence he lived. The Rousseau romantics that seem to dominate so many of the social science departments in so many universities had a field day with Otzi's corpse, conjuring up politically correct visions of his simple, rustic past.

Some of them seem to have been so keen to project onto Otzi what they wanted to see, they never got around to properly examining his remains. It was not until 2001, when someone administered a CT scan, that an arrow was found embedded in Otzi's back. He had head injuries and died due to violence. Further investigations showed traces of human blood on his weapons, indicating that he might have killed a couple of people shortly before he met his own demise. Otzi was no peaceful organic farmer. He killed, and then in turn had been killed.

The twentieth century, you might imagine, was a uniquely bloody era in human history, with world wars and genocide. However, violent as it was, you would have stood a much greater chance of being a victim of violence if you had lived in any previous century. As a rough rule of thumb, the further back you go, the more violent things were.

Among the kind of tribal society in which Otzi lived, before the creation of any sort of organized state, the homicide rates were horrific. It really does seem to have been, as Hobbes put it, 'a war of every man against every other man'.

Scientists have studied skeletal remains, recovered in different parts of the world, from pre-state societies and used them to estimate how many of those that lived in those places, at that time, were killed by violence. The results suggest intense levels of violence, over long periods of time. Almost 60 per cent of those who died in South Dakota in the 1300s were, it would seem, killed as a consequence of warfare and violence. In Nubia between 12,000 BC and 10,000 BC, over half of all skeleton remains showed signs of a violent death. In parts of India between 2140 BC and 850 BC, over one-third seem to have perished through conflict.

The evidence of human savagery is everywhere in the archaeological record. Recently in Germany, a Neolithic mass grave was discovered containing the grisly remains of twenty-six individuals showing evidence of violence – and possibly torture. Half a dozen of the victims were children. Among some North American tribes in pre-Columbian times, there are estimated to have been 1,000 deaths from violence per 100,000 people per year. Among societies without a state, the average homicide rate was 500 per 100,000 per year.

To put this into perspective, that would have made these

pre-industrial societies more than twice as bloody a place to be as either Germany or Russia during the twentieth century. After the emergence of organized states, violence seems to have declined but things were still pretty gruesome by modern standards. Using court and country records, the political scientist Ted Robert Gurr has calculated homicide rates in England since the Middle Ages. It shows that 'Merrie England' was in fact a rather murderous place. Oxford in the thirteenth century had a homicide rate three times above south-central Los Angeles at the height of the US crack cocaine epidemic of the early 1990s. The murder rate in England today is 95 per cent lower than it was in the Middle Ages.

Even though we do not have such accurate records for much of medieval Europe, what we do know suggests that murder would have been a much more everyday occurrence. So much so, in fact, that if you had been around then, you would almost certainly have had friends, family or acquaintances who had been victims of murder.

Early-modern Europe was a pretty violent place, too, when compared to the present day. The homicide rate in Italy was ten times higher in the eighteenth century than it is now. Even in 1900, it was four times what it is today. The homicide rate in Germany in the late nineteenth century was double what it is today.

Think of the most violent countries today; Colombia, with a homicide rate of 52 per 100,000 per year, or South Africa, with a homicide rate of 69 per 100,000 per year. London in the fourteenth century was more violent than Colombia today. Italy and the Netherlands in the early fifteenth century had higher homicide rates than South Africa does now.[46]

---

46 Pinker, S., *The Better Angels of Our Nature: A History of Violence and Humanity* (2012) p. 63.

THE ENGINE OF PROGRESS

After washing the mud off my hand axe, I took a photo of it in one hand, using my iPhone in the other. Two human tools a few feet apart, yet separated by a quarter of a million years of human progress.

One, the hand axe, is the product of one individual, or a small family group. Whoever made it, huddled where my vegetable patch now sits, did not really need input or know-how from anyone else to do so. A flintknapper I met to discuss how hand axes were made told me how, with a bit of practice, it's possible for someone to learn how to produce one from scratch in a few days, or weeks at the most.

But there is no one person you can meet to show you how to make an iPhone. Not even the late Steve Jobs would have been able to make an iPhone from scratch. The original team at Apple that designed the first iPhone might have put together a detailed blueprint, combining chips someone else built. They incorporated someone else's LED technology. Designers used someone else's plastic coating for the cover. And you, of course, select someone else's app with which to programme it. Your iPhone is a product of many different design teams, some standing upon the achievements of others scattered across the planet.

Quite unlike the hand axe, your iPhone is not, and never could be, the product of any one person's intelligence. It's the result of a broad pool of human knowledge, from how to mine the minerals that made the chips, through to the coding used for the apps. All that know-how could never fit inside one human head. That's the fundamental difference between the way we lived in the past – and lived for most of the past – and the way we have learnt to live. It's what explains how we got from hand axes to iPhones.

I bought my iPhone 5 in about 2015. It's an improvement on the iPhone 4 I had before. And way better than the BlackBerry

I had before that. Which was a big step up from my old Nokia. But to be fair to my old Nokia, that was a huge leap on from the time before that, in late 1990-something, when I did not have a mobile phone at all. In the space of a few years, my mobile phone got vastly better. So much so that I no longer use it just to make phone calls, but as an atlas, a camera and a way of accessing my bank account, too.

But hand axes never changed for tens of thousands of years. The Happisburgh hand axe, found on the East Anglian coast, is about half a million years old. It looks little different to hand axes that were being made hundreds of thousands of years later. If there was a hand axe Mark 5, as opposed to an older hand axe Mark 4, the improvement took tens of thousands of years to come about.

For most people that have ever lived, including those in my Essex vegetable patch, technology hardly ever changed from one generation to the next. Whoever made my hand axe used the same techniques and technology as someone would have done a thousand years before or after them. Or indeed ten or a hundred thousand years before or after.

In fact, the human species itself developed faster than the technology humans used. And that is because *Homo Heidelburgensis* seemed incapable of specialization and exchange. 'Somewhere in Africa more than 100,000 years ago', writes Matt Ridley, humankind 'began to add to its habits, generation by generation' thanks to the power of 'exchange... the swapping of things and services between individuals'.

This change was barely perceptible at first. There are a few fragmentary clues in the archaeological record – such as sea shells that have obviously been exchanged over long distances. But gradually, generation after generation, this knack of specialization and exchange began to gather pace. People started to become interdependent – to depend on the efforts of other people.

What has elevated the human condition in the past few hundred thousand years is our ability to work with other humans, allowing us to specialize and exchange. At some point in the past, our ancestors learnt how to specialize in producing one thing – and then to exchange it for things made by other specialist producers. No other species barters and trades. Some, to be sure, exchange favours. But none exchange one unrelated item for another. As Adam Smith put it, 'nobody ever saw a dog make a fair and deliberate exchange of one bone for another with another dog'. Barter, writes Matt Ridley, 'was the trick that changed the world'.[47]

Specialization and exchange unleashed the capacity for innovation. It allows us each to benefit from what Ridley calls 'an external, collective intelligence' far greater than anything we each might be able to hold in our own brain. Good ideas happen, shows Steven Johnson author of *Where Good Ideas Come From*, when people have a hunch – and when one hunch meets another. Rarely does invention take place in isolation. Ideas feed off one another. The engine of inventiveness, says Johnson, is connectedness. The more we are connected, the more innovation.

Slowly but surely humans stopped living in quite such Hobbesian isolation, and started to depend on each other. New technology gathered pace. By 30,000 years ago, humans had learned to make bone-tipped spears; 26,000 years ago, needles. Then bows and arrows. We tend to think of the Stone Age as a single epoch. But there was more invention in the last 50,000 years of the Stone Age than in the previous million years.

By the time that Otzi died, specialization and exchange were well established. Stone Age technology was giving way to metal working. Researchers were amazed to discover quite how sophisticated Otzi's clothing and equipment were. He wore

47 Ridley, M., *The Rational Optimist: How Prosperity Evolves* (2010), p. 65.

fur from five different kinds of animal. His shoes were so specialized, apparently, they were almost certainly manufactured by Chalcolithic-age cobblers. His tools and equipment were made from many different materials, and it's highly unlikely he made them himself. Others, perhaps in his extended family or clan, or even those in neighbouring valleys and beyond, would have created at least some of the things he had about him.

Otzi did not live in a state of simple self-sufficiency. And, despite the romanticism of those who dream of giving up city living and returning to a simpler existence, self-sufficiency sucks. American Andy George decided to make himself a chicken sandwich. Except he didn't just reach into the fridge for the bread, the tomatoes and lettuce, and the chicken breast. He decided to make it from scratch.

He planted a vegetable patch to grow the wheat for the bread, plus the pickle and salad. He travelled to the ocean to get seawater to boil for salt. He milked a cow to make the cheese and butter. He ground the flour to make the bread. Then he killed a chicken, before putting all the ingredients he had gathered together to make the sandwich.

The trouble is that it took him six months – and cost him $1,500 dollars. Thankfully, the rest of us wanting a chicken sandwich can walk into a sandwich shop and buy one for a couple of pounds. In fact, the cost of a chicken sandwich can be earned within twenty minutes if you are paid the minimum wage. If I tried to live a life of rustic self-sufficiency in my Essex vegetable garden, it would not be idyllic, but misery.

It is specialization and exchange that has made that shrinkage – from six months to twenty minutes – possible. It is what has given us iPhones where there were once only hand axes. It has elevated *Homo Sapiens* from the swamps to the stars.

But for most of the last few thousand years, we never really went anywhere. Economic historian Angus Maddison has shown that for most of the past 3,000 years there was very little change in per-capita income globally.[48] A person living in 1500 BC would have had, on average, more or less the same standard of living as someone alive in AD 1500. Ever since the Neolithic revolution – if not before – most people lived only a subsistence existence.

Technology, to be sure, did lead to a slow rise in output. There were incremental improvements in farming techniques and irrigation. Tools developed, as stone gave way to bronze and then iron. But these increases in output were offset by a corresponding increase in the number of people. Before 1800, observes the economic historian Gregory Clark, 'sporadic technologic advances produced people, not wealth'.[49]

Economic growth was extensive. Adding to human output meant adding to the human population. There was no per-person increase in output. Intensive economic growth, which would mean output rising faster than the population and living standards also rising, was almost unknown. Humans were, as that infamous eighteenth-century pessimist Thomas Robert Malthus (1766–1834) correctly spotted, stuck in a trap. The population grew faster than the food supply. If the population increased beyond a certain level, famine, war and pestilence would reduce the numbers again.

Despite all the derision that has been heaped on the poor Rev. Malthus ever since he wrote his essay in 1798, his analysis was basically correct. For most of human history, until AD 1800, we were indeed stuck in a state of Malthusian misery. In what has to be the most ill-timed piece of economic analysis ever, at almost the precise moment Malthus published his piece, we started to escape the Malthusian trap. Output started to grow faster than

48 See Maddison, A., *Contours of the World Economy 1–2030 AD: Essays in Macro-Economic History* (2007).
49 Clark, G., *A Farewell to Alms: A Brief Economic History of the World* (2007), p. 32.

the rate of population increase. There are about six times more people living on the planet today than when Thomas Robert Malthus published his theory, yet output per person has risen sixteen-fold.

It is the division of labour that has delivered us from Malthusian misery. It did not only elevate humankind materially, either. It was instrumental in what cognitive scientist Steven Pinker refers to as the Civilizing Process – not just a decline in violence, but a gradual change towards gentler, less coarse manners and pastimes.

Pinker attributes this Civilizing Process to two things; first came the establishment of orderly societies and an end of the predatory free-for-all. Then the rise of the market economy prompted a further decline in violence from its Middle Ages levels, as commerce and interdependence brought about a change in cultural mores.

When we lived in small, self-sufficient communities, we held human life in low regard. As we have come to depend on an ever-widening network of specialization and exchange, we have increased our empathy for one another. The greater our interdependence on others, the greater our regard for others. Seeing how specialization and exchange not only allowed us to escape Malthusian misery but made us more civilized in the process, why didn't it happen much sooner?

PARASITES

If specialization and exchange is the motor of human progress, how come it only revved up so recently? If humans were capable of specialization and exchange thousands of years ago, why did economic progress not start to accelerate towards an industrial revolution then and there? Why was progress so agonisingly slow?

It was isolation, suggests Ridley, that explains why progress was so sluggish and sporadic[50]. Ridley shows convincingly how small communities, cut off from a network of know-how, regress. Being interconnected and interdependent is, without question, one of the preconditions necessary for the specialization and exchange required to achieve intensive economic take-off.

But there is more to it than not being isolated. Each time we buy a chicken sandwich, we are getting what we want because we have, in effect, got lots of other people to work for us. An almost incomprehensibly complex nexus of specialization and exchange produces for us a simple chicken sandwich. Hundreds, if not thousands, of people co-operated – often unseen – to work for us and provide us with what we want. All those thousands of different people involved, who grow, harvest, transport and process all the raw ingredients that go into the sandwich, are working for us – and doing so by choice.

Everyone involved in the process that assembled your lunch did so voluntarily. From the farmer who sold his grain, to the shop worker who sold his labour putting the sandwich on the shelf, they served you because they stood to gain from doing so. The tragedy is that for most of human history, people have worked for other people not through this kind of voluntary exchange, but through force.

On the edge of the Egyptian desert, at Nazlet Khater, are the remnants of one of the oldest mines ever found. Discovered in the mine were the 40,000-year-old remains of an adolescent boy. Short and stocky, such is the evident wear-and-tear on his young body, it's likely he laboured hard in those mines, digging out chert under brutal conditions as a slave.

Slavery was widespread. There is evidence for it in almost every settled society, from the Pacific North-West to central Asia. From

---

50 Ridley, M., *The Rational Optimist: How Prosperity Evolves* (2010), see Chapter 2.

pre-Islamic Persia to pre-Roman Britain. And slavery has been remarkably persistent. As late as 1861, in the United States of America it was possible for one person to own others, and to take from their slaves the fruits of their labour.

Humans have developed a creative knack for specialization and exchange – what Ridley calls a habit of 'swapping things and services' – which drives progress. But humans also seem to have a tendency to parasite off other humans, which inhibits it.

Perhaps we are an inherently parasitic species, and living off others has been integral to the human condition since we abandoned hunter-gathering some 15,000 years ago. At first, we discovered how to parasitize other species; the agricultural revolution, when we learnt to live off plant and animal species.

Then with the rise of the first city-states, based on large-scale agriculture, new hierarchical societies formed, in which the elites farmed farmers.[51] For many millennia, peasants toiled on behalf of princes and pharaohs. Parasitism took many different forms but it always involved organizing human society on the basis of redistributive exchange: forcibly taking from one person to give to another, rather than allowing people to trade voluntarily for mutual gain.

The trouble is that an economic system run on the basis of redistributive exchange simply cannot generate the kind of gains to be had from a system of voluntary, or mutual, exchange. Small parasitic elites might have benefited by organizing society that way, but society in aggregate suffered.

Today, the web of productive activity that brings you a chicken sandwich is organized without any central direction. Of course, there might be a supermarket co-ordinating part of the supply

---

51 A controversial school of thought in evolutionary biology even argues that humans have domesticated themselves, with the human physiognomy showing many of the similar traits, such as reduced aggression and gracilization, evident in other domesticated animal species.

chain, but even that is only a small segment of the overall productive process that delivers you your lunch in a neat little cardboard box.

Yet instead of allowing such self-organizing systems of specialization and exchange to evolve, with all the complexities involved, for most of human history small elites have used a combination of command and custom (social norms) to direct production – and to take their cut.

Without free exchange, intensive economic growth is simply not possible. Why not? For a start, a system based on redistributive exchange tends to impoverish the most productive. If a farmer knows that he will have his grain taken from him, leaving him only the bare minimum required to feed his family, what incentive does he have to increase his yield?

Intensive economic growth means investing in order to expand production. A good harvest one year might give a farmer more time to clear some of the forest and increase the size of his field. Amazon today ploughs its profits back in order to expand the scope of what it sells. But what if you have a surplus-sucking elite hoovering up whatever it can? There is no surplus to invest – and therefore no chance of improved productivity.

If production is organized on the basis of command and custom, those self-organizing systems of specialization and exchange that are vital for innovation just do not develop. As Leonard Read described in his 1958 essay *I, Pencil*, even producing a simple pencil involves an extraordinarily complex process, which no one person can fully understand, let alone direct. No elite, no matter how powerful and determined, has yet existed with the wherewithal to produce even a pencil more efficiently than the self-organizing system of mutual exchange that makes them today. If command and custom cannot even produce pencils more effectively than spontaneous exchange, you perhaps start to see the problem.

Extractive elites do not just prefer redistributive exchange. They are often actively hostile to mutual exchange and those that engage in it. Humans might have been capable of specialization and exchange for many millennia, but progress was slow because predation and parasitism prevailed over production.

'Isn't that simplistic?' you interject. 'Not all economic interaction is either redistributive or mutual. Even in autocratic states, there must have been trade. Even in the most *laissez-faire* systems, there is redistribution.'

You are right. There's a spectrum. But every society that ever managed to sustain intensive economic growth did so only by staying close to the free-exchange end of the spectrum. No society on earth has ever sustained per-capita increases in output by hovering round the redistributive end of the spectrum – though many have maintained redistributive exchange for centuries without seeing any increase in per-capita growth.

There have been plenty of civilizations in the past but what do we mean when we talk of a 'great' civilization? Is a great civilization one that is better at biffing its neighbours, like the Romans? Is greatness a matter of strength? Perhaps it's a question of longevity. The ancient Egyptian and Chinese civilizations were great, in part, because they lasted for so many millennia. Maybe greatness also has something to do with size? Perhaps the Ottomans or the British were once great because they ruled over vast spaces? Or maybe it has something to do with sophistication? Civic administration, or technological precocity, or perhaps simply the ability to read and write?

By any of these standards, there have been plenty of great civilizations. It's just that almost all of them have been based on extortion. If it wasn't the neighbours being extorted and forced to pay tribute, it was the poor, miserable peasantry.

Many of the great civilizations of the past were patriarchic societies, ruled by a caste of parasitic priests and bureaucrats.

In the valleys of the Yangtze, Tigris, Euphrates, Nile, Indus and Mexico, a tiny elite lived off the toil of others. The masses were coerced into building pyramids, Great Walls, palaces and canals. They were forced, from one generation to the next, to pay such extortionate levels of taxation that they were only left with enough food to feed themselves – in a good year. In each of these societies, in the words of historian Marvin Harris, 'total submissiveness was demanded of underlings, the supreme symbol of which was the obligation to prostrate oneself and grovel in the presence of the mighty'.[52]

The 'greatness' of many patrimonial societies rested not on their ability to facilitate the human habit to specialize and exchange. It came instead from the scale on which they extorted and expropriated; a small elite siphoning off a steady surplus from a mass of peasant farmers from one generation to the next. Far from innovative, such civilizations often lasted for millennia precisely because their model of extortion hardly changed at all. Dynasties came and went but for the peasantry farming beside the Nile, or the Euphrates, or the Yangtze, life was pretty much the same in AD 1000 as it had been in 1000 BC.

But, just occasionally, a different sort of society has emerged. One in which our innate propensity to parasite off each other has been held in check, and instead that countervailing habit that we have – to specialize and exchange – has been unhindered. Production has been allowed to trump predation. Each time this has occurred – even if only briefly – the effect has always been extraordinary.

52 Harris, M., *Cannibals and Kings* (1977), p. 236.

7

WHAT IT TAKES
TO TAKE OFF

In around 496 BC, a small, unexceptional town in central Italy – Rome – was locked in a deadly struggle against her larger neighbours, the Latin League. Outnumbered, and betrayed by her former king – Lucius Tarquinius Superbus – Rome's army met her foe on the shores of Lake Regillus. And crushed them.

The battle marked a key moment in Rome's rise. She went on to gain mastery over not just the Latin tribes of central Italy, but the whole Italian peninsular, and in time a stretch of territory extending from Britain in the West to and Iraq and Egypt in the East. Even by today's standards, with jet travel and email, that's a mind-bogglingly large territory for one city in Italy to control.

As Rome was rising, many Romans attributed their success against the Latin League to the intervention of their gods. Pollux and Castor, it was said, had appeared at the decisive moment in the battle beside Lake Regillus, helping to rout the enemy. In gratitude, the Romans built a temple to them in the Forum.

It is not just the Romans who attributed their success to divine intervention. It's been a remarkably persistent idea. Two and a half thousand years on, the Victorian naturalist William Buckland argued that the enormous seams of coal that fuelled England's Industrial Revolution were a sign of divine favour. Throughout the nineteenth century, American statesmen talked of Divine Providence steering their republic towards a Manifest Destiny.

WHAT EXPLAINS SUCCESS?

Why do some societies flourish, while others fail? If divine determinism sounds foolish to us, it is not the only sort of determinism on offer.

Jared Diamond's bestselling *Guns, Germs and Steel*, for example, offers a kind of ecological determinism to explain the relative success of Eurasian societies. They had, apparently, access to an abundance of crops and animals suitable for domestication.

Others explain the success of societies through a kind of technological determinism. Early-modern Europe, we are often told, developed faster as a consequence of maritime technology, which opened new markets, or printed books, which drove science and secular knowledge.

Perhaps the most common kind of determinism is economic. A flourishing economy, we are often told, explains why a state rises, and a floundering economy, why it fails.

What determinists so often regard as the cause of development – domesticated crops and animals, technological innovation or improved irrigation, increased economic output – is really a consequence of something else altogether. What kind of plants and animals a society domesticates is as much a matter of their ability to innovate as it is a reflection on the local flora and fauna. Technological advances reflect how the innovative innovated, not necessarily why. That an economy grows is important, but it also raises the question – usually left unanswered by economic determinists – as to why one society's economy grows, but not another.

Nor do the determinists manage to explain why progress has happened when it has. Why, for example, after millennia of Malthusian misery, did some societies in northwestern Europe start to achieve intensive economic growth from the seventeenth century? Why not from the fifteenth, or the eighth? Why did societies in Asia start to take off fifty years ago, yet others in sub Saharan Africa twenty years ago?

In their account of *Why Nations Fail*, the economist Daron Acemoğlu and political scientist James Robinson argue that societies stagnate if powerful elites are able to rig things so that they can siphon off from the productive. Only when powerful elites are constrained and unable to extort from the productive, do the productive generate growth and innovation.

History has indeed been a constant conflict between those who produce and those who parasitize and predate. The former has long kept the latter fed. The latter have kept the former poor.

Progress comes, as we have seen, when the human habit of exchange is able to happen unhindered; when the hold of the parasites is broken. And for that to happen, I would suggest a society needs three specific conditions.

First, a society must be independent from any external parasites. In a subject society, any surplus is likely to be carted off. Economic exchange within a subject society is likely to be based on redistribution, rather than free exchange, meaning less of a surplus in the first place.

Second, power within a society must be dispersed in order to ensure that internal parasites do not emerge, either.

Third, although independent, a society needs to be sufficiently interdependent, and able to interact and exchange with the neighbours. Isolation has rarely been conducive to any kind of innovation.

If reining in parasitic elites is the key to progress, why did it only start to happen in northwestern Europe two or three hundred years ago?

Actually, it didn't. There have been previous societies – rarely and fleetingly – where the three conditions needed for human progress existed, and which flourished.

THE RISE OF REPUBLICAN ROME

Why did Rome rise? Obviously it was not a case of Pollux and Castor intervening. Nor, in fact, was Rome's epoch-defining ascent just a case of winning battles like the one at Lake Regillus and bashing the neighbours.

All those military campaigns and conquests tell us how Rome rose, not why. Ask any nineteenth-century historian to account for the predominance of Prussia in forging a unified Germany, and they will soon explain that Prussia prevailed not merely because of military victories – blood and iron – but economic take-off – coal and iron.

Talk to a foreign policy expert about America in the world today and they will soon make the connection between the US as a military power and her economic strength that underlies it. So why don't accounts of the rise of Rome focus on the economic ascendency of the city-state from the third century BC?

Partly because there's just not a lot of economic data. We know how much steel was being produced in nineteenth-century Germany or mid-twentieth-century America. We can't be so sure of the productive output of ancient Rome. But we do know enough to be certain that the Roman republic achieved that rarest of things: intensive economic growth.

Between 300 BC and AD 14, the population of Italy approximately doubled, from 4 million to about 7 million. If the Roman republic had been stuck in the Malthusian trap, like most societies on the planet, output would have increased only in line with population. But it didn't. While the population of Italy almost doubled over that time, total output almost quadrupled, meaning that wealth per person almost doubled. Economic historian Angus Maddison, with a precision that perhaps the data does not entirely justify, estimates that annual income per capita in Italy grew from the equivalent of $425 in 300 BC to $857 by AD 14.[53]

This might not seem like a terribly impressive increase by today's standards. Average income per capita in Italy today is $25,000 a year. But by historic standards, the level of intensive economic growth that Rome achieved was without precedent. 'Romans lived well,' writes Peter Temin in *The Roman Market Economy*. 'Better than any large group… before the industrial revolution.' Living conditions in Rome at their peak were better than anywhere until the rise of the Venetian and then the Dutch republics centuries later.

There might not be much hard evidence of economic output, but a pretty big clue as to what was going on has been found buried deep in the ice sheet in Greenland. Whenever humans smelt metals – especially tin, lead and silver – tiny microscopic amounts escape into the atmosphere. They are then blown far away, eventually settling back on earth. Some of these particles happened to land during a snowfall in Greenland all those years ago. And they remained trapped in the ice for millennia, concealed beneath countless later layers of snow.

When scientists drilled down into the ice sheet a few years ago, they found something remarkable and unexpected. The tiny traces of metal particles increased dramatically during the first, second and third centuries BC: clear evidence of increased human – Roman – industrial activity. Italy's wealth in the first and second centuries BC rose not as a consequence of conquest or booty, but

---

53 See Maddison, A. *Contours of the World Economy 1–2030 AD* (2007).

thanks to higher productivity – facilitated by voluntary, rather than redistributive, exchange.

The Roman republic enjoyed the three conditions necessary to make intensive growth possible; independence, dispersed power and interdependence.

Even in her early days, Rome was pretty effective at repelling external predators, seeing off the Latins in the sixth century BC, the Gauls (more or less) in 387 BC and Hannibal in 216 BC.

She was also networked, enabling trade and specialization. Evidence from coins shows that the economy was increasingly monetized, suggesting greater commerce. New roads created a regional, rather than a purely local, market. Sea lanes, too, radiated out from Rome. Citing evidence from ancient shipwrecks, the Cambridge professor of ancient history, Keith Hopkins, argued that there was a surge in maritime trade beginning in the fourth century BC, with Rome at the centre of a Mediterranean-wide network.

The low cost of transport encouraged regional specialization early on. By the middle of the third century BC, Roman fine pottery was being exported to Sicily, north Africa, Gaul and as far west as Cadiz. Rome also traded extensively with Athens, Alexandria and Antioch. During the late republic, a factory system in Italy was producing pottery, arms, bricks, pipes, tiles and even textiles. Significantly, they were producing for a mass market, not just individual or local consumers. There was a standardized, mass-produced oil lamp, and red slip pottery. Wool weavers in small factories were selling to distant markets.

Yet what made Rome truly remarkable was that she expelled her internal parasites – and then made sure they couldn't return. At Lake Regillus, Rome was fighting for her survival as a newly formed republic that had expelled the last of her Tarquin kings. She was not only fighting against the return of the last Tarquin king, but, as such, for the constitutional republic that she was to remain for the next half-millennium.

The Roman republic was from then on ruled by an oligarchy of its most prominent families – the patricians – seated in the Senate. She was to have elaborate constitutional arrangements – and at times a measure of democracy – in place designed to disperse power.

From 494 BC, the common citizens – the plebs – gained a role in political affairs. From 367 BC, the tribunes had the power to veto laws made in the Senate. They were elected by the tribal assembly, in which the common citizens had a majority. The Lex Hortensia, passed in 287 BC, gave the decisions of the tribal assembly the force of law. The common citizens subsequently not only had a say in politics, nor did their tribunes merely have the power to veto the decisions of the Senate. From then on, they could make laws directly.

Rome was administered by magistrates, elected usually for a single year. Care was taken to restrain the power of whoever held office. There were two consuls elected to ensure that no one man or faction held too much power. Rome might have been an oligarchy but it was an open oligarchy. Seated alongside the patricians in the Senate were the *equites*, or knights. They were often men who had made their fortune in business, and were in effect incorporated into the Senatorial elites. Many of Rome's leading heroes and statesmen – Cato the Elder, Marcus Cicero, Gaius Lutatius Catulus (naval hero of the Punic Wars) – were these new men, or *homines novi*.

Rome's institutions helped to hold power in check. But more important as a constraint against parasitism was its invention of the written law. Before 451 BC, Rome's laws had been a mixture of tribal custom and priestly command. But without writing them down for all to see, laws could be whatever the powerful wanted them to be. Half a century after expelling the last of the Tarquins, a written record of statute – the Twelve Tables – was drafted. It was to form the basic law of Rome for the next 900 years.

The written law, this greatest of Roman inventions, was not just a constraint against arbitrary rule. It had the effect of secularizing the law. The law in Rome after 451 BC was the preserve of lawyers, not parasitic priests. And the laws that were passed seemed to favour the productive, not any kind of extractive interest. Six years later, in 445 BC, plebs were free to stand for the highest magisterial office. Laws were passed to relax the penalties for debtors, making it easier to risk capital and do so with limited liabilities.

Roman law allowed bottomry loans – a kind of conditional loan whereby an investor funded a sea voyage on the understanding that if successful, they were entitled to a certain share of the profits. If, on the other hand, the ship was lost, the merchant loaned the money would not be liable for the loss. This allowed capital to be invested in the certainty that liabilities were limited.

Rome's constitution promoted voluntary exchange of not just capital, but also labour. 'Really? Weren't the Romans famous for taking slaves?' you might think. Yes, they were. Even in the early days of the republic, before the first big influx of slaves that followed the acquisition of Sicily, not everyone could sell their labour voluntarily. But, alongside slavery, Rome had a free labour market. There was a mass of freehold farmers – the *assidui* – and an even greater number of *proletarii* – men who owned no property but were free to work as labourers, craftsmen and artisans, paid according to what they produced.

There were many independent producers in Rome, in stark contrast to the highly regimented economies of Egypt and the eastern Mediterranean at the time. Individuals in the Hellenized East were deprived of the freedom to pursue personal profit in production and trade. Subjects of a king, they were forced to labour under a crushing burden of taxation, often dragooned to work in enormous collectives where they were little more than bees in a hive.

The Roman republic was simply not like that. Far from collect-ivizing agriculture, it had a free market in grain, too. 'I thought Rome redistributed grain from the provinces to keep its own citizens fed?' you interject. 'Wasn't there a massive tribute paid by the subject provinces to the ruling Romans?' That was to come. But in the early days of the republic, the vast quantity of grain imported into Rome to feed the city was purchased from willing sellers on the open market. Roman agriculture was efficient enough to feed a city of one million, easily the largest city ever to have existed until Beijing a thousand years later.

That agrarian efficiency released labour to live in the towns, further increasing productivity. The late Roman republic and the early empire had a level of urbanization not seen again until the eighteenth century. As the German scholar F. Oertel put it, a Roman 'bourgeoisie came into being whose chief interests were economic'. A productive class, in other words, who could not easily be extorted and exploited by a class of parasites – helping to keep the system of free markets going.

ANCIENT GREECE

In April 480 BC, around about the time that the Romans were trying to subdue the Latin League, the mighty Persian empire invaded Greece.

Persia was a superpower. Their empire stretched from the Indus to the Aegean. United under Xerxes, the Persians could command a vast pool of manpower, making her invasion force one of the largest ancient armies ever assembled.

And against her? The Greeks had no capital or unified authority. They formed a mosaic of small city states and statelets. Not even Athens was able to impose a unified command.

The situation must have seemed hopeless. Yet against almost unbelievable odds, the Greeks blunted the Persian onslaught.

Then they defeated the invaders, first at sea at Salamis and then on land at Plataea. The Persians were expelled.

As with Rome, military successes should not be allowed to overshadow all the other things that this remarkable civilization achieved. Greece's great achievements were not through force of arms. Ancient Greece achieved the most extraordinary cultural innovation, in everything from architecture and art, to philosophy and the way people think. Athens's Parthenon is to this day regarded as one of the architectural pinnacles of humankind. Athenian philosophers laid the foundations for what we now think of as Western thought. Much of what we today regard as having been passed on to us by the Romans, is in fact Greek in origin.

If we know that the ancient Greeks were capable of conjecture and critical thought in a way few other societies have been before or since, we struggle to find as much evidence about intensive economic growth. If information about the performance of the Roman economy is sparse, for archaic Greece it is almost non-existent. Almost, but not quite. The data that is available hints at a massive expansion in wealth there too, in the fourth and fifth centuries BC.

Life expectancy seems to have increased. Skeletal and dental remains suggest that people were in better health and that diet improved. Houses got bigger. Before the Peloponnesian War (started 431 BC), Athens enjoyed a per-capita level of consumption similar to the level in Rome under Augustus (27 BC–14 AD).[54] Athens under Pericles (461 BC–429 BC), like Rome under Augustus, enjoyed one of those rare and exceptional periods in human history that saw intensive economic growth.

Greece had those three conditions essential to allow the product

54 Goldsmith, R.W., *Pre-modern Financial Systems: A Historical Comparative Study* (1987), p. 19.

to prevail over the parasitic and ensure intensive economic growth and innovation.

The Greeks were independent; heroically so, fighting against Persian and other predators. Greek city-states were not only independent from outside overlords; the different *poleis* were independent from each other, too.

Ancient Greece had no capital or unified authority. No one state, not even Athens, was able to impose itself in perpetuity over the rest. Some 1,200 different *poleis* existed as independent entities between 650 and 323 BC. Greeks might have been united by a Pan-Hellenic identity and even mutual loyalty, which they showed when they joined forces as Greeks against a common Persian foe, as Herodotus tells us in his *Histories*. But they were independent from each other.

In the absence of political centralization, the Greek city-states were in constant competition with each other. This helped drive forward innovation and outward expansion. Between the fifth and fourth centuries BC, Athens was the largest and richest city in the Mediterranean – perhaps the world.

Power was not only dispersed among competing city-states, but within some of the most successful. It was, after all, the Greeks who invented the idea of rule by the people (*demos*) – democracy.

Rome's republican constitution might have seemed remarkable compared to the centralized monarchies of Persia or the Eastern powers but, seen through Greek eyes, it was not without precedent. Polybius, a Greek exile living in Rome, regarded the Roman republic's constitution as the perfect realization of Aristotelian political theory.

Of course, plenty of Greek city-states were run by tyrants and kings. Others were oligarchies or plutocracies. Indeed, the Greeks gave us the words to describe these systems of government. It was perhaps the sheer variety of states, free from each other, interconnected yet in competition, that helps account for the most remarkable rise of this otherwise nondescript peninsula at the bottom of Europe.

Independent they might have been, but the ancient Greek world was interconnected, too. Long-distance maritime trade around the Mediterranean had opened up, making the whole of the Mediterranean basin accessible. This brought people into contact with one another. Athens, the most prosperous city state, was open not only to trade, but to creative people from throughout the known world.

The Greeks traded far and wide. They established colonies as far afield as southern Italy, north Africa and the Black Sea. What we know of Greek contractual law shows that the rights of merchants over property were safeguarded. Athenian merchants of the fourth century BC, like those of Rome later, were able to use loans to finance maritime trade and to do so with limited liability in case of shipwreck. Risk, in other words, could be correlated with reward.

There was a transfer of technology, with the Greeks borrowing certain distinctive cultural features – many of which we now think of as definitively Greek (temples, statues, epic poetry and painted ceramics) – from others.

Independence, dispersed power and interdependence allowed the productive to trump the parasitic on the Greek and Italian peninsulas in antiquity. They also combined to produce the most remarkable human progress in some of the most inauspicious locations.

A MIRACLE ON A MUD BANK

Try to imagine the most unlikely place in which to prosper. A water-logged swamp off the northeast coast of tenth-century Italy might have seemed just about the worst piece of real estate imaginable. Venice was literally built in a backwater. There was very little farmland and few natural resources, besides sea salt and a few fish.

Yet on this mud bank between the tenth and thirteenth centuries was to emerge what the popular historian John Julius Norwich called, 'the richest and most prosperous commercial centre of the civilized world'.

The population of Venice grew rapidly. By 1050, what had been a fishing village a couple of centuries before was now home to about 45,000 people. By 1200, she was a city of 70,000. Before the Black Death, in the mid-fourteenth century, her population had swelled to over 120,000.

Had Venice, like much of the rest of humankind at the time, been stuck inside a Malthusian trap, any increase in its economic output would have been matched by the increase in its population. There might have been more Venetians but they would have remained poor. But Venice was special. It increased in both population and wealth per person. For several centuries, income per capita in Venice was far higher than anywhere else on the planet. She shone while all around her the Mediterranean was a sea of Malthusian gloom.

Intensive growth allowed Venice to punch above its weight. Despite being a tiny city-state 0.0005 per cent the size of the Holy Roman Empire and 0.0001 per cent the size of the Ottoman domains, Venice was often a match for these parasitic powers around the Mediterranean. Indeed, in 1204 she notoriously spearheaded the attack on Constantinople, with her aged Doge, Enrico Dandolo, leading the first successful assault on the walls of that great city in almost a thousand years.

How did she do it? The Venetians themselves attributed their successes to the blessing of their patron, St Mark. But it wasn't divine determinism that accounted for her success.

Venice was secure from external predators. Those muddy

islands might have seemed an unlikely place to want to live, but the neighbourhood across the water was far worse. Venice's almost impregnable lagoon protected her from marauders and invasion. It saved her from the Longobards, then Pepin and the Franks. It kept out the Huns and the Saracens (whose fleet once got to within sight of the city). It stopped the Normans far more effectively than any city wall.

But it was not just geography that kept predatory powers at bay. Venice had the great fortune to have been born – notionally at least – a child of Byzantium. She was, at one time, the most western point of that empire. This kept her free from the feudalism of the mainland, and beyond the reach of the Holy Roman Emperor. At the same time, she was overlooked by the distant court in Constantinople, and outside any meaningful kind of imperial control. By AD 810, Venice was in effect independent – and from then on she was able to avoid getting gobbled up by any of the big power blocs around her.

But even though she was an island, Venice was never insular. Her barges filled the waterways of northern Italy and the Adriatic. Because she began as a Byzantine province, Venice was born part of a wider Greek-speaking Mediterranean world. In other words, Venice networked with her neighbours. Even by modern standards, a very high proportion of economic activity in Venice was linked to trade, suggesting a very high level of specialization and exchange.

The city grew rich trading spices and manufactured Byzantine wares from the East. She gained trading rights in Constantinople and established a large Venetian quarter there. By 1140, she was importing raw cotton from the East, processing it and exporting it to be sold in Alexandria, Constantinople and Jerusalem. Trade functioned as an extension of Venice's resources. It allowed a few acres in an Italian lagoon to draw on the grain of the Po Valley, the timber of Dalmatia, the vineyards of Apulia, sugar and cotton from Cyprus, silk from China, and the metalwork of Constantinople.

But independence and interdependence aren't enough alone to account for Venice's economic miracle. The serene republic owes her success to a further factor: she was free from internal parasites, too. Venice might have been an oligarchy – never a democracy – but, for her first few centuries, power was dispersed amongst a merchant aristocracy. Think of Florence, and the name Medici comes to mind. The Sforza family are synonymous with medieval Milan, the Este with Ferrara and Modena, the Scaligeri with Verona. But there is no equivalent family in Venice. To be sure, there were plenty of distinguished Venetian families, like the Dandolo or Morosini, who produced plenty of heroes, villains and statesmen. But no single family or faction dominated in quite the way that the Medici and the rest did in other city-states.

In most northern Italian towns, the republican theory of the communes was soon subverted by tyrannical facts. *Il signori* took over. Yet when, in 1032, Domenico Orseolo attempted to set himself up as a Venetian *signore*, he was ousted. Tellingly, his replacement, Domenico Flabonico, was a silk merchant with staunchly anti-dynastic views. 'Although they are few compared to the whole population of the city,' observed the fourteenth-century jurist Bartolus of the Venetian aristocracy at the time, 'they are many compared to those ruling in other cities.'

After the attempted coup of 1032, on only two occasions over the next 700 years did the same family name appear consecutively on Venice's long list of doges. The power of the Doge – who henceforth was elected by the General Assembly, and subsequently a Ducal Assembly – was progressively eroded. Doges could no longer appoint cronies to any of the offices of state. Each new doge was required to sign a binding *'promissione'* contract before assuming office, which, in ever more elaborate terms, stipulated things they could no longer do.

The Venetian constitution was complex and elaborate, at times to the point of near absurdity. But it kept power diffuse. The Doge was held to account, and answered to the merchant interest. Neither the Doge, nor the Great Council, nor the Venetian Senate could make decisions without the approval of the others. Venice, almost uniquely in the medieval Mediterranean, had independent magistrates, courts and courts of appeal, as well as the rule of law.

The dispersion of power and the supremacy of mercantile interests amplified the gains of interconnection. They made the city an attractive trading hub. They facilitated voluntary exchange. By the late tenth century, the merchants had pushed successfully for a policy of free trade with Byzantium. They sought – and won – tax exemptions on Venetian goods from the Holy Roman Empire and Otto III. They even traded openly with the Saracens in north Africa.

Being independent, Venice could ignore the papal edicts banning trade with Muslims, as well as the ones that tried to outlaw charging interest on loans. When two producers controlled the market in tiles, cement and building material, the government broke up the duopoly and sold off the kilns. The Senate investigated unfair practices in the cotton trade with Cyprus. No one family was allowed more than one member on the key administration boards. As well as ensuring competition, Venice's government was, as historian Frederick Lane puts it, 'frankly and efficiently capitalistic'.

Venetian law actively encouraged exchange and early capitalism. *Colleganza* or *commenda* contracts, not unlike the system of bottomry loans in ancient Rome, allowed investors to put private capital into trade missions almost as a sort of *ad hoc* joint-stock company. They gave investors a measure of control over the venture into which they were putting their money and limited their liabilities.

Commenda contracts were so successful that they did not just facilitate private capital investment in private enterprise, but also allowed a measure of social mobility, reflected in official records of new investors. According to surviving government documents from the time, in AD 960 and then again in AD 982, between 65 per cent and 81 per cent of those acquiring a *commenda* contract were doing so for the first time.[55]

Independence from external parasites and dispersed power to safeguard against internal ones, plus interdependence with the neighbours; we can be certain that these three magic ingredients are essential for intensive economic growth, not merely because of what happens when they exist. We can also see what happens when they ceased to exist; regression.

---

55 Acemoğlu, A. and Robinson, James A., *Why Nations Fail: The Origins of Power, Prosperity and Poverty* (2012), p. 153.

8

REGRESSION

The collapse of the western half of the Roman empire was perhaps the most dramatic – and bloody – regression in human history. A highly advanced, technologically sophisticated civilization, capable of sustaining a large, relatively literate and urbanized population came to an end. The population of Italy and the western Roman empire plummeted. Reading and writing were largely forgotten.

Sometimes presented by revisionist historians as a sort of gradual passing of the old ways, and a gentle, incremental shift towards a new post-Roman order, the fall of the western Roman empire between the third and fifth centuries was anything but that. It was one of the bloodiest events in human history, with an estimated death toll of about eight million. To put that into perspective, if a similar proportion of the human population were to have been killed in the mid-twentieth century, it would have meant the deaths of 105 million people – far more than were killed in the two World Wars combined.[56]

56 Pinker, S., *The Better Angels of Our Nature: A History of Violence and Humanity* (2012), p. 195.

Civic order collapsed as warlords took over. Towns and cities emptied. A system of clearly defined laws was replaced by a world in which tribal custom – and the whim of the barbarian tribal chief – prevailed. But the barbarian invasions of the late fourth and early fifth centuries were ultimately a symptom of Roman decline, not a cause of it. The Romans had, after all, fought off far more organized foes, such as the Carthaginians.

ROME: PARASITES WITHIN

The seeds of Rome's collapse lay not in the arrival of barbarian predators from outside the empire, but parasitic ones within. Long before the Roman republic became an empire in 27 BC, power had become increasingly centralized. As Rome acquired overseas provinces, she outgrew her system of checks and balances, allowing an oligarchy to emerge.

Vested interests within the Senate enriched themselves by systematically looting the provinces. Sicily's governor, Verres, personally made three million *denarii* during his tenure, which some have suggested exceeded the entire tax take of the island. And Julius Caesar made himself a personal fortune as governor of Hither Spain. Others in the Senate grew rich from the proceeds of tax-farming businesses – *societates publicanorum* or *publicani* – which bid for the right to tax the provinces. Cicero estimated that, in his time, these *publicani* made average profits of 120 per cent.

A little like corporate banks today, these *publicani* enabled the state to spend right away, by providing investor cash up-front. Investors in the *publicani* were not, of course, issued with bonds. But like bondholders today, they were guaranteed a slice of future tax revenues. And, like the banks and government in our own time, there was a power nexus between the revenue-hungry government and *publicani*.

Publicani became a major investment vehicle for rich Romans, who bought shares in them. Investors were not disappointed. Having won the right to tax the provinces, the *publicani* systematically looted what they could. In 133 BC, the king of Pergamum – a Greek city that controlled most of what is today western Turkey – bequeathed his kingdom to Rome. The *publicani* promptly set about stripping it systematically. According to the author of *Rubicon*, Tom Holland, 'The aim was not only to collect the official tribute owed ... but to strong-arm the provincials into paying extra for the privilege of being fleeced.' Debtors might be 'offered loans at ruinous rates' in order to enslave him. 'Shipping sailed for Italy crammed with the fruits of colonial extortion.'[57]

There was a massive influx of slaves from Sicily and other newly acquired overseas territories. It was not unusual in the first century BC for 10,000 slaves to be auctioned at Delos in a single day. This huge supply of cheap labour helped further enrich the rich. Big landowners built up extensive farming corporations – the *latifundia* – using armies of slave labour. The freehold farmers could not compete. Many small independent farmers were forced to abandon the land, and drifted workless into the city. 'Roman society, once a community of free farmers,' writes the American historian Will Durant, 'now rested more and more upon external plunder and internal slavery.'

In 104 BC, the plebeian tribune, Marcius Philippus, when proposing a law to redistribute land, claimed that all the property in Rome was owned by fewer than 2,000 people. His claim might have been an exaggeration but wealth had become greatly concentrated.

Maddison estimates that by the death of Augustus in AD 14, the elite – defined as Senators, *equites* and *decuriones* – comprised 121,600 people, out of a total Italian population of seven million.

---

57 Holland, T., *Rubicon: The Triumph and Tragedy of the Roman Republic* (2003), p. 42–3.

Yet, by that time they took over half of total income in Italy. By any measure, this was an extreme concentration of wealth and far removed from the idea of Rome as an agrarian republic of freehold farmers.

The emergence of this oligarchy provoked a crisis. Politics in the late republic became a contest between rival interests battling over the spoils. There was, if you like, a first-century Roman version of our own twenty-first-century populist insurgency – and then all-out civil war.

The plebs elected first Tiberius Gracchus – a kind of cross between Jeremy Corbyn and Donald Trump – and then his brother Gaius as consuls to take on the vested interests. Like the New Radical left, the Gracchi brothers demanded more equality, land reform and a dole to help the poor. Like those of the New Radical right, they also raged against cheap migrant labour.

The response of the Gracchi to unjust redistribution that favoured the patrician elite was to demand a countervailing redistribution in favour of the plebs. And – despite both coming to a grisly end at the hands of patrician mobs – Tiberius and Gaius got their way. The corn dole that they instigated in 123 BC to feed the Roman poor remained in place until the very end of empire, and was even expanded as a form of welfare.[58]

But their achievement, in so far as they had one, was to ensure that it was no longer just the oligarchs that extorted the provinces. The poorer Romans joined in too. The corn dole that fed over a quarter of a million Romans a day by the time of Augustus was largely provided by Egypt – the personal possession of the emperor.Oppression and extortion of the provinces reached an epic scale.

---

58 The corn dole was started by Gaius Gracchus, with the *Lex Sempronia frumentaria* providing for subsidized corn rations. It was not until the *Lex Clodia* in 58 BC that corn became completely free to its recipients. To the grain ration was added in time oil, pork, wine and even gifts of money.

The plebs might have got their dole but the oligarchs prevailed. Sulla suppressed the plebeian faction and formally curbed the power of their tribunes. Democracy turned to oligarchy. The republic had ceased to exist long before Julius Caesar formally overthrew it in 49 BC.

At the battle of Actium in 31 BC, one of the warring oligarchs, Octavian, defeated his rivals. Calling himself Augustus, the *princeps* – or 'the first' – he established a military dictatorship. His successor, Tiberius, abolished the plebeian assembly. It might have been a relatively benign military dictatorship at first but power was now in the hands of one person, who more often than not asserted his claim to the job through force. The constitution Polybius described in such detail in the second century BC had gone forever – and with it the genius of Roman civilization.

The problems that the centralization of power was to produce were not immediately apparent. In fact, Roman grandeur was all the greater once she became an imperial power. More than that, given the violent disorder that had gone before, the rule of Augustus, even in the eyes of republican traditionalists, must have seemed like an improvement. Augustus encouraged trade and abolished tax farming – making the collection of taxes less arbitrary and less of a disincentive to commerce.

The early empire, wrote the Russian historian Michael Rostovtzeff, was a period of 'almost complete freedom for trade and splendid opportunity for private initiative'. But with power so centralized, the seeds of destruction had been sown. Stagnation set in slowly. According to the economic historian Raymond Goldsmith, there is 'no evidence of an upward trend in income per head over the first two centuries of empire'.[59]

Under the empire, Italy no longer lived through mutual

59 Goldsmith, R.W., *Pre-modern Financial Systems: A Historical Comparative Study* (1987), p. 35.

exchange by trading with far-flung parts of the Mediterranean. She became a parasite, living increasingly off redistribution. The empire became a military machine, which needed feeding. This was done partly through conquest and plunder – the Roman empire expanded to reach its greatest territorial extent under Trajan (AD 98–117) – and partly by pauperizing the provinces.

But whatever spoils it might have yielded in the short term, redistribution couldn't sustain the growth produced by mutual exchange. Intensive growth didn't just stop; it went into reverse. The military machine of empire put constant upward pressure on taxes. Because power was not dispersed to those who were expected to pay them, they rose steeply. Extortionate taxes often became simple extortion. Caligula achieved what the Gracchi had failed to do when he seized the estates of many of the richest Roman landowners.

Property rights became progressively less secure, as confiscation became an established practice. Increasingly, big fortunes were not made through mutual exchange, or selling to a market, but by being the beneficiary of one of the increasingly frequent rounds of land expropriation. Wealth was increasingly concentrated. Goldsmith estimates that the wealthiest 3 per cent in Italy accounted for a quarter of all income.[60]

A change of emperor could mean the sudden loss of a family estate. Or, if you backed the right horse, gaining one. Many of the elite, therefore, had a vested interest in the imperial succession. Perhaps unsurprisingly, contests to succeed to the purple became increasingly violent. From AD 180 on, it was rare for an emperor to die peacefully.

Pressure to provide money to the army was unrelenting. So much so, in fact, that Nero took the decision to debase the currency,

60 Goldsmith, R.W., *Pre-modern Financial Systems: A Historical Comparative Study* (1987), p. 36.

reducing the silver content of the *denarius* to 90 per cent. Cutting the amount of silver by 10 per cent meant that the authorities were a little better off for every debased coin they issued – and the person who received that coin, 10 per cent worse off. It was a way of transferring money from the citizen to the state.

Rather like Nixon would do when breaking the link between the US dollar and gold two thousand years later to help pay for a vast military machine, Roman emperors routinely debased the currency by reducing its silver content. Emperor Trajan reduced the silver content to 85 per cent. Marcus Aurelius (AD 161–180) to 75 per cent. By the reign of Septimus Severus (AD 193–211), it was down to 50 per cent. By the middle of the third century, 5 per cent.

This debasement of the Roman currency caused massive inflation. By the reign of Diocletian (AD 284–305), prices were rising so fast that he issued an edict to try to control the price of many goods throughout the empire. Like our own elites, that of Rome not only manipulated the money supply to enrich a few. They also started issuing cheap credit. Tiberius gave out low-cost loans to crony companies involved in public works projects.

Rome ultimately became an economic empty shell, receiving taxes, grain and goods from the provinces, but producing almost nothing herself. 'The mob of Rome and palace favourites produced nothing, yet continually demanded more, leading to an intolerable burden on the productive classes.'[61]

Evidence from shipwrecks suggests a dramatic fall in sea-borne traffic. Goods were transported only according to central command and under duress, not traded freely. No longer trading with others but extorting from them, and without a sound currency to underpin trade and investment, Italy deindustrialized. The big manufacturing concerns that had existed in the first

---

61 See essay 'How excessive government killed ancient Rome', Bruce Bartlett, Cato Institute.

century BC were gone by the third century. There was no longer a mass market for many goods as there had been. In the western empire – the eastern part seems to have fared better – regional specialization and exchange dried up.

Again, evidence from the Greenland ice cores – showing a fall in the amount of lead and silver released into the atmosphere – testifies to this industrial decline. Manufacturing did not return to the level it had reached in the first century AD until the thirteenth century AD.

Romans had once been innovators, capable of taking new technology and using it to great effect. It is striking that there was an almost total absence of technological innovation during the period of empire. Even where there was invention, new ideas never seemed to be widely applied. Businesses, which had been in private hands, were increasingly corralled into 'collegia' – cartels. Workers were organized into restrictive guilds. By the third century AD, there was no longer a free labour market. Imperial decrees forbade workers from changing jobs or moving from one workplace to another – something that, in the first century AD, only slaves were prevented from doing.

Trade fell precipitously, and inflation in the third century AD is estimated to have been 15,000 per cent, making monetary exchange increasingly difficult. With the monetary economy breaking down, normal taxation became harder and harder to levy. The Roman state began to demand taxes in the form of goods and services. The tax contribution, moreover, was calculated according to military need.

This was not the only way in which the late Roman economy began to take on many of the attributes of feudalism, long before any Goths showed up. Agricultural workers became semi-servile coloni. Like slaves, they were increasingly bound to the land and to a landlord. As this proto-feudalism took hold, they were, like vassals, prevented from selling their own property without their landlord's permission.

With ruinous tax rates, little incentive to trade and few gains to be had from specialization, landlords turned their estates into increasingly self-contained units. Without comparative advantage and the division of labour, the gains that those engines of human progress had yielded over previous centuries simply disappeared.

To grasp the full scale of this economic calamity, consider the fact that, by AD 400, the number of people living on the Italian peninsula had plummeted by about a third, from seven million in AD 14 to five million – the smallest total since 200 BC. This decline happened *before*, not as a consequence of, the barbarian invasions that were to come.

'It is clear', writes Maddison, 'that there was a significant decline in per-capita income in all the west European provinces.' In fact, income per capita in Italy in AD 400 fell back where it had been in 300 BC, *700 years before!* The economy had returned to localized self-sufficiency.

As the Belgian Medievalist Henri Pirenne puts it, mourning the end of Roman specialization and exchange, 'the minting of gold had ceased, the lending of money at interest was prohibited, there was no longer a professional class of merchants, oriental products... were no longer imported, the circulation of money reduced to a minimum... Civilization had regressed to the purely agricultural.'

By the time that those external predators – the Goths and the Vandals – showed up, they were helping themselves to what Rome's own parasites had left behind.

HOW VENICE SANK

Giorgia Boscolo became Venice's first female gondolier in 2009. Breaking with centuries of tradition, 34-year-old Giorgia was finally allowed to do something previously only men had done – ferry paying customers around Venice's waterways.

A triumph for feminism, you might think? Only sort of. Giorgia was only allowed to paddle a gondolier on certain days of the week. Provided no male gondolier was available to do the job. And only once she had completed extensive and laborious training procedures.

It's easy to read this story as a clash between twenty-first-century egalitarianism and quaint Venetian tradition. Except Venice was never traditionally in the business of restricting trade like this. When Venice was the wheeler-dealing capital of the world, there was no guild of gondoliers. Guilds only became compulsory in Venice in 1539. Those rules and regulations that stipulate who can row what kind of gondolier, built to what specification and under what conditions, aren't as old as we imagine.

At some point, the productive – long paramount – had been made subservient to a parasitic interest. This subtle, yet profound, shift turned what was once the centre of innovation, ambition and enterprise into a crumbling museum.

How did it happen? The change was not dramatic. There was no sudden transformation, followed by a swift collapse. Decline by its nature tends to be a slow, steady rot. Indeed, in terms of art and architecture, Venice's most lavish and exuberant decades happened only after a gilded – or should that be 'guilded'? – elite had taken over. Like Medici Florence or imperial Rome, perhaps it takes the proceeds of parasitism to commission the greatest art.

Like Rome, Venice was also a republic that acquired an empire. The great inflow of wealth from overseas possessions upset the republic's internal equilibrium. It was not so much the raw inequality that was problematic but the fact that this new source of wealth allowed a faction within the body politic of the republic to outgrow and circumvent the safeguards against the predominance of any one group.

After sacking Constantinople in 1204, Venice took over various prize territorial possessions in the eastern Mediterranean that had previously belonged to Byzantium. A new class of colonial administrators grew rich running them. Trade from Cyprus, especially from sugar produced on slave estates, enriched a small number of families. Much as the acquisition of Sicily and Pergamum had enriched a faction within the Senate, a small number of Venetians benefited from the acquisition of these new imperial possessions.

At the end of the thirteenth century, a rich clique within Venice launched a constitutional coup. Previously an open oligarchy, in 1297 there was what is known even today as *Seratta* or closure, after which membership of the Great Council was restricted to political insiders. Soon membership became hereditary *de jure* as well as *de facto*.

A new executive body, the Council of Ten, was created in 1310. It became chief executive and judicial body of the state, answerable only to itself. Centuries of trying to restrict the danger of an overbearing executive by constraining the Doge was undone. From 1315, the merchant aristocracy became a closed shop, literally. If your name was registered in the *Libro d'Oro* – or Gold Book – you were part of the oligarchy and could hold office and take part in administrative matters. If you were not on the list, you were not allowed in.

And you were not just excluded politically, but economically too. The number of *colleganza* contracts involving non-nobility – those not named in the Gold Book – dramatically declined. Economic historians Diego Puga and Daniel Trefler have shown that before the *Seratta*, between 1073 and 1203, 40 per cent of those involved in *colleganza* contracts in the city were not nobles. There was space for *nouveaux riches* – and wannabe *nouveaux riches*.

Between 1221 and 1240, the *nouveaux* even seemed to be taking over, with a small majority of non-nobility engaging in *colleganza*-based trade. But after the oligarchic coup, the proportion of commoners trading under *colleganza* contracts fell dramatically. Between 1325 and 1330, a mere 5 per cent were non-nobles. Between 1339 and 1342, none.

In 1324, the *Capitulare Navigantium* law entered into force, stopping poorer merchants from trading. From then on, only the rich and politically connected were able to engage in long-distance trade and commerce. Indeed, the parasitic would force the productive to carry them – literally. Rules were imposed on private carriers requiring them to have a noble on board, who was automatically granted a certain amount of stowage space for goods traded in his own name, even if they were carried at someone else's cost.

Alongside the internal restraint of trade, the elites imposed protectionism. Statutes were introduced preventing foreign-born merchants – and their capital – from investing in *colleganza* ventures. By the fifteenth century, rules insisted that Venetian trade had to be carried on Venetian ships. A series of ever more protectionist Navigation Acts followed.

And with protectionism came nationalization. From 1325, galleys had to be publicly owned, with merchants bidding to have space aboard them. Somewhat like our regulated markets today, trade still happened but it was increasingly based on obtaining permission. Relations with officialdom in the naval yard and industrial hub of the city, the Arsenale, suddenly became more important than that with customers – who were forced to buy from a restricted range of suppliers.

But, as a manufacturing hub, the Arsenale became a shadow of its former self. In the early fourteenth century, it had been the largest industrial centre in Europe and the site of innovation in ship design. But soon it was producing only a few dozen antiquated galleys totally unsuited to carrying goods on the long-distance ocean routes that the Dutch and English had opened up.

Indeed, far from trying to adapt to the new nautical technology transforming shipping in northwestern Europe, Venice's rentier rich restricted innovation. Ship construction in the Arsenale was nationalized shortly after the *Serrata*. While new, faster, ocean-going ship types were designed and built in Holland and England, such as the Dutch *fluyt*, the Arsenale continued to churn out the same sort of ponderously slow, less manoeuvrable galleys. Perhaps with only one state-owned boat-builder, there was simply not the sort of scope for the kinds of innovations happening elsewhere.

Venetian naval technology might have been sufficient to defeat the Turks at Lepanto in 1571, when galleys were pitched against galleys. But northwestern Europe had by then developed an entirely new kind of naval technology, with ships able to undertake long-distance ocean voyages, all of which left galleys, partly powered by rowers, increasingly obsolete. 'The *Serrata*', say Puga and Trefler, 'marked the beginning of the end of Venice's maritime power.'

Venice's slide from free-market capitalism to crony corporatism brought restrictions on manufacturing and labour, too. Before the thirteenth century, guilds had been expressly forbidden from boycotting customers and had never been permitted to exclude new workers from joining.[62]

That all changed long before Giorgia Boscolo had had the temerity to want to row a gondola. Guilds became compulsory and they were no longer open to anyone. They acted as a restraint on trade – as Giorgia was to discover – in the interests of allowing a privileged few a means of earning a living free from competition.

By the fifteenth century, there were detailed rules specifying what kind of apprenticeships textile workers had to have undertaken, and restricting who could work and in what capacity. Increasingly, Venetians were no longer free to sell their labour to whom they wished. In fact, workers even lost the right to leave. Skilled craftsmen of the Murano glassworks and shipwrights of

---

62 A statute of 1219 specifically forbade guilds from price-fixing and other restrictive practices.

the Arsenale were forbidden from emigrating. In 1460, it was decreed that caulkers attempting to leave Venice to sell labour elsewhere were liable to face six years in prison.[63]

The result of these constraints was that Venice lost her innovative edge – and not just in shipbuilding. In the sixteenth century, for example, silk merchants imposed restrictions on silk processors in order to protect their own interests – but in doing so prevented Venice's silk looms from adapting new techniques.

In the absence of opportunities for productive investment, the elite increasingly ploughed their capital not into trade or manufacturing, but into large estates on the *terra firma* mainland. So much so, in fact, that in 1677, a law was passed to try to stop this from happening.

Under the weight of parasitism, innovation gave way to stagnation. Once a place where outsiders came to make their fortune, Venice became a city where 'every man owed his position to what his father had been, from *stevedore* to customs house, through to the privileged craftsman of the Arsenale, and the secretariat in government bureaus up to nobles in the Senate and the Council of Ten'.[64]

Like our own emerging oligarchy, Venice's did not content itself with simply restricting trade in order to feather its own nest. They also helped themselves to public money. Bureaucracy expanded to provide employment to the well connected. A law passed in 1490 seems to suggest that most of the nobility in Venice by that time were living on the public payroll, enjoying some sort of sinecure. Sinecures permeated the Arsenale and the military, rendering both increasingly ineffective. The American Medievalist Frederick Lane blames the string of naval and military defeats that Venice suffered on the incompetence of over-promoted oligarchs.

63 Cipolla, C., *Before the Industrial Revolution: European Society and Economy 1000–1700* (1993), p. 189.
64 Lane, F.C., *Venice: A Maritime Republic*, p. 427.

As in our day, a class of quangocrats called the *Barnabotti* lived almost entirely at public expense. And, like our own public-sector elite, at times they lived quite lavishly. By the seventeenth century, they consumed over 200,000 ducats of state spending each year. In the last days of Venice as an independent state, more nobles were on the state payroll than there were members of the Grand Council.

To fund the sinecures, the parasites had to take from the productive. So taxes soared. In 1340, tax revenues yielded 250,000 ducats, 1.15 million ducats by 1500 and 2.45 million ducats by 1600. Unlike the Roman elite, the Venetians did not bother with debasing the currency. They simply imposed forced loans on those who were not politically well connected through a sort of compulsory bond-purchase scheme.

The guilds, too, became a kind of tax-farmer for the state. Once required to provide the government with a compliment of gallery rowers in times of crisis, the guilds began to pay a *galeotti* levy in lieu of this, which morphed into a tax. Perhaps it was in return for this that the guilds got rules and regulations that protected their interests.

The enrichment of the Venetian elite was not down to the free market. On the contrary: a small elite enriched themselves by restricting the market. In fifteenth-century Venice, capital was concentrated as a consequence of crony corporatism. When Napoleon finally did what no invader had achieved in a thousand years and launched a successful invasion across the lagoon, he snuffed out not a proud maritime nation of adventurers and entrepreneurs, but a grubby rentier republic.

Commenting on Venice's decline, many historians note how, from the sixteenth and seventeenth centuries, Venice lost her share of the market in Mediterranean textiles. The Dutch and the English producers simply undercut what Venice sold. The advent of Dutch and English competition might explain how Venice fell behind, but not why. The reason Venice's textiles were so hopelessly uncompetitive – why no Venetian producer, despite the head start of several centuries, seemed capable of making the sort of innovations in textile production that seemed to come so easily to her rivals – was, in large part, the restrictive practices of her guilds.

Parasitic vested interests caused Venice to stagnate, and then slowly decline. In other societies, parasites prevented take off in the first place.

CHINA: TAKE-OFF STALLED

'Of all the civilizations of pre-modern times,' writes the historian Paul Kennedy, 'none appeared more advanced, none felt more superior, that that of China.'[65]

Her fertile river valley, the Yangtze, was highly productive. China had invented printing by the ninth century, and gun powder by the eleventh. By then she had a unified canal system too, creating transport links and opening China to the possibility of specialization and exchange. The wheelbarrow, stirrup, compass, paper, porcelain and silk were all Chinese innovations.

In the twelfth century, China started to operate enormous blast furnaces, producing vast quantities of iron, and had invented water-powered machines to spin hemp. Indeed, when Venice's most famous son, Marco Polo, visited China in the late thirteenth century, she was far more technologically sophisticated than Europe's most advanced state at the time.

By the fifteenth century, China had twice as many people as Europe, a good number of large towns and cities, and almost all the ingredients that are said to have generated industrial take-off in northwestern Europe 400 years later. But it did not happen.

65 Kennedy, P., *The Rise and Fall of the Great Powers* (1987), p. 4.

Instead, she went backwards. Someone living in China in 1900 would have been on average a third poorer than someone living in China in 1500. China might have had a water-powered textile machine in the fourteenth century but she never produced a Richard Arkwright, whose water frame powered England's early industrial take-off. The compass guided not Chinese ships into European ports, but Portuguese and Spanish vessels on great voyages of global discovery.

China might have led the world in porcelain production in the sixteenth century, but she never managed the kind of mass production of what Europeans called 'China' that Josiah Wedgwood achieved in the eighteenth century. Paper and printing might have been Chinese inventions, but there were precious few new publications produced in China to add to the sum of secular knowledge.

China might have had a unified, hierarchical administration run by a well-educated Confucian bureaucracy, but they did not preside over progress. On the contrary, China failed precisely because she was presided over by these surplus-sucking, innovation-stifling parasites.

The Chinese state expropriated and oversaw, regulated and repressed. It took over any activity seen to be lucrative, prohibited what it could not control, fixed prices and extracted bribes. A class of omnipotent bureaucrats produced rules to govern every aspect of commerce, trade, production and indeed life itself, from the cradle to the grave.

Under the Ming, wrote French sinologist Étienne Balázs, 'no private undertakings nor any aspect of public life could escape official regulation...' There were 'clothing regulations, a regulation of public and private construction (dimension of houses)... all regulated'. There were state monopolies on salt, iron, tea, education and the use of the printed word. The Ming even banned all overseas trade.

Just as the European Union has thus far failed to produce an Amazon, or a Google, PayPal, Facebook, Apple or Airbnb, all that regulation in early-modern China meant that the sort of innovation happening elsewhere passed the Middle Kingdom by. China was a 'culturally and intellectually homeostatic society'.[66]

As in our own time, all those rules and regulations were introduced to serve vested interests. The mandarinate sought monopolies to ensure it reaped the proceeds of production. Officials set the price of commodities. Merchants were registered and taxed. Peasant farmers were heavily taxed to the point of subsistence existence. Any surplus was taken by the ruling elite.

By the end of the nineteenth century, China's population of 400 million was toiling to support a parasitic elite of 7.5 million, or 2 per cent of the population, who consumed almost a quarter of total national product. Despite all the initial promise, parasitism prevented China from taking off. In the mid-twentieth century, China was as poor and underdeveloped as she had been a thousand years before.

THE MIDDLE EAST AND INDIA: EARLY PROMISE ARRESTED

Early Islam's capacity for wealth creation was remarkable.

Carved out of the wreckage of the eastern half of the Roman empire, the early Abbasid rule conferred on the conquered territories many of the conditions needed to induce intensive economic growth.

The Middle East achieved a brief period of intensive economic growth and innovation, and the Arabs under the early Abbasids grew rich through production, not plunder.

66 Landes, D., *The Wealth and Poverty of Nations: Why Some Are So Rich and Some So Poor* (1998), p. 33.

By AD 1000, Abbasid Baghdad was one of the richest places on earth. Per-capita GDP reached $650 per year in today's money – substantially above the measly $427 in Europe at the same time.

The Abbasid empire formed what was in effect a giant single market. Within it, there was something of an agricultural revolution between 700 and 1100, with big advances in irrigation and the adoption of new crops, such as sugar, rice and cotton. Early Islam, argues the historian Benedikt Koehler, encouraged enterprise and free markets. While European rulers and pontiffs in the early Middle Ages were in the business of decreeing what constituted a 'fair' price, Muhammed – himself once a merchant – had declared prices to be 'in the hands of God'. It's no coincidence, Koehler reminds us, that many of the words we use today when we talk about trade – tariff, check, carat – are Arab in origin.

Under the early Abbasids, the Middle East enjoyed a new monetary regime and a legal system that allowed trade centres – *funquqs* – charitable trusts – *waqfs* – and an Arab version of the later Venetian *commenda* contract – *qirad* – which allowed capital to be invested on trading ventures and liability limited. In fact, Koehler argues, it was the other way round; the *commenda* was really a Venetian version of the *qirad* contract. The Venetians, he shows, got their idea for *commenda* contracts from the Arabs. Capitalism in northern Italy, he goes on to suggest, or rather the institutional arrangements and legal ideas that made it possible, did not arise in a vacuum. These ideas, rather like the new system of what we mistakenly sometimes refer to as 'Arabic' numerals, slowly taking hold in Europe, came via the Muslim world.

It is certainly the case that the Arab *qirad* and the Venetian *commenda* contracts, were – like the Roman system of bottomry loans before them – a strikingly similar answer to the problem of how to ensure capital could be invested, risks managed and liabilities limited. Whether each approach arose independently of one another or, as Koehler claims, the Venetians were emulating the Arabs with whom they traded in the East, the more important point surely is that such arrangements – be it bottomry, *qirad* and *commenda* contracts – could only have arisen in a society where the rights of the productive were relatively secure.

Of course, as we now know, parasitism in the Middle East eventually overwhelmed the productive from the tenth and eleventh centuries on. Having relied on a land tax, the Abbasids started to auction the right to collect it through a form of tax-farming in order to extract what they could, as quickly as they might, from the peasantry, who were paying over between 40 and 50 per cent of their produce to the tax collectors.

In time, like the Romans, the Abbasid elite resorted to expropriating property to get the surplus they required. The Abbasid empire became just another extortion racket. Innovation stopped. Per-capita incomes fell. Egypt, under the successor regime of the Ayyubids, moved from tax-farming to feudalism – with military service expected in place of set taxes. After 1171, trade became overtly protectionist.

If in the tenth century, the world's leading scientists might have written in Arabic, they did little thereafter to enhance technology in the Muslim world. The Muslim world began to regress to an almost European level of backwardness. By 1429, the Mamluk regime in Egypt, which maintained power through a slave army, was debasing the currency and banning exports of certain commodities altogether. All the characteristics of parasitism were there.

The Ottomans, who ruled over much of the Middle East from the fifteenth to the eighteenth centuries, were even worse. Their empire was a plunder machine. Taxes were so extortionate that their rule actually depopulated large swathes of territory, reducing parts of the Middle East and Europe to primitivism. Incomes per capita in the Ottoman empire in AD 1600 were below what they had been under Roman rule a millennium and a half before.

It is estimated that during the reign of the sixteenth-century sultan Suleiman the Magnificent, the fifty highest-ranking Ottoman officials received 15 per cent of total expenditure.

These are some of the most extreme instances of wealth inequality anywhere in human history – and it certainly was not a surfeit of capitalism that was to blame. About the only road open to personal enrichment within the Ottoman empire by the sixteenth century lay in purchasing a public post – and using it to extort. Trade depended on concessions granted by the authorities. The sultan seized whatever assets he pleased, including those of the nobility. State confiscation and despoilment were commonplace. There were, in effect, no property rights.

Such predation and parasitism did not encourage any progress at all. By the eighteenth century, Egypt had a per-capita income far lower than it had been in the eleventh century. India ought perhaps to have had even greater potential than Egypt and much of the Middle East. She had people – lots of them, being one of the most populous states in the Middle Ages. India produced innovations, in everything from ideas about maths to the production of cotton. But Indian society came to epitomize hierarchy and parasitism, with an inflexible, extortionate caste system that held her back.

'Century after century the standard of living in China, northern India, Mesopotamia, and Egypt hovered slightly above or below what might be called the threshold of pauperization,'[67] wrote the American anthropologist Marvin Harris in *Cannibals and Kings*.

The Mughal elite in India, rather like the Ottoman elite, luxuriated in water gardens and harems, surrounded by slaves, servants, jewels and splendour. They had zero involvement in any kind of productive activity and lived a life of luxury at the expense of the oppressed farmers and traders. They milked rural India as a parasitic warlord class.

67 Harris, M., *Cannibals and Kings* (1977), p. 156.

Lesser nobles were subject to 100 per cent death duties, their estates becoming the personal property of the emperor on their death. Jagir estates were awarded by the emperor to cronies for short periods, encouraging them to extract as much as they could out of the peasantry in as short a period as possible.

According to the French physician François Bernier, who lived at the court of the seventeenth-century Mughal Emperor Aurangzeb, property rights were so insecure that nominal land owners would not so much as bother to clear a ditch or repair a house for fear it would be confiscated. Like the Romans, the Mughals debased the coinage as a means of extortion. Trade monopolies were awarded in return for bribes. Membership of guilds became, in effect, hereditary and part of the caste system. Only those born to produce and sell certain things could do so.

There was almost no innovation in northern India under the Mughals. Indeed, it was not until the nineteenth century that Gutenberg's idea of a printing press came to India. The colossal mass of ordinary Indians existed in a state of crushing poverty. Parasitism induced sclerosis. Per-capita income remained unchanged for a century and a half after Akbar – the third Mughal emperor, whose reign ended in 1605 – before falling further in the late eighteenth century.

At the time of Emperor Akbar's death, three-quarters of the land tax, approximately two-thirds of total revenue, went to the army – and that was long after Akbar had stopped waging external wars. The emperor and his top 122 officials received about one-eighth of national product. That is to say, 0.0006 per cent of households took 12.5 per cent of total wealth.

None of this concentration of capital was due to a surfeit of capitalism.

It was only after India's external parasites were ejected in 1947, and her own elite interfered less in trade and exchange in the

1980s, that India began finally to enjoy sustained, rapid intensive economic growth.

NORTHERN ITALY IN THE EARLY MIDDLE AGES: STOP, START, STOP

If China, the Middle East and India were held back by parasitic elites, signs of early promise snuffed out, they at least never managed to regress quite as far and as dramatically as Western Europe did between the fifth and tenth centuries.

Predation and parasitism destroyed civilization across Europe. The reason we call this period the Dark Ages – and know so little about it – is that literate society in many places ceased to exist. Only centuries later, in what we now know as the Middle Ages, do we start to see much evidence of advancement – most notably in northern Italy.

Of course, Venice was not the only northern-Italian city state that started to flourish in the early Middle Ages. From the eleventh century, other settlements in northern Italy – notably Milan, Florence, Cremona, Pisa and Genoa – started to enjoy those pre-conditions for progress; independence – as the power of the emperor over city-states waned; dispersed power – as the communes adopted republican constitutions; and interdependence – as trade picked up.

The manorial system, which I have suggested started to take shape in the last century before the collapse of Roman authority in Western Europe, began to disintegrate in northern Italy in the mid-twelfth century. This hints at the end of complete self-sufficiency, with greater monetary trade and therefore more specialization, exchange – and wealth.

Italy also started to see innovation, with the invention of the mechanical clock and spectacles, as well as improvements in the design of ships, artillery and windmills. There was, at the same time, financial innovation, with the advent of bills of exchange and banking allowing greater trade. Medieval Italy experienced a marked increase in consumption and productive investment, too. The late Italian economic historian Carlo Cipolla recounts how, in the eleventh century, the opening of a new mill was a major deal in the neighbourhood. A couple of centuries later, mills were commonplace.[68]

Markets and regional trade fairs also expanded across much of Europe. There was a massive expansion in textile processing before 1350, using imported cotton, silk and know-how from the East. Lucca had water-powered silk works by 1200. In Milan, there were an estimated 6–9,000 cotton workers by 1348, and even more in Florence and Genoa.

It seemed in some ways as if northern Italy in the twelfth and thirteenth centuries was almost on the verge of the kind of textile revolution that England underwent 500 years later. But it never happened. The pull of the parasites was just too strong. Take-off stalled – just as it did in China and elsewhere.

During the fourteenth century, to an even greater extent than happened in Venice, power in the other northern-Italian city-states was concentrated in the hands of a few. Consuls, who had administered many city-states in the communes' republican tradition, were replaced by *podesta* magistrates, who often became hereditary. While Venice moved from an open to a closed system of oligarchy, most other Italian city-states ended up in the hands of a tyrant, or *il signore*. Perhaps what made Venice exceptional is that she was able to stave off the parasites a little bit more effectively and for a little bit longer than many of the other city-states around her.

The *signore* elites that emerged in most medieval Italian city-

---

68   Cipolla, C., *Before the Industrial Revolution: European Society and Economy 1000–1700* (1993), p. 219.

states found it easier to enrich themselves through taxation than via the difficult business of commerce. Tax revenues in city-states increased dramatically as the parasitic princelings milked the merchants. Annual expenditure in Siena, for example, rose from a modest 6,300 lira in 1226 to a crushing 347,000 lira by 1328. This was a massive addition to the burden that the *signori* imposed on merchants and the productive. Often the parasitic elites had to resort to forced loans, where a wealthy merchant found himself becoming the owner of a virtually worthless IOU, in return for lending the civic authorities a large sum of ready cash.

Taxes were then spent in ways that rewarded parasites: interest payments on loans – so bondholders did well; increased military spending – so mercenaries, or *condotti*, did well. In Venice, defence expenditure meant generous contracts awarded to vested interests not especially good at converting financial strength into naval muscle – so suppliers might have done well, too.

The emergence of parasitic *signori* allowed a tiny elite to accumulate capital in the Italian cities. In 1427, for example, the richest 10 per cent in Florence had 68 per cent of the wealth. The poorest 60 per cent, a mere 5 per cent.[69] Rather like in our own time, it seems to have been bondholders in particular who did well.

The *signori* were not the only parasites in the communes. As in Venice, guilds restricted voluntary exchange as well. They compelled producers to use established techniques, impeding innovation. They set quality standards, preventing producers from supplying lower-cost products to a potentially wider market. They made sure only certain kinds of apprentices could make certain kinds of products, or work in certain trades. They even had the right to seize the goods of any rivals threatening to offer the customer a better deal.

69 Ibid., p. 11.

So, as happened in Venice, textile exports across northern Italy collapsed. The proto-industrialization that seemed to be gaining momentum in northern-Italian cities fizzled out. In the early 1500s, the number of woollen workshops in Florence fell from 270 to 60. Its nascent industry lost market share to Dutch and English competitors unhindered by anti-competitive practices.

Having been at the forefront of economic development and innovation in Europe between 1000 and 1500, Italy stagnated. The country might not have seen the absolute decline in per-capita income that China experienced over that period but, nevertheless, between 1500 and 1800, Italian income per capita flatlined.

We must add northern Italy to that long list of places – including China under the Ming, the Middle East under the Abbasids, and India under the Mughals – where even the most promising progress came to grief as a consequence of small parasitic elites.

EUROPE: A GRINDINGLY SLOW ESCAPE

Historians of the Middle Ages seem to report finding a 'renaissance' wherever they look. Some have claimed to have spotted a Carolingian renaissance in the eighth and ninth centuries. Others say they found one in the tenth century, while several medieval renaissances are alleged to have happened in the twelfth century. Perhaps these apparent discoveries tell us more about the tendency specialist historians have to overstate the significance of 'their' period of history than they do about the past.

During the Middle Ages, some progress took place. There were improvements in farming, with the adoption of a heavier, wheeled plough and the use of crop rotation. Milling technology improved, with more water mills and new designs of windmill. But the Middle Ages need to be put into perspective. Between 1000 and 1500, per-capita output in the West rose from $426 to $754 in today's money. Or by 77 per cent stretched out over half a millennium.

There might have been some intensive growth but it was grindingly, painfully slow. We have experienced more economic expansion in the past three decades than there was in half a millennium of the Middle Ages. Indeed, growth in the Middle Ages wasn't just slow from a modern perspective but by the standards of the Roman republic. Per-capita income in Italy doubled over a period of 300 years between 300 BC and AD 14 – more than the increase in output over 500 years in the Middle Ages.

By 1500, Europe might have progressed in relation to other parts of the world but it was by no means clear that she was ahead – certainly not militarily. She endured a series of military defeats: Wahlstatt in 1241, Nicopolis in 1396 and the Siege of Vienna in 1529 – following which the Balkans were lost to the Ottomans.

E. L. Jones, the famous Australian scholar, wrote about the 'European miracle'. But before the sixteenth century, if not the nineteenth for many, it was an extraordinarily slow-moving miracle. In fact, progress was so slow during the Middle Ages that, after 500 years of successive renaissances, Europe's per-capita income was still below what it had been in Italy in the first century AD.

Europe had not made enough progress between the tenth and fourteenth centuries to escape Malthusian constraints. The Black Death in the mid-fourteenth century was a brutal manifestation of this fact. From 1348 to the 1650s, a series of catastrophic plagues reduced Europe's population by between a quarter and a third. War and famine played their part, too. In 1500, Europe's population of 60 to 70 million was lower than its estimated 80 million in 1300. For all the progress of the Middle Ages, there was no miraculous escape from age-old constraints.

But, despite this, Europe in the Middle Ages was one of few places on the planet where there had been any intensive economic growth over the preceding two millennia. Why was it that Europe made progress, albeit so slow? Because she was steadily starting to escape the grip of the parasites.

If you study a map of Europe in 1500, you will see it consisted of a mosaic of states and statelets. In contrast to China, or the empires of the Mughals, Abbasids or Ottomans, Europe was never unified politically.

'There existed no uniform authority in Europe which could effectively halt this or that commercial development,' writes Paul Kennedy. 'No central government whose changes in priorities could cause the rise and fall of a particular industry; no systematic and universal plundering of businessmen and entrepreneurs by tax gatherers, which so retarded the economy of Mogul India.'[70]

The closest thing to any kind of pan-European authority, the papacy, was weak. As we have seen, Venice could simply ignore the papal ban on overseas trading with Muslims in a way that Chinese traders couldn't ignore similar bans under the Ming. Without a single political authority imposing uniform policy, there could be – to use modern management-speak – systems competition, like there was in ancient Greece.

If one prince taxed trade too highly, or imposed too many obligations on merchants, they would move. If one king repudiated his debts, he would find it hard to get a loan again. Good ideas and innovation could spread. Semi-autonomous cities in the Middle Ages were a distinctively European phenomenon. There was no equivalent of Dutch burghers or Italian communes in Japan, India or China, beyond the jurisdiction of the emperor or local warlord.

Harvard economist and historian David Landes, author of *The Wealth and Poverty of Nations*, recounts the story of how the Count of Flanders in the twelfth century marched into Bruges to reclaim a runaway serf. The townsfolk drove him and his

70 Kennedy, P., *The Rise and Fall of the Great Powers* (1987), p. 19.

henchmen out. Fragmentation did not prevent parasitism, but it was a restraining influence. During the Middle Ages, it is possible to see, very gradually, the slow emergence of a market economy, greater respect for property rights and the restraining influence of law.

There was a gradual 'widening of the market that promoted specialization and division of labour', according to Landes. And it meant that 'the world of Adam Smith was already taking shape 500 years before his time'.[71]

It's no coincidence that progress happened where the parasites were at their weakest. 'Market activity was greatest in areas of half-hearted control such as borderlands between feudal units or pairs of political authorities.'[72] Or on inaccessible mud banks, such as Venice. Or in that other swampy corner of Europe, known as the Netherlands – home of the world's first industrial revolution.

71 Landes, D., *The Wealth and Poverty of Nations: Why Some Are So Rich and Some So Poor* (1998), p. 44.
72 Jones, E. *The European Miracle: Environments, economies and geopolitics in the history of Europe and Asia* (1981), p. 91.

9

THE MIRACLE
OF MODERNITY

With the exception of Venice, republican Rome, and maybe ancient Greece, almost everybody else who had ever lived before the seventeenth century had only a subsistence existence.

Where riches had been accumulated in the courts and harems of kings and emperors, it had been through extortion. The tiny few who were rich became rich by taking from everyone else. In this world of Malthusian gloom, progress flickered only sporadically. But, starting in the Netherlands, something extraordinary happened, which would ultimately make prosperity, rather than poverty, the norm for billions of people the world over. What changed?

DUTCH BOOM

The Dutch economy was the first modern economy in the world. Over three generations in the seventeenth century, Dutch per-capita income increased by a greater amount than it had during all the previous generations who had ever lived.

But, at first glance, Holland's emergence was unlikely. Like Venice, the Netherlands was a soggy backwater, with few natural resources. Yet, as with Venice, those key conditions that allow intensive economic growth to take hold all happened to be in place.

Firstly, the Dutch achieved their independence from foreign rule, ousting those archetypal parasites, the Spanish branch of the Habsburgs, during the Dutch Revolt, which began in the 1560s. Although it looked for a time in the 1580s and again in the 1620s as if they might get gobbled up again, their independence was finally recognized in 1648.

Secondly, power was dispersed within the new republic. The Union of Utrecht in 1579 created an awkward amalgamation of seven different autonomous provinces, unified under a central administration in the form of the Stadtholder and States General. The central authorities had responsibility for a common defence, foreign and, to some extent, fiscal policy. But there were so many constraints on the power of the executive that the contemporary Dutch thinker, Hugo Grotius – perhaps a little fancifully – compared the United Provinces with the Roman republic, with its ornate system of checks and balances.

At a local level, there were drainage boards, or *waterschappen*, with independent tax-raising powers. Towns were, to a large degree, self-governing. The rebellious Dutch had long had a free peasantry, with feudal obligations having disappeared much earlier. In 1538, William the Silent, the leader of the Dutch revolt against Spain, had observed that 'there are no feudal goods in the countryside... for all the lands are freely owned'.

With the end of the Habsburg menace, heavy taxes disappeared, as did the granting of special commercial privileges. With towns run by local merchants, after 1590, guild restrictions were removed and restrictive practices abolished.

Finally, the new republic was interconnected by virtue of geography, sitting at a confluence of waterways. Rivers linked her to Germany and the European interior. The sea linked her to the Baltic, Scandinavia, England, France, Spain, the Mediterranean and beyond.

Her ocean-going *fluyt* ships opened up new markets, as she began to trade in salt, fish, wine, grain and timber – and, from the sixteenth century, spice, cloth, silk and copper. Longer-distance voyages were launched to Brazil and the Far East. War, meanwhile, meant a large influx of migrants, who poured into the United Provinces bringing know-how, entrepreneurial flair and capital – which helped the textile trade in particular. By the 1590s, one in ten people in Holland was an immigrant. Over half of the largest depositors at the Bank of Amsterdam were Walloons.[73]

This combination of independence, free internal markets, international trade and new capital transformed the Netherlands from a backwater into a booming economy. The Dutch grew rich by processing tobacco, weaving silk, refining sugar, and making everything from bricks to watches, glass to guns, maps to beer. And all for a mass market.

As the Dutch accumulated more capital, they invested it – intensifying the boom. In 1602, Holland became home to the world's first modern stock market: the Amsterdam Stock Exchange. Moreover, capital was invested in new industrial technology. Italian innovators had done little more than toy with the idea of water-powered frames. The Dutch pioneered new windmill technology, which alongside a plentiful supply of peat, provided the energy input for their industrial take-off. By the early 1600s, there were thousands of windmills, including industrial ones used to power timber saws, grain presses, paper mills, textile frames and even the production of dyes.

Consequently, Dutch productivity increased and production

73 Cipolla, C., *Before the Industrial Revolution: European Society and Economy 1000–1700* (1993), p. 268.

rapidly expanded. There were three sugar refineries in Amsterdam in 1603. By 1660, there were sixty. Leiden produced 30,000 pieces of cloth in 1585. By 1665, she was making 140,000 a year. Dutch workers were producing so much more efficiently than anyone else that they commanded high wages.

Urbanization – in part, enabled by a free labour market – intensified the gains of industrialization and trade. By the seventeenth century, the Netherlands was easily the most urban country in the world, with over half her population living in towns and cities.[74] Dutch ports became great centres of shipping and commerce. So much so, in fact, that a Venetian diplomat lamented how Amsterdam was 'the image of Venice in the days when Venice was thriving'.[75]

Indeed, like Venice, Dutch greatness lay in the precocity with which people learnt to earn a living through specialization and exchange. Specializing in finished goods while trading for other products, including raw materials, is what made the Netherlands wealthy. Already, by 1567, Italian traveller Lodovico Guicciardini marvelled at how the Dutch consumed more bread, finer wines and textiles, and had higher-quality furniture, despite not themselves producing much in the way of grain, wine, flax, wool or wood.[76]

Whereas almost 60 per cent of people in the UK were still engaged in agriculture in 1700, only 40 per cent of the Dutch were by then, with approximately a third of the workforce in industry.[77] It was a triumph of what the English economist David Ricardo would call comparative advantage, as resources

---

74 Kennedy, P., *The Rise and Fall of the Great Powers* (1987), p. 68.
75 Cipolla, C., *Before the Industrial Revolution: European Society and Economy 1000–1700* (1993), p. 267.
76 Ibid., p. 265.
77 For more detail about urbanization, and the transition from agriculture to industry, see Wrigley, A., 'Urban Growth and Agricultural Change: England and the Continent in the Early Modern Period', *The Journal of Interdisciplinary History* (1985), pp. 683–728.

were allocated to those sectors in which the country was most internationally competitive.

Describing what made the Dutch so wealthy, Daniel Defoe (1660–1731) wrote that it was because they were '... the carryers of the World, the middle Persons in Trade... they buy to sell again, take in to send out; and the greatest part of their vast Commerce consists in being supply'd from all parts of the World, that they may supply all the World again'.[78]

Because Holland's gains were made possible by an absence of parasitism, prosperity wasn't concentrated but shared. Dutch living standards soared. Per-capita income in 1500 was at about the European average of $761 (using Angus Maddison's constant prices, again) – which was below the standard of living enjoyed by people in Italy in the last days of the Roman republic. A century later, in 1600, Dutch incomes had almost doubled to $1,381. By 1700, they were almost $2,130.

Nor were the social benefits of the Dutch golden age confined to economic prosperity. Science and learning flourished, too. There were twelve university-type institutions within the republic, including the University of Leiden. In the seventeenth century, it is estimated that twenty-five out of every thousand young men had had a university education. Nowhere in Europe was this percentage higher until the First World War.

Despite the unprecedented progress that took place in Holland, the Dutch economic miracle is sometimes forgotten. Why? Perhaps because, although the Dutch were the first to modernize, they were not the mightiest. For a brief period, the Dutch navy had a string of successes and Dutch armies held their own against the French and Spanish. But she simply was not numerically large enough to become a first-rate European power.

Moreover, Holland's achievement, as home to the world's first

78 Defoe, D., *A Plan of the English Commerce* (1728).

industrial revolution, might have been rather overlooked because her accomplishments were so overshadowed by the industrial take-off enjoyed by her neighbour: England.

ENGLAND, THEN AMERICA

The English, too, had those three magic ingredients – independence, dispersed power and interconnectedness – necessary to induce intensive economic take-off. And, unlike the Dutch, she had coal, rather than wind and peat, to power it all.

Long since independent, the English had a history of imposing constraints on their kings. The Common Law tradition meant that the law was determined by what had gone before, not the whim of the current monarch. Most famously, in 1215 King John had had his wings clipped by the barons who forced him to sign Magna Carta.

Yet it's important not to overstate the extent to which the power of English kings was limited. For all the charters and supposed constraints, the Tudor strongman, Henry VIII, had freely expropriated and extorted in the 1540s, debasing the currency and seizing what he wanted, just like any other parasite. England remained a relatively poor and backward island off the coast of Europe.

It was not until the extraordinary upheavals of the seventeenth century that monarchical absolutism came into conflict with the insurgent power of Parliament. The victorious Parliamentarians defeated Charles I in battle before beheading him in 1649. Eventually, in 1688, they imported a Dutch monarch with what they hoped would be a Dutch appreciation of monarchical minimalism.

Just as the Venetians had once presented their new Doge with a *promissore* contract, curbing his power, King William of Orange was bound by the new Bill of Rights, passed by Parliament in 1689.

The Act of Settlement, passed in 1701, placed further constraint upon executive power, preventing a monarch from waging non-defensive wars without Parliament's permission and limiting the king's ability to appoint whomever he wanted to public office.

It is no coincidence that the Glorious Revolution was followed by the Industrial Revolution. The former was the essential precursor of the latter. England's new Whig elite might have been an oligarchy but they were a far cry from the absolutist monarchy of the old order. Increasingly, producers were protected from the parasitism of the ruling classes.

At the start of the seventeenth century, there had been over 700 monopolies sold by the crown. Awarded by the king in return for money, they controlled the manufacture and sale of everything from soap and starch to bricks, buttons, coal and iron. In 1623, early on in its struggle against absolutism, Parliament had tried to abolish these restrictions with the Statute of Monopolies. By the end of the seventeenth century, almost all had gone.

A series of seventeenth-century court cases removed many of the medieval restrictions on labour and diminished the power of the guilds. Already, from 1614, an apprentice in one trade was free to work in another.[79]

Tax extortion became a thing of the past. At the beginning of the seventeenth century, a Stuart monarch had imposed ship money – theoretically a tax to fund the navy – on the merchant class. By the end of the seventeenth century, Parliamentary approval was required before any taxes could be imposed. Taxes were also removed from production. The hearth tax, which had been an impost upon the productive in some of the nascent cottage textile industries, was abolished in 1689 with the arrival of the new, pro-the-productive regime.

79 Jones, E. *The European Miracle: Environments, Economies and Geopolitics in the History of Europe and Asia* (1981) p. 99.

In 1694, the Bank of England was established. This helped ensure that credit was not restricted to the king's cronies, as had happened before. Records from one London bank in the early decades of the eighteenth century show that capital was increasingly allocated to merchants and businessmen that needed it, not simply lords and aristocrats with the political connections to demand it.[80]

Consequently, production and trade were free to grow. As Adam Smith noted a century later: 'In Great Britain industry is perfectly secure; and though it is far from being perfectly free, it is as free or freer than in any other part of Europe.'

Britain also had the third ingredient needed for intensive growth. It was interconnected – both internally and externally. New turnpike roads and canals cut the cost of transport, not only making it easier for producers to bring their goods to market, but also facilitating regional specialization. The ability to access a wide variety of goods through exchange enabled cities to specialize in the industry in which they were most competitive – exploiting comparative advantage, just like the Dutch. Daniel Defoe could see the signs of specialization everywhere in his *Tour Through the Whole Island of Great Britain*: metal goods in Sheffield, woollens in East Anglia, cotton in Manchester, potteries in Cheshire, glass-making in the Midlands.

It wasn't only England's internal trade network that improved, either. England accessed a vast international network, too. Like the Dutch, she traded with the Baltic and Scandinavia, and with France and Spain. Her commerce with the world beyond Europe expanded too, especially with the West Indies, north America, India and the Far East.

Wider international trade enabled even greater specialization

---

80 Acemoğlu, A. and Robinson, James A., *Why Nations Fail: The Origins of Power, Prosperity and Poverty* (2012), p.195.

at home. By the start of the eighteenth century, raw cotton was being imported and processed in Lancashire and the north. By the 1790s, there were hundreds of cotton mills, with over 500 textile businesses in Manchester alone.

The combination of both fewer restrictions on the free exchange of goods, labour and capital, and a growing web of trade links made the Industrial Revolution possible. Investment flowed into productive new technology. Labour was divided efficiently, based on market demand. The import of raw materials from around the world freed up resources for specialization in manufacture.

By exploiting her comparative advantage in industry, England became the wealthiest society the world had ever known. If Holland had been the richest place on the planet at the end of the seventeenth century, by the end of the eighteenth it was England. By the late nineteenth century, she accounted for almost a quarter of the world's manufacturing output.

Between 1760 and 1830, the UK accounted for two-thirds of Europe's industrial output growth, and her share of manufacturing production shot up from 1.9 per cent to 9.5 per cent. By 1860, her output share was up to 19.9 per cent; by 1880, 22.9 per cent.[81] The UK produced over half the world's iron by 1860, and half its coal. Her energy consumption by 1860 was five times that of the US or Germany, six times that of France, and 155 times that of Russia.[82]

The United Kingdom by 1860 was responsible for a fifth of the world's commerce, and two-fifths of the world's trade in manufactured goods. But if the English had shot up the development ladder, overtaking the Dutch, there were soon a host of others scrambling up behind them – starting with the recently formed United States of America.

81 Kennedy, P., *The Rise and Fall of the Great Powers* (1987), pp. 149–51.
82 Ibid.

In 1776, the American colonies did what the Dutch had done a century and a half before. They ejected the external parasites – not the Habsburgs but the Hanoverian George III – and established a free republic. Then, in 1787, they adopted a constitution that dispersed power. Instead of the *ad hoc* arrangements put in place by the post-revolutionary Dutch and English, the US Founding Fathers drafted a deliberate and sublimely crafted charter, which harked back to the Roman republic.

During the century that separated the two revolutions on either side of the Atlantic, the works of the Greek scholar Polybius, which described in detail the Roman republican system, had been rediscovered and widely reprinted. The US Founding Fathers who met in that Philadelphia court house in the summer of 1787 to draft their constitution had read Polybius. They were familiar with the Roman republican tradition in a way that the Dutch and the English at the time of their upheavals were not.

It's why they built a Senate and a Capitol Hill on the banks of the Potomac. Although the Dutchman Grotius had compared the hodgepodge constitution of the United Provinces to that of the Roman republic, it was nothing like it. That's not just my view. It was the view of James Madison and the other American Founding Fathers who, unlike the English revolutionaries of 1688, rejected the Dutch approach for its 'imbecility'.[83]

Polybius gave the Founding Fathers a sense of the intricate checks and balances that could be put in place to ensure that no one faction predominated. Power in the fledgling American republic was to be shared between the constituent states and a federal authority. Instead of two consuls presiding over the American republic for a year, they opted for a single president for four years. The executive branch of government was constrained by a powerful legislature and judiciary. No one faction or party,

83 See Publius, *The Federalist Papers (1787–88)*, no. 20.

Madison and his colleagues hoped, could ever dominate. They put in place safeguards not only against another George III, but against the emergence of an American Caesar or rabble-rousing *signore*.

Parasitism in America may not have ended with the American Revolution. Slavery continued on a vast scale for almost another century, only ending as the result of civil war. But the United States' constraints on the power of the ruling classes, and protections for freedom, were unique. And the economic results were astonishing.

The fledgling republic did not just prosper. Within a century of its birth, it had become the greatest economy on earth, with its citizens consistently enjoying some of the most elevated living standards anywhere. So much so, in fact, that in every decade since the establishment of the American republic, millions – at times, tens of millions – have moved from every corner of the planet to live there and enjoy the fruits of its remarkable intensive economic growth.

By the early twentieth century, the United States had overtaken the United Kingdom economically. By mid-century, she accounted for approximately 40 per cent of the world's economic output. Like golden-age Holland, the United States does not stand out only as an economic powerhouse either. America's contribution to science and learning are without precedent. At the forefront of the Industrial Revolution of the nineteenth century, America today leads the way in the digital revolution.

JAPAN AND GERMANY FOLLOW

The idea that intensive economic take-off started in 1800 with the world's first industrial revolution in England is far too simplistic. As we have seen, there was a cumulative process of specialization and exchange, which had already started to lift living standards in the Netherlands from the sixteenth century.

If it is obvious to us with hindsight that a process of intensive economic take-off was underway in the late eighteenth century, it was not always evident to contemporary observers, not least to the likes of Thomas Robert Malthus. Rather than seeing the process of intensive economic growth as a phenomenon particular to certain countries, perhaps a better way of thinking of it is as a web of specialization and exchange. The web was initially small and confined to only a few.

As the seventeenth century became the eighteenth, more people were drawn into the web, which became more complex. In the nineteenth century, it was not only the Americans who became part of it, following Holland and England up the ladder towards intensive economic growth; other European states, notably Germany, followed and even, in the last few decades of the century, Japan.

Almost everything about Germany in the early nineteenth century discouraged specialization and exchange. Agricultural workers were tied to the land. Society was divided into status groups – or *Stande* – which reserved certain vocations to people born into certain backgrounds. Merchants were awarded trade monopolies but were not allowed to own land. Industrial crafts were the exclusive preserve of trained craftsmen and their apprentices.

In large swathes of Germany, an almost medieval division of society into distinct orders – lords, peasants, clergy, merchants and artisans – still prevailed. Early-nineteenth-century Germany was ruled by a parasitic elite, who extorted what they could from both peasants and merchants. Trade was constrained by an extraordinarily complex array of tolls and taxes on roads and rivers that made it difficult to carry goods. There were thirty-eight different tariff systems in Germany in 1815, as well as thousands of local river tolls, fees and charges.

But as the nineteenth century progressed, much of this was to change. In 1809, Prussia abolished serfdom, freeing labourers to earn money for a living. Landowners lost out – at least in the western part of Germany, if not in the east where traditional servility continued until well into the twentieth century.

The Napoleonic invasion, in the first decade of the nineteenth century, might have caused turmoil, but it swept away many of the mini-statelets – and, with them, the barriers to trade. From 1834, the German customs union, or *Zollverein*, allowed many of the local tariffs and charges to be abolished. Taking away from local feudal overlords their means of extortion was a slow and painful process, and it was only completed with German unification in 1871 when local jurisdictions were simply dissolved.

Unification also put the final nail in the coffin of restrictive guilds who, with the advent of a central authority, were no longer able to impose constraints on local urban economies. Germany's mosaic of local economies started to merge into a unified economy. Attempts to re-impose constraints on competition and trade failed. Within the German customs union, goods and services could be moved around freely for the first time.

The removal of internal feudal parasites, in tandem with the growth of a trading network, opened up Germany to specialization and exchange. The result was rapid industrial growth in the last three decades of the nineteenth century. By the end of the century, Germany, like the US, had in many respects overtaken the English.

Something similar was underway in Japan, too, where the end of the old feudal constraints allowed a sudden transformation. For several centuries, the Japanese peasants had been horrifically put upon. The Keian edict of 1649 specifically forbade farmers from eating any rice that they grew, ordering them instead to live off millet and vegetables. The surplus that they produced went to a feudal elite, the *samurai* and the *daimyo*, while the farmers themselves endured a subsistence existence.

Japan was also cut-off from the world, fiercely opposing any outside influences – including commerce. For much of the sixteenth and seventeenth centuries, Japanese citizens were forbidden from travelling overseas on pain of death, and what little trade did occur – the Dutch were virtually alone with a trading station in Japan – was tightly controlled.

Not surprisingly, with parasites lording it over the productive and trade limited, living standards in Japan in 1850 were virtually unchanged from 1600. Having been the third most populous state on the planet in 1600 (China and India were ahead), the population flatlined and did not increase until the mid-nineteenth century.

But then in the mid-nineteenth century, Japan had a revolution: the Meji Restoration of 1867. The Tokugawa clan, who had run the country as a collection of fiefdoms for centuries, went the way of the Habsburgs and the Stuarts. And just like England's upheavals in the seventeenth century, or German unification in the nineteenth, the end of the old feudal order helped erode monopolies and restraint.

Feudal fiefdoms, *han*, were abolished and became not the private preserve of feudal overlords – *daimyo* – but prefectures overseen by central government. Japanese peasants no longer had to pay 40 per cent of their produce to parasitic *samurai* and overlords, but instead taxes to the imperial government. The *samurai* might have attempted a counter-coup in 1878, when they assassinated one of the chief architects of the change, Okubo Toshimichi. But their days as an elite, able to live at the expense of merchants and peasants, were over.

Even before the overthrow of the old order, Japan had started to open herself up to outside influences after centuries of self-imposed isolation. In 1868, the radical *rangakusha* officials, who supported the new order, opened Japanese ports to foreign trade. In 1871, a delegation was sent to Europe and America to assess how modernity had elevated those societies. They returned full of enthusiasm for reform, and Japan consciously set out to imitate what was seen to have worked in the West.

Consequently, Japan began to industrialize – and specialize. Between 1886 and 1894, thirty-three new mills were founded, mostly in the Osaka area. By the end of the century, Japanese mills were producing 355 million pounds of yarn. By 1913, production had almost doubled – amounting to a quarter of the world's cotton yarn output.

To be clear, even at the outbreak of the First World War, Japan remained something of an industrial pygmy in comparison to many Western states. Her output was not much greater than, say, Italy's. But significantly, Japan was the first Asian state to begin to catch up with the West. And that was because she was the first Asian state to have the three key ingredients to achieve intensive growth: she had overthrown her own internal parasites, she had consciously opened herself up to a global commercial network, and she had kept herself independent from those external European predators that annexed almost every other Asian state.

THE REST OF ASIA, AFRICA AND THE WORLD

By the late 1950s, most Asian states had achieved their independence, ejecting their external parasitic overlords. Then – starting with Singapore, Hong Kong and South Korea in the 1960s and 1970s – successive Asian states opened themselves up to world trade, investment and influence. They were able to join that network of global interdependence that today envelops almost all of humankind. Intensive growth took off.

China and India followed suit in the 1980s, then Vietnam and Indonesia in the 1990s. To be sure, both China and India delayed their take-off until the last two decades of the last century because they continued to have problems inflicted by their own internal elites. China's Great Leap Forward and Cultural Revolution caused famine, misery and chaos. In Nehru's India, a policy of permits and autarky – or economic self-sufficiency – meant three decades of stagnation.

But in both those states, the key moments came in the late 1970s (China) and early 1980s (India) when the elites stopped trying to command development and let change happen organically. China started to take off not because her ruling Communist Party got things right, but because they got out of the way.

Matt Ridley shows how the decision to decollectivize Chinese agriculture was not made on the basis of a concerted strategy from the top. On the contrary, it happened through voluntary exchange among ordinary people. After appalling agricultural performance, some villagers – a man called Yen Jingchang, according to Ridley – agreed to allow each other to work for themselves and retain the fruits of their own labour. The practice spread and by the time Deng Xiaoping formally allowed family farms, the policy was simply recognizing what had become a reality for many on the ground.

Similarly, from 1978, when the Communist Party started to decentralize control over state-owned enterprises, they paved the way for those who ran them to benefit from their performance. Yet this was not rooted in any new dogma but happened because those who took over the Communist Party wanted to repudiate the dogmatic Gang of Four.

What ensured the extraordinary intensive economic growth we have seen in China over the past three decades is not some grand plan, but rather the absence of interference from grand planners. In the last two decades, Africa, too, has started to climb the development ladder – as the key ingredients that enable intensive growth have started to come together.

Like their counterparts in Asia, African countries gained their independence from external, European parasites. But independence on its own was not enough. Post-colonial Africa exchanged European elites for local – arguably more extractive – despots. For thirty or forty years after independence, many African states failed as a result. But over the last twenty years, local elites have been reined in. Where there were autocrats in Africa there are now democracies, and where there were dictators, autocrats.

At the same time, Africa's commerce with the rest of the world has increased thanks to the digital revolution. Now that parts of Africa can be as interconnected through the worldwide web as anywhere else, tens of millions of Africans have begun to join the global economy. Independence, internal freedom and global trade are enabling Africans, finally, to break the Malthusian trap.

As more countries have begun to gain from specialization and exchange, only a tiny handful of societies remain impervious to progress. They are the ones that remain the preserve of parasitic elites – the Congo or Tajikistan – or cut-off from the rest of us – North Korea.

It's an extraordinary story, isn't it? What a tiny number of Dutchmen and women started to do in the seventeenth century – specialize and exchange – almost all of humanity is now doing. But there is, of course, another side of the story. The march of modernity has not been a tale of constant progress.

10

WHEN PARASITES
STRIKE BACK

Stefan Zweig was born into a wealthy middle-class family in Vienna in 1881. His father had made money in textiles, and they were typical of the kind of prosperous bourgeois family that the Industrial Revolution had created during the second half of the nineteenth century.

Zweig graduated in 1904 from the University of Vienna, a distinguished seat of Western rational thought, before embarking on a career as a writer. During the 1920s and 1930s, indeed, he became one of the most popular writers in the world.

Everything about that world for the first few decades of Zweig's life suggested progress and permanence. It was, he later wrote, a 'golden age of security'. Vienna, his home, had been 'an international metropolis for 2,000 years'. But the world for Zweig, and for millions of others whose lives had been enhanced in almost every conceivable way over the previous few generations, fell apart.

Jewish, Zweig was forced to 'steal away from Vienna like a thief in the night'. His books, once beloved by millions, were burnt.

He found exile in England and the New World. But millions of Jews who did not flee were murdered in the years that followed. Millions perished.

In 1942, Zweig killed himself in despair. Europe – where the miracle of modernity had begun – had become a continent of savagery. Zweig's *The World of Yesterday*, the manuscript of which he sent to his publisher the day before he took his own life, is a lament for the past – and a timeless reminder to us that there is nothing inevitable about improvements in the human condition.

Zweig's story is proof that modernity is no guarantee that the productive will always be free from the parasitic, or that tyranny is impossible. Dramatic regressions have happened not just in antiquity, but within living memory. The history of Germany and Japan in the first half of the twentieth century illustrates how dystopian an economically advanced society can become when the conditions that make progress possible disappear, and a parasitic oligarchy retakes control.

TOTAL TAKEOVER: GERMANY AND JAPAN

Those living in Vienna at the end of the nineteenth century, like those in Rome in the first, or those in Venice in the thirteenth, might well have imagined themselves to be at the zenith of creation. But far from being unassailable, their sophisticated societies proved deeply vulnerable. Productive civilization is a more fragile thing than we perhaps care to understand.

The Second World War's aggressors, Germany and Japan, had both achieved rapid economic progress in the nineteenth century by sweeping away feudal princelings and opening up to global trade. They had modernized not just economically, but socially, too. Yet, for all their advances, neither had the safeguards in place to prevent the takeover of an extreme nationalist oligarchy.

Never a democracy, late-nineteenth-century Germany was ruled over by an increasingly aggressive clique of – often Prussian – *junkers*, or landed aristocrats. Emperor Wilhelm II reasserted his royal prerogatives and, after his chancellor, Bismarck, left office, he became much more hands-on.

The emperor was surrounded by a clique of ultra-conservative, militaristic army officers, who egged each other on towards disaster. Emboldened by success in war against Austria in 1866, then France in 1871, and their acquisition of an African empire in the 1880s, the newly united Germany forcefully challenged the balance of power in Europe, ending in war in August 1914. It was to become the most lethal conflict the world had yet endured.

If the consequences of that catastrophe were not bad enough, out of the post-war chaos that followed, there emerged an even more aggressive gang: the Nazis. After Hitler assumed power in 1933 internal critics of the regime were brutally suppressed and supposed enemies of the state ruthlessly persecuted.

Nazi despotism didn't stop at abolishing democracy and dissent; it relied on an assault on private property and economic freedom, too. The Nazi regime financed public works and rearmament by deficit spending. Industries, such as the Junkers aircraft company, which the new elite thought useful to possess, they simply expropriated.

While never implementing quite the kind of totalitarian command economy that existed in the Soviet Union, the Nazis did operate a corporatist command economy. An elaborate bureaucracy was created to oversee much of the economy and regulate imports. A system of wage and price controls was imposed. Big business interests, such as IG Farben, entered into agreements with the government to produce what was required at a fixed price, using resources often allocated by permission.

Nazi Germany's wars of conquest, from 1938 onwards, imposed their parasitism across the continent. German administrations were forced on occupied territories. Eastern Europe and France were run as a massive estate, producing for the greater good of the Fatherland. As the war progressed, parasitism became mass dehumanization. Millions of workers were enslaved. The most extraordinary atrocities were committed. Millions of Jews, Gypsies and others were murdered on an industrial scale.

In Japan, which came to be Nazi Germany's most powerful ally, the productive were overwhelmed by the parasitic in a similar way. The Meji Restoration might have ousted the parasitic Tokugawa clan, but far from leaving in place any sort of liberal order, it centralized power – leaving the stage set for takeover by military-industrial mobsters.

As Japan industrialized in the first three decades of the twentieth century, economic power was increasingly concentrated in the hands of the *zaibatsu* – meaning literally 'wealth-clique'. These were family-controlled industrial conglomerates, with monopolies and banking subsidiaries attached. Rather like many of the big businesses in 1930s Germany, the *zaibatsu* entered into agreements with the government. They predominated in mining, chemicals, metals and the merchant fleet, and supplied the army with the weapons to wage war.

Like the Roman *publicani*, they even acted as an adjunct of the state, collecting taxes on its behalf. In return, they had close ties with the government and Imperial Army chiefs. They helped influence the policy of establishing an empire of extortion – or what they called the East Asian Co-Prosperity Sphere – and encouraged the army to invade China and Korea.

Under the Meji settlement, the Japanese army was only accountable to the emperor, not the civilian government. Indeed, during the 1920s, civilian administrations came to depend on the backing of an increasingly nationalistic officer corps that ran the army. By the 1930s, the army was in effective political control. In October 1941, Hideki Tojo, a Japanese general, took over as prime minister. Less than two months later, he gave the order to launch the unprovoked assault on Pearl Harbor.

Japan, like Germany, imposed a command economy over the territories that it conquered. The neighbourhood was annexed, and millions killed. The survivors were set to work for the greater good of the conquerors. Japan and Germany are the terrifying proof that modernity is no guarantee against parasitic take-over.

Could it happen again? Should we worry that, like the world of Stefan Zweig, all that is civilized and certain could disappear?

COULD OLIGARCHY OVERWHELM AGAIN?

'America', insists the writer Andrew Sullivan, 'has never been so ripe for tyranny.' He's not alone. A flurry of political pundits have suggested much the same. In the *Chicago Tribune*, for instance, Richard Longworth explained that if America had the temerity to elect Trump, it would turn the country into an autocracy.

Suddenly, Sinclair Lewis's long-forgotten 1935 novel, *It Can't Happen Here* – about the rise of an American fascist president – is being quoted by newspaper columnists. One contributor to the *New Yorker*, Adam Gopnik, has even implied that Donald Trump could be the new Hitler. And that was before Trump won the election. Since then, there has been the most extraordinary outpouring of hyperbole implying that he was a dictator, by a *commentariat* that was almost universally hostile to him.

The New Radicals are not *Führers* in the making. It's offensive at many levels – not least to Stefan Zweig's generation – to suggest they are. These kinds of claims perhaps tell us more about the preconceptions of pundits than they do about where we are headed.

Looking for historical precedents to explain Trump and the rise of the New Radicals, others have gone back much further than the 1930s.

The BBC's *Newsnight* produced a clip at the time of Trump's inauguration, full of quotes from Plato's *Republic*, implying that Trump might be some sort of tyrant in the making. Others, such as Gideon Rachman writing in the *Financial Times*, have suggested he is the new Nero – a Roman emperor who became a byword for arbitrary rule and avarice.

Could they be right?

Those who try to paint the New Radicals as oligarchs or tyrants in the making have it 180 degrees the wrong way round. We are not witnessing New Radicals being elected as a new oligarchy, but as a populist reaction against an emergent oligarchy. The danger is not that the New Radicals play the historic role of oligarchs, but of anti-oligarch insurgents that end up making the tyrannical alternative attractive and much more possible.

The New Radicals are not about to produce any sort of Caesar – in America or Europe. If you want to find a historic precedent, they are perhaps our age's equivalent of the Gracchi in Rome.

Trump-like, Tiberius Gracchus sent a shudder through the Roman patricians in the Senate when he was elected by the plebeians.[84] Yet far from reviving the lot of the small-hold farmers who elected him, his main achievement was to instigate a system of subsidized corn consumption that exacerbated the agrarian crisis. His corn dole became a handy way for future emperors to consolidate their power, once Egypt, the source of much of the corn, became their personal property. Out of the chaos of the conflict between the *optimate* and *plebeian* factions that followed the Gracchi, consolidating power in the hands of one ruler started to seem like a good idea.

84 Trump-like, too, Tiberius Gracchus was elected on a promise to do something about the cheap migrant labour flooding into Italy and taking small farmers' jobs – which created an agrarian crisis, a sort of ancient unemployment crisis caused by cheap foreign labour.

A millennium and a half later, a handful of families in Venice concentrated power with the creation of the Council of Ten. But it was the inept insurgency of Bajamonte Tiepolo, a sort of Venetian version of a New Radical being populist but not popular, that made the case for creating this strong executive agency to safeguard the republic. Initially with a mandate of just two months, it was to become central to the governance of the republic for almost 600 years.

The anti-oligarchs often end up justifying oligarchy – and there is precisely such a danger today. The very odiousness of some New Radicals makes 'Davos Man' – otherwise insufferable – attractive. In Greece, the folly of Syriza and Yanis Varoufakis made the Troika seem rather sensible. Suddenly, having unelected technocrats writing the budget, instead of elected politicians, felt like a better deal.

When the Front National is in with a chance of governing in France, perhaps leaving government in the hands of the technocratic *énarques*, who preside over France irrespective of who is president, doesn't seem so bad. In America, to what problem can Donald Trump be the answer? If he is the anti-oligarch, oligarchy for many suddenly seems less threatening.

During the recent EU referendum in Britain, the Remain campaign was supported by a long list of grandees – from central bankers to Goldman Sachs to the Confederation of British Industry. The entire establishment lined up on one side to tell people how to vote. And they came perilously close to getting their way. Why?

Because for a while UKIP seemed to be the only advocate for an alternative. It was only when Eurosceptics with a wider appeal took back control of Euroscepticism that the Leave side pulled ahead. Even so, other self-proclaimed insurgents did their best to defend the establishment they pretend to oppose. The anti-capitalist campaigner Paul Mason claimed that while he wanted

Britain to leave the European Union, he would be supporting Remain because he so disliked Boris Johnson. Or Michael Gove. Or was it Nigel Farage? Based on such petty personal preferences did he cast his vote on one of the great issues of our day.

Owen Jones seems to have spent most of his life willing some sort of populist revolt. Yet when it came, he was on the same side as Goldman Sachs because he did not want to be on the same side as UKIP. It's all a bit absurd. Many of those who ought to come out on the side of the political insurgents instead direct their ire at those they call 'populist'. No wonder the new oligarchy keeps advancing.

But perhaps a more likely precedent is not Rome in the first century BC, nor Venice in the fourteenth, but rather the Dutch republic in the seventeenth.

DUTCH DECLINE: A MORE REALISTIC SCENARIO?

The Dutch produced the world's first modern economy. What happened also provides us with a template of what can happen when oligarchy gradually re-emerges.

The Western world is not on the verge of a new dictatorship. Dutch-like, it may be in the process of being taken over by stealth. The instructive example for our times is not the modern-day tyranny of Nazi Germany or imperial Japan, nor imperial Rome, but rather the steady regression of eighteenth-century Holland.

The Dutch boom of the seventeenth century came to an abrupt end in the eighteenth. Per-capita income fell precipitously and there was dramatic deindustrialization. Leiden, which had churned out vast quantities of cloth in the 1670s, was producing less than half the amount by 1700. Production collapsed almost completely in the eighteenth century. The silk industry in Haarlem, Amsterdam and Utrecht disappeared. Tobacco-processing plants, cotton presses and shipbuilding collapsed. Towns decayed.

An index of Dutch industrial output, set at 100 in 1584, peaked at 545 in 1664 – and slumped to 108 by 1795.[85]

What caused this Dutch decline? Conventional accounts, Trump-like, put it down to foreign competition. It's true that, like the US today, other countries were able to produce many things, from ships to textiles, better than the Dutch. But being overtaken is usually a symptom of failure, not the root of the disease. Holland, after all, didn't just decline relative to its neighbours, but in absolute terms. To attribute its regression to foreign competition is to mistake the effect for the cause. The question is: why were the Dutch less able to compete?

'It was a lack of coal,' insist some historians. Unable to adapt their wind-powered industrial revolution to coal and steam, so the theory goes, they fell behind. Perhaps not being close to coal seams did not help, but the Dutch had plenty of peat. And coal, of course, like raw cotton, can be imported. Those early English competitors at the start of the eighteenth century weren't yet using coal and steam either.

Others have attributed Dutch decline to the protectionist barriers thrown up against the Dutch, particularly by the French and the English. England's Navigation Acts of the 1650s and French tariffs of the 1660s did hit the Dutch hard. But none of these restraints imposed by outsiders against Dutch trade were as harmful as what the Dutch imposed upon themselves.

There had long been a tension within the United Provinces between the centralizing, Stadtholder 'Orangist' faction and the States Party (or Republican faction). Slowly but surely, the former prevailed and the republican principles unravelled. The House of Orange gradually seized control. The office of Stadtholder, which was not supposed to be hereditary, became so. By 1636,

---

85 Landes, D., *The Wealth and Poverty of Nations: Why Some Are So Rich and Some So Poor* (1998), p. 445.

Louis XIII of France was addressing the Stadtholder, Frederik Hendrik, in terms normally reserved for a fellow monarch. The States General, or parliament, followed suit the following year. In 1641, Frederick married his son off to Charles Stuart's daughter, thereby ensuring his family entered the ranks of major-league Euro monarchy.

But, for a few brief decades, it seemed like the momentum was moving in the other direction. From the sudden death of the young William II in 1650 until 1672, the Republican faction held power. Over a period of twenty years, they saw to it that there was no Stadtholder, with all his monarchical presumptions, in office.

What enabled the Orangist faction to centralize power permanently was the crisis of 1672. And what helped produce that year of disasters, what the Dutch call the *Rampjarr*? The sheer ineptitude of their anti-oligarch insurgents.

Opposed to the Orangist takeover, and elected to office on a wave of anti-Stadtholder feeling, was Johan de Witt. A sort of Dutch version of Tiberius Gracchus or Bajamonte Tiepolo, de Witt blundered. Not the first, nor the last, New Radical to discover that it is easier to gain office by expressing outrage than it is to govern effectively, as councillor pensionary he failed hopelessly to marshal the state defences against invasion.

Gracchi-like, de Witt and his brother came to a grisly end, murdered not by the Stadtholder-supporting elite, but by an angry mob of peasants enraged that he had failed to make the Netherlands great again. Trump should take note.

With de Witt went his era of 'True Freedom', and the idea that power might be dispersed. Republicans were ousted and the Stadtholder, William III, was restored in all his hereditary glory.

Under the Orange oligarchy the Dutch exceptionalism that had elevated this nondescript corner of north western Europe came to an end. The Dutch state became just another European monarchy.

As with the others, the king and his cronies held power. Their patronage became prevalent. Dutch exceptionalism was over. The Dutch republic, like the Roman and Venetian ones before her, came to acquire an empire. And, like the Romans and Venetians, she set about squeezing what she could from her overseas possessions. In 1621, the Dutch East India Company (VOC) invaded the Banda Islands – then the world's main producer of spices – murdering most of the population as they did so. There they imposed a plantation system, with over sixty separate estates on the islands, each overseen by a Dutchman. The locals were rounded up and forced to work in conditions scarcely distinguishable from slavery.

Even as the Dutch in Amsterdam and Leiden were flourishing thanks to the voluntary exchange of goods, capital and labour, in the Far East the VOC was amassing wealth through the age-old method of extortion. The VOC made most of its money not by trading freely, but by imposing restraints on trade. It grew rich almost entirely thanks to its ability to maintain monopolies in spices, rice, sugar and coffee.

From that overseas extortion flowed great wealth – into the hands of a tiny few. Like the Roman governor Verres in Sicily, or Julius Caesar in Spain, or the Zeno, Morosini or Dandolo families in Venetian Crete, fortunes could be accumulated quickly by those willing to work for the VOC in the Far East. A governor general, nominally paid 700 florins a month, could take home 10 million. A junior merchant who bought himself a post that paid 40 florins a month could make 40,000.[86] Those who invested in the VOC by buying its bonds expected the state to ride to the rescue as and when any overly aggressive foreigners threatened to disrupt their enterprise of exploitation.

It's worth looking in a bit more detail at what happened within

86 Ibid., p. 141.

the Dutch republic, since much of it seems to have a certain prescience.

The Dutch elite profited from the proceeds of not just VOC bonds but government bonds, too. During the late seventeenth century and eighteenth century, the Dutch state accumulated a monumental amount of debt. So much so that the republic – like London or New York today – became a major market in sovereign debt and bonds. The damage this vast bond issue did to the Dutch republic is sometimes underestimated. It has often been pointed out that this ability to borrow explains why the Dutch were able to defeat France and Spain, their less financially versatile opponents. But while the issue of bonds allowed the Dutch state to marshal the resources to stave off external predators, the creation of all those bondholders installed a new breed of internal parasites.

Government borrowing created a class of 'regent rich' who had a vested interest in the accumulation of public debt – and in living off the returns. By 1713, 70 per cent of tax revenues in Holland went on servicing the debt – or, to put it bluntly, the bondholders. As a parasitic elite grew rich, taxpayers and producers lost out. To repay a few rich bondholders, taxes rose sharply and were highly regressive. Consequently, capital became increasingly concentrated in the hands of the Orange oligarchy – but not, *pace* Piketty, as any kind of consequence of free-market capitalism.

Tax rises, in turn, hit the Dutch economy hard. Because the Dutch acted as Europe's middlemen, higher duties simply encouraged their European customers to start dealing directly with each other. Duties in the port of Amsterdam, for example, were about five times what traders were charged in Hamburg. Unsurprisingly, by 1750 Hamburg did twice the trade of Amsterdam. Higher taxes also pushed up Dutch wages, pricing Dutch manufacturers out of what was an increasingly international market.

Indeed, even though the negative effects of these tax hikes were known at the time, reversing them wasn't an option. In 1751, the Stadtholder, William IV, commissioned an investigation into the economic decline. *The Propositions* that it published in 1751 recognized the effect of higher taxes in driving away trade. A bold programme for reform, it called for the removal of trade restraints and tariffs, making the republic a 'free port' open to what we would call free trade.

The Propositions was an acknowledgement that the Dutch were hit less by the protectionist barriers thrown up against them by others than by the restraints they had imposed on themselves. Yet rather than revive free exchange, the Dutch moved in the opposite direction; still more protectionism. In the same year that *The Propositions* was published, the States General issued an edict forbidding skilled workmen from emigrating. Whereas in the seventeenth century, skilled workers from across northwestern Europe had freely gone to Holland to sell their specialized skills, by the mid-eighteenth, they were being forcibly restrained from doing so. A free-wheeling republic had become a restrictionist, rentier state.

There were simply too many vested interests behind the restraints and tariffs. *The Propositions* were ignored. Dutch decline continued. Like the Roman oligarchy, the Dutch elite didn't stop at fiscal extortion but engaged in monetary manipulation, too. They did so not by debasing the amount of gold or silver in the currency, but by inflating the number of claims on the currency held by the Bank of Amsterdam.

For the first 150 years of its existence, the Bank of Amsterdam was a 100 per cent reserve bank. The amount of loans and credit it extended corresponded with the amount of currency it held. Indeed, there was an earnest ritual each year whereby the city's four new burgomasters visited the bank's vaults on assuming office and 'compared their content in cash with deposit entries in the books and with great solemnity declared under oath that the two coincided'.[87] But by the mid-1700s the Bank of Amsterdam was extending much more credit than it had in its reserves.

Fractional reserve banking gave another boost to the bond market. It made credit cheap and plentiful, with interest rates famously low. Low enough, in fact, for borrowers to borrow more to buy bonds. It also enabled a boom in what today we'd call financial services. The Dutch had a Chamber of Marine Assurance and a thriving insurance market, while their Bourse was the world's first modern stock exchange.

But cheap credit came at a cost. First, it encouraged malinvestment. With more money to be made by buying bonds than by trading, money moved out of commerce and industry. The historian Charles Wilson cites the example of one Dutch entrepreneur, David Leeuw of Amsterdam, who over a period of thirty-four years moved his money out of trade and into bonds.[88] There were thousands like him.

Worse was to follow when the credit boom turned to bust. Rather like our own financial crisis of 2007, the Dutch credit-bubble burst – with catastrophic consequences. A bit like Lehman Brothers folding in 2008, in 1763 a firm called Neufvilles went under, taking with it 9.5 million guilders of investors' money. A decade later, the credit market fell apart. The magic money-tree machine stopped.

By the end of the eighteenth century, the Dutch discovered that they had not only deindustrialized, but were bankrupt, too. The Dutch state soon defaulted on its debts. Several historians, seeking to account for the republic's decline, have made rather trite observations about how Dutch merchants lost their entrepreneurial spirit. Their commercial classes, it is suggested,

---

87 See de Soto, J.H., *Money, Bank Credit and Economic Cycles* (2006), p. 105. De Soto is quoting Adam Smith's *Wealth of Nations*.
88 Wilson, C., *Economic History and the Historian* (1969), p. 45.

lost their drive and dynamism. As an explanation, we should take this sort of generalized observation with a large pinch of salt.

But what is unquestionably the case is that in order for intensive economic growth to happen, the surplus that wealth-creators create has to be free to flow back into the business of wealth-creation. From England's Arkwright in the eighteenth century to Amazon today, it is this ploughing of the surplus back into production by the productive that generates transformative gains. Dutch producers stopped being so productive not because of any change of heart about commerce, but because the surplus that they produced began to be diverted away from further production and to the parasitic.

Vested interests raising public spending and debt to unsustainable levels. Easy money and a credit boom. Power within the republic centralized. The Dutch story will, for some, have an all too familiar contemporary resonance about it.

IS IT INSTITUTIONS?

Why do some societies succumb? Why are vested interests able to emerge and overwhelm certain societies, but not others? And why does it happen when it does?

It's all because of institutions, explain Acemoğlu and Robinson, in *Why Nations Fail*. When institutions are extractive, they explain, small elites are able to rig the system and live at the expense of everyone else. When, on the other hand, institutions are what they call inclusive, the surplus cannot be siphoned off – and intensive growth is possible. Societies stagnate or flourish, according to their thesis, as a consequence of the type of institutions they have.

Acemoğlu and Robinson certainly make a powerful case. Drawing on the history of all sorts of societies from central America in the sixteenth century to central Africa today, they show how parasitic elites can help ensure some societies remain in a state of Malthusian misery. Rome rose and Venice, they show, flowered because for several glorious centuries there were no extractive elites able to wreak ruin. In the first half of the twentieth century, Japan and Germany were overwhelmed by tyrannical, extractive cliques.

This sort of institutional determinism is even used to try to account for the state of America and Europe today. Francis Fukuyama has suggested that America's institutions are in a state of 'decay'. It is, he suggests, the failure of Congress and other bodies to get to grips with public policy making that accounts for astronomical levels of public debt and the power of various vested interests and lobby groups in Washington.

While Acemoğlu and Robinson are absolutely right to recognize the connection between extractive elites and a society's ability to flourish – or fail – they are wrong to attribute everything to institutions.

For a start, you don't need extractive institutions to extort. Indeed, you don't need institutions at all. Acemoğlu and Robinson cite extractive institutions as being a decisive factor in states such as Sierra Leone, Liberia and Zimbabwe. Yet at the time they are writing about, such states hardly had any functioning institutions – extractive or otherwise.

Extractive institutions are not the primary cause of extortion, but the means through which it is sometimes done. Extractive institutions are a consequence, rather than a cause, of oligarchy. In late republican Rome, oligarchy did not emerge because the Senate overturned the position of the elected tribunes and the Tribal Assembly. The tribunes and Assembly lost their powers because an oligarchy emerged.

In Venice, it was not the closure of the Great Council to new members – the *Serrata* – that explained the emergence of oligarchy. The emergence of a closed oligarchy lead to the closure of the Great Council. Power was not concentrated because of the creation of the Council of Ten. The new Council of Ten reflected a concentration of power that expressed itself in such new institutional arrangements.

If it was institutions that accounted for the emergence of parasitic elites as Acemoğlu and Robinson suggest, surely two societies with similar sorts of institutions and almost identical elites would fare much the same? But we know of two separate states, with almost identical institutional arrangements, which took very different trajectories.

Not long after assuming mastery of the Dutch state in the 1670s, William of Orange took the throne of the English one, too. In 1688, King James II of England was ousted, and the Dutch monarch installed upon the throne.

After 1688, the Dutch and English not only had the same monarch, but the same sort of elite – think of it as an Orange oligarchy – in charge. And they also had the same sort of charter companies, central banks, stock exchanges, guilds and municipal corporations.

Yet on one side of the channel, the Orange elite managed to extort the productive and stall a nascent industrial revolution. On the other side of the channel, the Orange elite were restrained, and England took off.

WHIG ENGLAND

If institutions explain the extent to which a society is preyed upon by parasitic elites, why didn't eighteenth-century England succumb?

It's not just that England had similar institutional arrangements to the Dutch. The Orange elite in England were as prone to predation and parasitism as any other. A couple of years after securing the English throne, William invaded Ireland, dispossessed the Irish landowners of their property and did all he could to turn the island into a Protestant estate. The new Orange overlords behaved much as the Dutch had done in the East Indies – invading, killing and taking. From 1691, a draconian penal code was imposed on Catholics, often preventing them from owning property.

England's Glorious Revolution was, according to not just Acemoğlu and Robinson but Niall Ferguson and many others, a seminal moment in the move towards modernity – not only for England, but the world. It marked a key moment when extractive elites were constrained. While that is all true, the idea that the Glorious Revolution heralded a liberal system of government, free from parasitic self-interest, is simply false. At times, the English oligarchy behaved more like Robert Mugabe's ZANU-PF.

After 1688, it is sometimes suggested, England's Parliament was so full of disparate interests, no one faction could prevail. True. But surely the same could be said of the Roman Senate or the Venetian Great Council or the Dutch States General? The composition of such assemblies is not enough to explain why some societies succumb to narrow interests, and others don't.

At home, despite the various interests in Parliament, the oligarchy did what all oligarchs try to do, rigging the rules to enrich themselves. The protectionist Navigation Acts, introduced in the 1650s to ensure that only English ships carried English trade, were retained. On top of them, a new series of protectionist laws – the Calico Acts – were passed in the early eighteenth century, which banned not only the import of cotton from India, China and Persia, but even the wearing of it.

William of Orange brought with him a court full of cronies. Eighteenth-century England was full of sinecures for sale. Politics was often really a matter of patronage and graft, what came to be called the 'old corruption'.

Oligarchy emerged in the late Roman republic, Venice and Holland as a fabulous new source of wealth flowed in, enriching a tiny extractive elite. Rome's new riches came from Sicily and the newly acquired provinces outside Italy. Venice's mega-riches flowed in from the territories she took off Byzantium. Holland's came from trade with the East.

England, too, saw new trade and territory generate fabulous wealth for a few. The newly acquired Irish estate enriched a powerful faction of Anglo-Irish peers.[89] The East India Company created a new class of super-rich nabobs.

It is perhaps all the more remarkable then that Whig England did not end up like those others, succumbing to extractive elites. Of course, like every oligarchy the Whig elite clung onto its powers and privileges as long as it could. But slowly and incrementally, the parasitic class lost control.

As early as the 1690s, efforts were made to break up the East India Company monopoly. By the end of the Whig era, the East India Company had not only lost monopoly. Its autocratic chief executive, Warren Hastings, responsible for some of the worst excesses in India, was put on trial.

Whig England might have been full of corruption and sinecures. But the point is that the 'old corruption' was called out for what it was. In the nineteenth century, John Wade's *Extraordinary Black Book*, rather like the Guido Fawkes blog site today, detailed the wrong-doings of officialdom and courtiers. What was treated as the normal prerogative of those in power elsewhere became unacceptable in England. In 1854, the Northcote–Trevelyan reforms removed the system of sinecures and patronage, creating a system of civil-service appointment based on merit.

The nineteenth century saw political reform. The vote was progressively extended. After the Great Reform Act of 1832, the

---

89 Indeed, they were strong enough almost two centuries later to veto Gladstone's Home Rule Bill, prolonging an ancient conflict by yet another century.

Whig elite no longer determined the composition of the House of Commons. By the end of the century, most working men had the vote. Unlike the Roman Gracchi brothers, or the Dutchman de Witt, the English radical insurgents Richard Cobden and John Bright did not end up murdered by a mob – but elected to the House of Commons.

The reformers' demands for economic change were met, too. Between 1815 and 1870, successive governments removed many of the restrictive practices that the oligarchs had imposed. The Corn Laws were repealed in 1846. The West India Sugar Acts broke up the sugar trade cartel. The Navigation Acts were repealed. The slave trade, once the mainstay for some transatlantic English traders, was outlawed.

Even in Ireland the tide of parasitism receded, albeit slowly. The laws on property ownership had already been relaxed in the 1770s. The protectionist – and sectarian – rules, which ensured that only (Protestant) guild members could be involved in the running of town corporations, were watered down. Catholic emancipation came in 1829. Laws allowing tenants the right to buy the land they farmed were introduced in the 1870s.

If it is not institutions that explain why some societies succumb to extractive elites, while others do not, what does? To answer that, we need to consider what it is that enables parasites to prevail in the first place.

PART III
SUBVERSION

11

WHY PARASITES
PREVAIL

For half its life cycle, the parasitic lancet liver fluke lives inside a cow. For much of the other half, it lives in cow poo.

It's easy to work out how the fluke gets from its first home inside a cow to its second in a cow pat. But how does this tiny little parasitic worm manage to get back into the cow to complete its life cycle? It finds an unsuspecting host – an ant. And it gets inside its mind, literally.

The fluke infects the ant, and then alters the neurochemistry of the ant's brain – particularly the part that controls locomotion. This causes the ant to climb to the top of a tall blade of grass, and stay there.

Why? So that the ant, atop the grass blade, gets eaten by a passing cow, allowing the fluke to get back to where it wants to be.

And it's not only liver flukes that alter the behaviour of their hosts in this way. Neuroparasitologists have discovered a whole myriad of ways in which parasitic organisms do not merely siphon resources off their host, but manipulate their minds to make them behave in ways that serve the parasite.

There is a species of hairworm that makes crickets and grasshoppers drown themselves in order to get into water, where they need to be to breed. A kind of wasp has been discovered that manipulates orb spiders to build them cocoons made of finest spider silk.

When such parasites manipulate their hosts' behaviour, they do so by releasing neurochemicals into the host organism, which mimic the hosts' own neurochemistry. This isn't, of course, the only way that parasites manipulate their hosts' behaviour. Often they do so by deceiving their hosts' sense of self-interest.

An adult warbler instinctively spends every day-light hour finding grubs to feed its fledglings. Its frantic feeding behaviour is intended to ensure its young grow as fast as possible, maximizing their chances of survival. But cuckoo chicks are, of course, masters at deception. Tricking the warbler into believing that it, the cuckoo chick, is part of its brood, it takes advantage of the warbler's feeding instinct, getting fed a steady supply of grubs – and killing off its smaller warbler step-siblings when Mum and Dad are not looking.

Human parasites are also in the business of manipulation and mind control – not through neurochemistry, but by deception. They use an ethical sleight of hand to deceive their human hosts, making the population serve its own interests while believing they are acting in self-interest. More than that, extractive elites often promulgate a deceptive image of reality to manipulate their hosts' behaviour to serve their own ends.

MIND CONTROL

A thousand years ago in India, those that produced wealth – the farmers and merchants in the Vaisyas caste – paid extortionate taxes, often having to hand over most of their harvest to the elite. The priestly Brahmin and warrior Kshatriya castes, meanwhile, lived tax free.

It was obviously unfair, right? Yes, to our twenty-first-century way of thinking. But not according to the belief system of the time. Ancient Hindu ethics held that the upper caste had belonged to a lower caste in a previous life. It would be unjust, or so they argued, for someone having paid high taxes in a former life to be expected to pay them again in this one.

As for the lowly Vaisyas, provided they paid their taxes on time, they would be reborn into the upper castes in the next life, and be able to enjoy their tax-free status then. Since they would be tax exempt in the next life, was it not fair that they pay them in this one?

Laughable? Absurd? Perhaps to our contemporary way of thinking, but the way that people think – like the neurochemistry in an ant's brain – can be manipulated. Our sense of right and wrong, what is fair and just, are not constant, but malleable. Many millions have lived and died – and not just in medieval India – believing that it was their lot in life to serve an elite – wittingly or otherwise – as part of some divinely sanctioned cosmic order.

To be sure, when small, powerful elites lived at the expense of everybody else, they frequently did so using nothing more subtle than raw force. From Tamerlane to Genghis Khan to the Vikings, history is full of marauders who lived off the plunder of others, and they had little need of much in the way of manipulation. But if you are looking to live at someone else's expense long term, plunder is not perhaps a sensible strategy. Why? For the simple reason that once a population has been pillaged, there's not a lot left to take. So while small groups of powerful people have frequently pillaged, they often settled down to a life of more subtle extortion instead.

Keeping power over a much larger group requires more than the threat of force. If the oppressed rose up, they could overwhelm their oppressors. So, human parasites had to convince their hosts of their right to rule – often by invoking some sort of higher authority. 'When plunder becomes a way of life for a group of men living together in society,' noted nineteenth-century French thinker Frederick Bastiat, 'they create for themselves in the course of time a legal system that authorizes it and a moral code that glorifies it.'

Think of those patrimonial societies which existed, often unchanged, for thousands of years in Egypt, China, Iraq, India and Mexico. They might have been separated by wide seas and many centuries, but from the cities of the Aztecs to those of the Egyptians or Sumerians, these societies had some strikingly similar features: a small, powerful priesthood presided over a mass of toiling farmers, aided by a caste of warriors.

Temples were often the political centres from which the state was administered. From pharaonic Egypt, to ancient Mesopotamia, to Confucian China, those that created the wealth – farmers and merchants – had their wealth taken from them in the name of a divinely ordained order. This sort of patrimonial parasitism was, if you like, sanctified. Peasants were expected to yield much of their harvest to their overlords, often leaving them little more than a subsistence existence.

Of course, force was available to ensure that the producers handed over their harvests. Non-payment of taxes was often regarded as insurrection and treated as such. Slavery or serfdom might have been the means of extortion, but such systems were not only underpinned by fear of the whip or worse. If slaves and serfs were never willing participants in the process of their own extortion, they were often surprisingly – to our way of thinking – passive and pliant. I can think of few major slave revolts in recorded history: Spartacus's in the first century BC, the Zanj revolt in what we now call Iraq in the ninth century, and the slave rebellion in eighteenth-century French Haiti.

Those who laboured for their overlords did so because the moral codes by which they lived made them much more passive about it than we might imagine. The priestly elites had implanted in the minds of their human hosts a bogus altruism, which demanded self-sacrifice in the interests of the divine – sometimes literally for the poor Aztecs. In each of those ancient patrimonial societies, the creation myths might have differed but always the story contained the same constant: man had been created to serve the gods – or at least their priestly representatives on earth.

The gods were lords, and the priests' and emperors' masters. Sin was defined as man seeking to live on his own terms – or, almost as bad, failure to hand over half of the harvest.

Elites have constantly invoked a set of ethics that legitimize and sanctify the transfer from the productive to the parasitic. The Abbasids and Ottomans invoked the Koran to justify a *djizya* tax on the unbelievers in order to pay for their life of luxury in their harems. The Christian church, too, invoked all manner of theological justification for the tithe or for leaving your estate to the church. When the Japanese peasants fed the *samurai* warrior caste, they did so because it was their divine duty to provide for them.

MERCHANTS MALIGNED

Who do you most admire? Steve Jobs, the driving force behind the laptop on which I type this? Richard Branson, the smiley entrepreneur who will fly you across the Atlantic? Mark Zuckerberg, a zillionaire before he turned thirty? Or the guy at the end of the street where you live who has just opened a new coffee shop?

In productive societies, the productive tend to be admired and well treated. Today we – albeit at times grudgingly – respect entrepreneurs. So, too, in early-republican Rome, where the self-made men and merchants – the *equites* class – were respected. They shared the Senate with patricians as equals.

Likewise, in the early-medieval period Venice was a city of merchants, run by and for the merchant interest. So, too, in many northern-Italian city-states before 1350, and in the towns and cities of Flanders in the seventeenth century. Traders and middlemen were free to live under merchant-made laws and were not beholden to the whims of kings and extortion of emperors.

In Britain, the city fathers who built Glasgow and Birmingham during the nineteenth century at a time of industrial take-off were merchants and businessmen. The city halls they erected were temples to trade; the exquisite details that decorated them, a celebration of commerce. Contrast that to the way that merchants and middlemen were treated in most pre-industrial societies.

American academic Deirdre McCloskey has noted how in productive societies merchants have been able to trade and exchange without being despised or persecuted. But in most pre-modern societies, she notes, 'the sneers of the aristocrats, the damning of the priest, the envy of the peasant, all directed against trade and profit ... have long sufficed to kill economic growth'.[90]

In AD 301 the Roman Emperor Diocletian issued an edict that raged against merchants and middlemen with their 'unbridled passion for gain', threatening with the death penalty those who did not sell at the prices he preferred. In Edo Japan, Brahmin India and Confucian China, society was divided into castes or classes, with merchants always firmly at the bottom. In Japan,

90 Deirdre McCloskey, 'Bourgeois Shakespeare Disdained Trade and the Bourgeoisie', talk given to the American Economic Association, 4 January 2015.

they were forced to live in their own urban quarters and without legal rights. In China, merchants were made to wear distinctive clothes so as to stand out as objects of contempt. In 7 BC, Emperor Ai banned them from owning land or becoming a state official.

Merchants were endlessly told what prices they might charge, then were blamed for not supplying at the preferred price. They were taxed and regulated. They were ordered to extend credit and loans – and often found their debtors unilaterally cancelled the forced loan. After the *signori* took over the northern-Italian city-states and started to predate on the productive, merchants began to be seen as menial and were excluded from the upper echelons of society.

Merchants and middlemen were despised in medieval Europe and by the Ottoman elite. Ethnic groups associated with trade and exchange – Jews in fifteenth-century Spain, Asians in 1970s Uganda – were demonized, persecuted and even driven out by the elites. Parasitic elites found it handy to vilify those they wanted to extort. It's less obviously unjust to help yourself to what the productive have produced if you can somehow convince yourself – and your subjects – that what they have was acquired through immoral means.

But it goes beyond even that. Parasites prefer a world in which there is redistributive exchange; where products and resources change hands as a consequence of political fiat and favours, rather than the agreement of two consenting parties. They therefore need to denigrate mutual exchange and demonize those who engage in it. They needed an ethical framework that legitimized extortion.

Historians have often observed how the emergence of merchants and middlemen curtailed the power of kings. In thirteenth-century Italy, fifteenth-century England or sixteenth-century Flanders, the emergence of merchants – and their cities – checked the reach of, variously, the Holy Roman Emperor, the Tudor monarch and the Habsburgs.

It was the very autonomous nature of free exchange, undirected by anyone, that threatened those who would rather that they controlled the allocation of resources. Once free exchange established a toehold in the northern-Italian city-states (albeit briefly) and then Holland and England, the power of emperors and kings waned. Elsewhere, those engaged in specialization and exchange in pre-industrial societies were all too often vilified by the elites. It's precisely why those societies remained pre-industrial. Incidentally, I suspect this antediluvian contempt for those engaged in mutual exchange accounts for the rather odd insult Napoleon hurled across the Channel at the English, when he called us 'a nation of shopkeepers'.

Ethical systems and parasite creeds that elevated redistributive exchange over and above free exchange inhibited specialization and exchange. The princes and priests prevailed and such societies remained grindingly poor.

SELFISH PARASITES

'But it makes no sense,' I hear you say. 'Surely if a small minority were wrecking a society's chances for everyone, the rest of that society wouldn't stand for it?'

Extractive elites might create moral codes that denigrate free exchange in order to enable their own extortion. But it's not as if humans are hardwired to intuitively appreciate what produces progress.

Part of the problem is that even without being conned by a deceptive image of reality, a host population often simply can't see the problem. For a start, states in the hands of extractive, ruinous elites can appear successful and strong – at least for a while. Rome as an empire was greater and grander in almost every way than Rome as a mere republic had ever been. As an oligarchy sapped Italian society's productive strength, for several centuries

Rome more than compensated for that by helping herself to the produce of others outside Italy.

The Roman elite amassed wealth by redistribution, and amidst the triumphs and imperial splendour, that aggrandizement would have seemed immediate and impressive. The loss of intensive economic growth through mutual exchange happened much more gradually. Rome seemed more resplendent and imposing in AD 100 than she had in 100 BC. It would have been easy to believe that Roman exceptionalism lay in conquest and empire, rather than in a carefully devised republican tradition of dispersed power.

For the Venetians and the Dutch, in many ways their glory days – if measured by the exuberance and splendour of the elite – came after the closed oligarchy had emerged. In fact, many of their greatest artistic and architectural achievements happened precisely because there was a wealthy, extravagant elite on hand to hose money on such things. Beneath the decadence and glitter, decline might have set in but it would not have been perhaps so apparent.

We don't even need to look back that far to see the seeds of decline being mistaken for progress. In 1980, Zimbabwe became an independent state. Far from allowing her to achieve the sort of take-off that the Dutch achieved after the 1580s, or the Americans after 1776, Zimbabwe ended up simply swapping one parasitic elite for another, even more extractive one.

As a consequence, Zimbabwe's GDP per person fell by almost half between 1980 and 2010. Zimbabweans ate better on the day they achieved independence than they did thirty-three years later, when they had a lower daily calorie intake. Indeed, Zimbabwe is one of the few places on the planet that is poorer today than it was in the early 1980s.

But even despite such unequivocal decline, there were many both inside and outside Zimbabwe who could not see the destructive consequences of Mugabe's government, even when the country was well on the way to ruin. Imagine how much harder it must be to discern a more gradual decline, spread out over decades and generations.

Even after two and a half centuries of intensive economic growth, the conditions that enable progress are still not always obvious. Those things that elevate us – mutual exchange and inter-dependence, self-organization in society – all seem to go against our instincts.

Self-sufficiency would have come naturally to the person who made my Essex hand axe. It sometimes seems that as a species we have been hardwired to want self-sufficiency. Although I might type this on a computer designed in California, assembled in China, using chips from Japan, while sipping coffee from Kenya, the idea that we are better off by being dependent on the neighbours for essential supplies can still seem unnatural.

It's easy to get a cheap cheer on *Question Time* by promising to 'save British steel'. It's harder to explain that the price paid by buying more expensive UK-made goods is lower living standards in Britain. Ideas like comparative advantage – the insight that we would be better off to specialize in making the things we make best, and then trading with someone else – are counter-intuitive. They are hard to grasp.

In the first half of the seventeenth century, the Ming rulers of China had not only reduced the country to a state of ruin. They found that they faced a well-organized threat in the form of the Manchu on their northern border. Even after generations of misrule, with all the resources and manpower at their disposal, you might imagine that they would have been able to organize themselves sufficiently to resist these outsiders. But they didn't. Why not?

Partly it was because Ming China was riven by internal unrest. But fundamentally, the ruling dynasty was unable or unwilling to take the steps needed to raise enough tax revenue and spend it efficiently enough on a big enough army. At almost every stage of that process were various vested interests, which would – and did – prevent it from happening.

Members of the elite enjoyed tax exemptions that they were unwilling to forgo. Imperial revenues were spent on a vast number of officials, who siphoned it off. Ming China was so beholden to vested interests, it was unable to do what was necessary to save itself.

Vested interests are inherently selfish. Parasites aren't interested in the wellbeing of their hosts. Just because it brings ruin to the rest of society doesn't mean they stop. Extractive elites don't mind if, as a consequence of elevating the parasitic over the productive, society flounders.

What does sometimes restrain extractive elites, however, is reason.

12

REASON

Reason – the power of the mind to think, understand and explain things logically – is what has robbed the extractive elites of their power. It is this that subverted the idea of a universe arranged by grand design – and in doing so, undermined the claims of those who seek to hold power over the rest of us as grand designers. Thanks to reason, those deceptive images of reality, so long promulgated by the parasites, were revealed for the falsehoods they always were.

It is this that has elevated the condition of human kind, for no longer inhibited by extractive elites, our propensity to specialize and exchange has been able to happen uninhibited, production trumping parasitism.

SELF-ORGANIZATION, THE ENLIGHTENMENT
AND OTHER SUBVERSIVE THOUGHTS

In pre-modern times, the rule of the extractive elite usually rested on the same fundamental falsehood: that the world, and all that was in it, was part of some deliberate cosmic order. From pharaonic Egypt to medieval Europe, ancient Mexico to Mesopotamia, there was always a top-down description of the world – and from that, 'a top-down prescription by which we should live'.[91] It is this that ultimately enabled the productive to be extorted and subservience made a form of virtue.

But what if the world was actually seen to be self-organizing? What if all about us was not some product of divine design? If there is no grand plan, where does that leave those who claim authority as grand planners? This idea of a self-organizing world was deeply subversive.

If the idea of self-organization were to catch on, those who hold authority by invoking some higher purpose or authority would find that it crumbles. The bogus ethics and parasite creeds used to denigrate the productive and sanctify extortion fall apart. The power of the parasites to manipulate our minds comes to an end. And this is precisely what started to happen in early-modern Europe, even before the eighteenth-century Enlightenment.

An essential precursor to the Industrial Revolution in Europe and America was a revolution in the way people thought. But just as the Industrial Revolution was much more incremental than is often understood, the Enlightenment of the eighteenth century was the culmination of a much more incremental process of change in the way people saw the world, which had started long before.

Renaissance humanists, like the Dutchman Erasmus, had begun to revive rationalism, not just the supernatural, as a way of explaining the world. In the sixteenth century came a religious revolution in northwestern Europe: the Reformation. Martin Luther (1483–1546) insisted that man's relationship with God was direct. It could be defined 'by faith alone', he proclaimed, not through the hierarchy of the Church. While not a rejection of

91 Ridley, M., *The Evolution of Everything* (2015), p. 8.

the divine itself, Luther and co. unleashed ideas that undermined the claims of those purporting to be the divine's representatives on earth.

If religious communities could be self-organizing as Luther proclaimed, why stop there? Why not a self-organizing society, with no all-powerful kings? Why passively accept your status as part of a divinely ordained order? So subversive were these ideas in undermining the assumptions on which the existing order rested that tens of thousands of German peasants rose up during the Peasants' Wars in the early sixteenth century – the largest anti-oligarchy insurrection until the French Revolution.

The Reformation presented a challenge to the notion of a single canonical set of truths defined by the authority of a Catholic church. In so doing, it presented a broader challenge to the idea of any kind of canonical truth, defined by a single source of authority. This slow erosion of the hierarchical order influenced the way political thinkers thought, too. Even those notionally looking to defend the status quo.

Thomas Hobbes, the author of *Leviathan*, which was published in 1651 amid the turmoil of the English Civil War, never set out to be an anti-oligarchy radical. On the contrary, his book was, on the face of it, a stout defence of a strong sovereign. Powerful kings, Hobbes argued, were an essential bulwark needed to save society from the kind of chaos that had gone before.

But in making his case, Hobbes was to suggest things that were to prove every bit as unsettling to the old order as anything Luther wrote. In arguing for a strong monarch, Hobbes argued that life in the past had been solitary, poor, nasty, brutish and short. It was parasitism, he implied, that had held humankind back, since in that pre-historic past there had been 'no place for industry' in a world where 'the fruits of these were uncertain'.

In claiming that kings should get the credit for establishing the order that enabled us to advance, Hobbes was arguing that progress was a consequence not of divine providence, but our own political economy. It was the way we organized ourselves that counted. So unnerving was the implication of this in a world in which the idea of divine providence had been accepted uncritically, that Hobbes's enemies even accused him of atheism.

Hobbes was no advocate for a self-organizing society. For him, rather a strong sovereign was the answer to the problem of parasitism that had plagued civilization in the past. But like Luther, he unleashed thoughts that went far beyond him. Hobbes opened the way for others, like John Locke (1632–1704), to go even further, holding unfettered kings to be part of the parasitic problem.

Like Hobbes, Locke believed in natural rights and equality. He specifically refuted those ideas, widespread at the time, that civil society should be founded on divinely sanctioned order. He rejected the divine right of kings and argued that government had to have the consent of the governed – the implication being that if it did not, it could be legitimately ousted.

It is no coincidence that where such subversive ideas burnt brightest the challenge to the old order came first. Protestant Holland, home of Erasmus and Spinoza, rose against the Habsburgs in the sixteenth century. England, the country of Hobbes and Locke, overturned the claim of kings to rule by divine right in the seventeenth.

Nor is it any coincidence that where people were rich in reason, rather than necessarily cotton or coal, the productive freed themselves from the parasitic and the world's first modern economies emerged. Intensive growth and technological innovation followed. Subverting the claims of extractive elites to shape and order society by design proved to be an essential prerequisite for human progress.

Just over a hundred years ago, the German sociologist Max Weber asked if there was a connection between Protestantism and economic growth. Noting how intensive economic take-off had happened first in seventeenth-century Holland and then eighteenth-century England, *The Protestant Work Ethic and the Spirit of Capitalism* argued that industrialization was down to a particularly protestant attitude towards industry and thrift.

It is not an argument with which I have much sympathy. Apart from anything it ignores antiquity almost entirely, and overlooks the emergence much earlier of a kind of proto-capitalism in northern Italy. There were not many Protestants in medieval Venice. Nor even much in the way of any proto-protestants, such England's John Wycliffe (circa 1320–1384) or Prague's Jan Hus (1369–1425). There is a connection between the reformation and intensive economic take-off, but not the way Weber imagined.

The Netherlands and England experienced take-off not because of any doctrinal developments or identifiably distinct ethics per se. But rather because one of the consequences of the Protestant revolt was to weaken the hold of extractive elites, freeing innovation and exchange to be less hindered. The Reformation played a part in promoting the idea of self-organization.

Like the Reformation, the Enlightenment is also best understood as a rebellion. It was, as the physicist and philosopher David Deutsch puts it, a rejection of authority in regard to knowledge.

For many centuries before the Enlightenment, it had been believed that everything worth knowing was known, and was enshrined in authoritative texts: the Bible or the Koran, the Torah or the teachings of Confucius. The Enlightenment was a consequence of people starting to appreciate that knowledge is acquired cumulatively. Certainty of knowledge, and the old insistence on authority, was replaced by criticism.

Out of this sense that not everything that could be know was known came the idea that there could be progress. And that progress was not just possible, but desirable.

From Adam Smith's observations about moral sentiments in

the eighteenth century, through to the Darwinian discoveries of the nineteenth, more and more people started to see the world as a product of self-organizing agency, with neither purpose nor extraneous design.

Newton and others made advances in scientific insight, which started to show that the world was arranged by a set of rules that could be understood and explained, not by cosmic design or divine orchestration. There was less and less of the supernatural about things.

Reason gave people in many parts of Europe a yardstick against which to assess the claims and creeds of the temporal and spiritual elites who had lorded it over them. These insights are, in a way, the very essence of modernity. They are what separates the pre-modern from the modern.

Yet here's the most extraordinary thing: many of these insights aren't very new at all. The world was first understood in such a way not in early-modern Europe, but in archaic Greece over two and a half thousand years before.

AN EVEN OLDER INSIGHT

To be sure, the ancient Greeks often invoked the supernatural to explain things. Plato himself reasoned that society worked by imitating some sort of intended cosmic order. Aristotle believed that there was intent within all matter. Neither the Sceptic nor the Stoic schools of Greek philosophy can be seen as a repudiation of the idea of divine design. And alongside philosophical attempts to explain human affairs, there was always the Oracle at Delphi.

But there was at the same time a strand of Greek thought that rejected any notion of divine design: the Epicureans, named after the great Greek thinker Epicurus (341–270 BC). The Epicureans understood that the world and all that was in it was not the product of some grand godly plan but was self-arranging. Gods, in so far as they existed, the Epicureans argued, were distant and uninvolved in the affairs of humankind.[92]

The influence of this way of thinking on wider Greek culture is reflected in its stories and texts. In *The Iliad* and *The Odyssey*, those two early Greek tales, outcomes are attributed to the actions of gods. Yet by the time Herodotus wrote his *Histories*, events are explained in terms of human agency and action.

The Epicureans themselves were perhaps the product of some even older strands of Greek thought. Xenophanes (570–475 BC) had rejected mythological accounts of why things were the way they were. Anaxagoras (510–428 BC) had argued that reality was composed of physical ingredients blended together in different ways to produce different substances. In about 400 BC, long before any eighteenth-century scientist, Democritus (460–370 BC) suggested that the tiniest matter was made of atoms – and that everything in existence consisted of various combinations of either atoms or a void. '*Nothing exists except atoms and empty space*,' he insisted. '*Everything else is opinion.*'

Epicurus drew such ideas into an overarching philosophy, one which saw the world as having emerged spontaneously, a consequence of atoms unceasingly grouping and regrouping. The world and everything in it was spontaneous and self-organizing. Two thousand years before Hobbes wrote *Leviathan*, Epicureans showed an interest in the prehistoric state of nature, and the evolution of laws and civilization. They understood that humans have emerged out of a primitive past – and had done so not by divine providence but their own agency.

The Epicureans developed not just a different conception of the world, but a distinct ethical system for those who lived in

---

92 Interestingly, when Erasmus sought to distance himself from the Protestant agitators, he accused them of being little more than Epicureans.

it, too. They believed that the purpose of life was the pursuit of pleasure – by which they meant not sensual hedonism, but self-interest. If there was a higher purpose we were ordained to serve, it was ourselves.

Epicurean ideas, like so much Greek thought, took root in republican Rome. *On the Nature of Things,* a six-part poem written by Lucretius (99–55 BC) in homage to Epicurus,[93] articulates ideas that are so thoroughly modern it is hard to believe that anyone thought that way two thousand years ago. Yet lots of them did.

Long before Charles Darwin, Lucretius suggested that nature endlessly experiments, and that the natural world is a product of evolutionary, organic process, not grand design. Lucretius, like Hobbes many centuries later, saw that man was once a primitive savage, lifted out of a miserable existence. 'He anticipated modern physics,' writes Ridley, arguing that everything is made of different combinations of a limited set of tiny particles, moving in a void.[94] *On the Nature of Things* is but one tiny surviving fragment of a lost Epicurean intellectual tradition that was once widespread around the Mediterranean in antiquity.

'Just when the gods had ceased to be', wrote Gustave Flaubert of this period of Roman history, 'and the Christ had not yet come, there was a unique moment in history… when man stood alone.' Flaubert might have over-simplified and got the timeline a little askew, but he had a point. For a few fleeting centuries, Roman man did indeed stand free from the fallacy that extraneous agency was responsible for the design, maintenance or moral regulation of the world.

There is so much in the way that the Epicureans thought that

---

93 Lucretius is fawning in his praise of Epicurus, referring to him as the 'glory of the Grecian race'. He goes on to lay it on thickly, writing that 'it is you I follow, tracing in your clearly marked footprints my own firm steps, not as a contending rival, but out of love, for I yearn to imitate you'.

94 Ridley, M., *The Evolution of Everything* (2015), p. 9.

seems thoroughly modern that some contemporary historians have actually argued it was the rediscovery of Lucretius's work in the library of a fifteenth-century German monastery that sparked the Renaissance.[95] Others have made a similar point, but suggested that Erasmus and other Renaissance humanist thinkers came to Epicurus independently of Lucretius.

Yet others argue that, irrespective of anything found in any dusty old texts, scientific discovery in early-modern Europe was undermining the notion of divine design anyhow. Whether it happened through a process of discovery or rediscovery, what is clear is that the idea that order could emerge spontaneously – the idea of a self-organizing world – which had existed in the ancient Greek and Roman worlds, re-emerged in early-modern Europe. This insight that the world is self-organizing rather than a consequence of divine design almost seems to be a prerequisite for progress.

Europe only exceeded many of the economic, architectural and technological achievements of the Romans with the recovery of the idea – slowly, imperfectly and painfully – that the world was not just a consequence of divine design.

REASON RETREATS

If you need to invoke the idea of some extraneous agency to secure society's submission, the idea that there is no over-arching higher purpose is deeply dangerous. So it was that in later antiquity, the Epicurean insights came to be seen not as civilized but subversive. Roman emperors took to declaring themselves godly. If they were to be the empire's grand planner, they needed to invoke a sense of the world as a product of a grand plan.

95 See Stephen Greenblatt's brilliant, thought-provoking book, *The Swerve: How the World Became Modern* (2011).

Cicero attacked Epicureanism as troublesome. It was a movement committed to undermining an idea of the divine that the state increasingly wished to encourage. From the third century, the Roman elite became increasingly hostile to the Epicurean tradition. If, like a succession of Roman emperors, you are trying to organize a huge empire and levy taxes to pay for large numbers of legions, the Epicurean insistence that law and justice need legitimizing in terms of the benefits they bring to those who submit to authority is not just a nuisance. It's intolerable.

As Flaubert understood, once Christianity became the official religion of the empire, such ideas receded. Indeed, they were driven out, treated almost as sedition. Epicurean thought faced a barrage of hostility in tracts, sermons and letters by Augustine, Ambrose, Lactantius, Jerome and many others. With great dishonesty but devastating effectiveness, early Christian propagandists portrayed a belief system that had emphasized frugality and simple living as being all about the pursuit of sensual pleasure. It's a misrepresentation that persists to this day.

Why don't we know as much about the Epicurean school of Greek thought as we do of others? Perhaps it did not get passed down to us in quite the same way, owing to the fact that it cannot, like Plato or Aristotle, be accommodated as easily with the teachings of the early Christian church.

A philosophy that acknowledged humans as their own agency was grotesquely misrepresented as some kind of cult of decadence by those who would rather we submit to their notion of an extraneous agency. In the fourth and sixth centuries, new monotheistic religions arose which insisted on the world as being a product of divine creation, unique and deliberate. They taught of a grand celestial order, in which every human was merely a part. Instead of espousing our own agency, these creeds emphasized the need to submit to the agency of the divine. The idea that the world was a product of self-organizing agency, without intention or purpose, was snuffed out. For the next thirteen centuries, what had been Roman Europe was preyed upon by parasites, who organized society for their own intent and purpose. It produced the Dark Ages. Society reverted to a subsistence level as parasitic warlords extracted what they could from the productive.

The parasites have waged a long war on reason. They not only extinguished Lucretius's ideas in the first and second century. So successfully were the insights that had arisen in ancient Greece erased, it was not until the fifteenth century that the teachings of Democritus, Epicurus and Lucretius were known about, other than via their detractors. They tried Giordano Bruno for embracing the philosophy of Lucretius at the very end of the sixteenth century, before burning him – and then the books of Spinoza – in the seventeenth century. They raged against Darwin in the nineteenth. They invoke a bogus altruism today, which insists that public policies that make a claim over others are somehow selfless virtue.

There is nothing inevitable about reason. Even when long established, it can be driven from the minds of men and women.

REASON AND TAKE-OFF

But of course the idea that progress is possible, knowledge cumulative and humans have their own agency did re-emerge in early modern Europe. And so, too, did intensive economic growth based on specialization and free exchange – something that had been almost entirely unknown in the interceding centuries.

There is a striking coincidence between intensive economic growth within certain societies and those same societies rejecting the idea of single, canonical truth, handed down by authority. Intensive economic growth is never just a measure of increased material output. Rather it reflects, too, our capacity for innovation – and an increase in how much we know.

A society can only come to know more if it has a capacity for conjecture and criticism, rather than adherence to absolutes as defined by authority. In both antiquity and the early-modern era, it seems that we only came to know more if we were able to accept that there was more to know.

In that unique moment in Roman history of which Flaubert wrote, 'when the gods ceased to be and the Christ had not yet come', the productive trumped the parasitic for several precious generations. There were all manner of innovations. Power was constrained and Rome flourished in a way no other society was to do for the next millennium and a half.

As we saw in Chapter 7, Italy's per-capita income of $857 in the first century AD was higher than for any large, settled society until sixteenth-century Holland. It had still not been exceeded in Asia by 1950 or most of Sub-Saharan Africa in 1990. Rome, with over a million inhabitants in the first century AD, was the largest city on earth until China's Hangzhou in the Middle Ages. Roman art and architecture, engineering and technology represented an unmatched pinnacle of human attainment until the early-modern era.

Indeed, so many of Rome's achievements were unmatched until the seventeenth century – when many of those insights, once commonplace in antiquity, were rediscovered.

The Dutch, where the idea of self-organizing religious communities was well established, called time on the Habsburg parasites. It's not just that they seemed to have had enough of foreign rule. Ideas of self-organization meant that in the aftermath they dispersed power – often chaotically – within the different provinces. The Dutch not only abolished the Habsburgs' tolls and tariffs, under the influence of Hugo Grotius, who invoked a new theological justification for free trade, they consciously – indeed, aggressively – embraced economic liberty.

The effect of such ideas was even more liberalizing in England. While Hobbes had seen a strong sovereign as an essential safeguard against primeval predation, John Locke saw society as capable of self-direction. It was man, not the monarch, who was the agent for our advance. 'Society is produced by our wants and government by our wickedness,' he wrote; 'the former promotes our happiness positively by unifying our affections.'

Exiled in the Netherlands in the early 1680s, Locke returned with the new regime in the wake of the Glorious Revolution. His ideas helped shape what came next. From 1689, the Bill of Rights acted as a kind of contract of constraint between the crown and subjects. The former agreed to abide by a set of rules that protected the interests of the latter. Monopolies, phased out during the seventeenth century, were not reintroduced. In fact the courts began to rule against guilds, and in favour of a free labour market.

Locke's ideas perhaps had an even greater influence in America, shaping the post-revolutionary settlement there to an even greater degree. After 1776, conditions were created that were even more conducive to economic freedom, free exchange and the dispersal of power. Instead of England's rather muddled approach, the Founding Father's drafted a constitution explicitly and deliberately designed to disperse power and ensure maximum economic freedom.

Perhaps the power of the mind to think, understand and explain things logically should be seen as a sort of inoculation. It has enabled some societies to fight off parasitic infections. Without any intuitive understanding of what produces progress, people in every epoch seem vulnerable to extractive elites and the parasitic creeds they promulgate, which manipulate our behaviour to serve their interests. But our ability to reason seems to have enabled certain societies to fight off this kind of parasitic infection – and flourish.

Of course, sometimes a vaccination can trigger a very different reaction. A strong dose of reason, far from liberalizing certain societies and freeing them from parasitic infection, seems to have given rise to a new type of tyranny and an even more extractive elite.

13

REASON BECOMES TYRANNY

The eighteenth-century Enlightenment gave rise to rational liberalism. An intellectual movement that emphasized reason and individualism over tradition and faith, it was a force for liberation from the parasite creeds of the past.

But the 'Age of Reason' also produced an intense illiberalism. The forces that it unleashed might have torn down the old order, but they also proved capable of elevating a new tyranny in its place.

ILLIBERAL INSURGENCY

In much the same way that many pundits today like to bracket the Brexit vote in Britain with the election of Donald Trump in America, many contemporary observers saw the American and French revolutions, separated by a mere six years, as part of the same phenomena. And to be fair, the stark differences between these two movements – perhaps like the two elections of 2016 – only became more apparent with time.

Unlike those earlier anti-oligarchy insurgencies in the Nether-lands, then England and America, the French Revolution did not create a liberal order under which the conditions conducive to free exchange could exist. Far from it, in fact.

France in the late eighteenth century was an absolutist state. Her king, Louis XVI, and his courtiers lived a life of rent-seeking luxury. A few titled families owned vast estates, on which a mass of peasants toiled. Taxes and tolls were excruciatingly high for all but aristocrats. With no one to curb the excesses of the extractive elite, the elite had extracted more than the tax base could bare. France was broke, and the state weak.

At the same time, dangerous new ideas about universal rights had started to percolate, undermining deference for order and hierarchy. The effect was explosive. In July 1789, a Parisian mob stormed the Bastille and the *ancien régime* fell. Feudalism was abolished, and new rights and a republic proclaimed.

But what came next was quite unlike anything that had happened in America. To appreciate the contrast, take a moment to consider the fate of Thomas Paine, a man who tried to straddle the two revolutionary movements.

Born in England in 1737, Paine had emigrated to America just in time to take part in the insurrection there in 1776. His pamphlet, *Common Sense*, brilliantly articulated the case of the rebel colonies against the crown. He was widely read and, after the war, went on to become one of the Founding Fathers of the new republic. Excited by news of what was happening in revolutionary France, he moved there, becoming a French citizen and getting elected to the new Assembly. But as Paine discovered to his cost, the two uprisings had very different aftermaths.

Following the revolution in America, Thomas Paine sat down in an old court house in Philadelphia to help draft a new constitution. Amongst his fellow Founding Fathers during that long, hot summer of 1787 there were plenty of bitter arguments and debates. But the ring-leaders of the revolt did not attempt to cart each other off to the guillotine as they were to in France. There was no terror, with a Jacobin faction systematically slaughtering Girondins, before turning on themselves. Paine in Paris only narrowly escaped with his life. Just imagine if Benjamin Franklin in America, as Robespierre was to do in France, had tried to have him executed?

Wouldn't it have been absurd if George Washington had declared himself Emperor of America? What if a Washington dynasty not only established itself as the hereditary government of the United States, but, after a series of invasions, installed puppet princelings to rule over Canada, Brazil and Mexico? Yet that was more or less the outcome of the French Revolution. The Napoleonic Wars that followed were, in terms of the numbers killed, amongst the bloodiest episodes in human history.[96]

Even Paine eventually recognized that the French revolt was nothing like the rebellion in America. Once a staunch supporter of the French uprising, he came to describe Napoleon, who had spoken the language of liberation and rights as he invaded neighbours and imposed new princelings, as a charlatan.

The French Revolution has far more in common with what happened in Russia a century of so later, than anything that happened in either America, England or the Dutch republic before.

Russia in the late nineteenth century was also an impoverished – still largely agrarian – state, with a mass of – recently freed – serfs labouring to support their landlords. Russia, too, suffered as her extractive elites waged ruinous wars, while living beyond the means of those who were supposed to supply a surplus. And as in France, a set of new ideas started to circulate, which eroded the old order.

96 Pinker, S., *The Better Angels of Our Nature: A History of Violence and Humanity* (2012), p. 195.

The effect was equally explosive. In February 1917, the Winter Palace in St Petersburg, like the Bastille before it, was stormed. As in France, the first set of relatively moderate reformists that took over was itself overtaken by some much more radical and determined revolutionaries. In place of the Romanov rent-seekers came the Bolsheviks, who assumed control of not only the military, but almost every aspect of the economy, expropriating all private property.

In terms of toppling the old order, both the French and Russian revolts were supremely successful – more so perhaps than anything that happened in England, America or Holland. But as an anti-oligarchy movement, each proved to be a disastrous failure. One form of tyranny was merely replaced with another. France went from the dictatorship of the Bourbons to that of the Bonapartes, Russia from the Tsar to Stalin.

Why are some anti-oligarchy revolts liberalizing in their effect, creating the conditions for human prosperity and progress, but not others? If the eighteenth-century Enlightenment produced liberal rationalism, one might expect that the later revolutions in France and Russia, which were influenced by new ideas, would have been all the more liberalizing in their consequences. In fact, it was the earlier ones that were. Why?

POWER CONCENTRATED

The hallmark of a successful insurgency against oligarchy is that it disperses power. By that measure, most anti-oligarchy revolutions – even if they successfully topple the old order – have failed.

In the aftermath of the French Revolution, power was put in the hands of a few; first the Committee of Public Safety, then a military dictator. In Russia, the Bolsheviks placed executive power in the hands of a politburo. Soon, it was in the hands of one man, Stalin.

It's not just the French or Russian revolutions that failed in this way. Japan's Meji restoration, which took power away from a parasitic, feudal family – the Tokugawa – ended up concentrating power in the hands of an imperial clique. In England, Cromwell's insurgency, it should also be remembered, concentrated power in his Commonwealth. Even the revolt of the Gracchi ended not in a revived Roman republic, but with power in the grip of Sulla, then Caesar and finally Augustus.

Contrast all of that with the way in which the Dutch revolt of the sixteenth century, or the Anglo-American ones of the seventeenth and eighteenth, dispersed power. Each of these revolts in their own way helped to create those conditions conducive to human progress. External parasites were ejected. Power was dispersed as a safeguard against internal predation. The productive were left free to engage in specialization and exchange.

Of course, when the English Parliamentarians cut the head off Charles I, they did so in much the same brutal manner as the French who killed Louis XVI. When the American's captured Yorktown, it was no doubt with the same derring-do that the Bolsheviks stormed the Winter Palace in St Petersburg. But it was not the actual act of ousting the old order that mattered. It's what came after that counted.

After England's revolution, the Bill of Rights of 1689 limited the power of the crown. Many taxes on the productive were abolished in the immediate aftermath of the takeover. The creation of the Bank of England ensured that credit was not in the gift of the politically powerful, but available to the commercially credible. There was even an effort made to end the privileged positon of the East India Company.

England might be ruled by a new oligarchy – the Whigs. But power was steadily constrained. In 1701, the Act of Settlement constrained the king's ability to nominate his favourites as ministers, without the approval of the electorate. The monarch could no longer wage aggressive wars or levy taxes without the consent of the taxpayer.

In America after victory at Yorktown, instead of replacing George III with an American monarch, the American's drafted a constitution with elaborate checks and balances on an elected president. Power was dispersed, with individual states retaining considerable autonomy. The Founding Fathers did away with many of the trappings of patronage, such as peerages and titles. They drafted a constitution and a Bill of Rights as an appendix to it that safeguarded property rights, restricting the ability of those with political power to constrain trade and commerce.

If liberal revolutions were the ones that dispersed power, while the illiberal ones were those that centralized it, that still does not really explain why. What was it about certain insurgencies that left power diffuse, while others concentrated it?

The Anglo-American revolts, Acemoğlu and Robinson and others would be quick to point out, meant open institutions, or at least the opening up of existing institutions. The Dutch had a States General, and provincial authorities in place. After England's Glorious Revolution, Parliament was full of disparate interests. After the American, Congress and the courts prevented the concentration of power. By contrast, in the wake of the French and Russian revolutions came institutions that concentrated power, like the French Directory or the Soviet Politburo.

That is all true. But if it is institutions that explain why power is either dispersed or concentrated, what accounts for the different kinds of institutions? Why, to use the language of Acemoğlu and Robinson, are some institutions made inclusive, but others extractive? They do not seem to have much of an answer.

They seem to imply that good, inclusive institutions arose almost by accident, as random ripples in the flow of history. Extractive institutions get replaced by good, inclusive ones because of 'critical junctures' in history, they say. Inclusive institutions arise when 'propitious existing institutions' are already in place, they claim. And 'some luck' they suggest 'is key, because history always unfolds in a contingent way'.

Critical junctures? Propitious institutions already existing? Luck? Having advanced the idea that institutions were the primary causation when it comes to human progress, at the last moment Acemoğlu and Robinson seem to retreat into a sort of random determinism. Perhaps they are not really so far away from all those others who attributed it to the divine or the saintly, the fauna or the flora.

Extractive elites, in their account, do or don't get their way depending on whether or not there are positive or negative 'feedback loops'. It all seems a bit mechanistic.

Nor, actually, is Acemoğlu and Robinson's explanation especially new. Thomas Jefferson got there two centuries ago when he asked, 'What has destroyed liberty and the rights of man in every government which has ever existed under the sun?' His answer: 'The generalizing and concentrating all cares and power into one body, no matter whether of the autocrats of Russia or France, or of the aristocrats of a Venetian senate.'

What we ought to instead ask is why Jefferson and the rest thought the way they did, given that it was the way they thought that made them put in place all those elaborate arrangements to prevent power falling into the hands of any one party, person or faction.

In their account as to why oligarchy waxes or wanes, Acemoğlu and Robinson put so much emphasis on institutions that they leave little room for the influence of ideas. They make no mention of Hobbes or Rousseau, and only one tangential reference to John Locke. It feels a little bit like trying to account for the Russian Revolution without mentioning Marx. To understand why different insurgencies have achieved such different outcomes, we have to properly appreciate the ideas that animated the uprisings.

DIFFERENT IDEAS ABOUT PROGRESS

One of the essential insights of the Enlightenment is that progress is possible. If progress is possible, it is however possible to come to a number of very different conclusions.

On the one hand, you can believe that progress is not just possible, but has actually happened. Like Hobbes and Locke (or indeed Epicurus and Lucretius, long before any European Enlightenment), you can believe that the human condition is elevated; that we have risen from some kind of primitive, almost animal-like past. And like those thinkers, you might argue that it is human agency, either in the way we organize ourselves, or our increased interdependence, that accounts for our elevation.

Or, you can take the view that progress – while *possible* – has been frustrated, that it needs a bit of a nudge. Like Rousseau, you might argue that far from our current condition being elevated, it was man in our pristine past who enjoyed an elevated existence – and that we have since been corrupted. Our increased interdependence, and the advancement of science, he wrote in his *Discourse on the Sciences and the Arts*, had produced less happiness. Private property, he asserted, was the root of humanity's failing, and inequality its result. The division of labour, he insisted, far from being the engine by which we were elevated, was rather part of a process of degeneration.

You could even, like Marx, go even further and argue that the division of labour is not only a cause of unhappiness, but has lead to exploitation and class struggle – which has inhibited our progress.

And the second insight of the Enlightenment was that the world could be understood as being run not on the whim of the gods, but according to a fixed set of rules that could be understood. This insight, too, could lead people to different places.

For some, it reinforced the idea of a self-organizing world, free from the intervention of the divine. But for others, the fact that the world could be understood as operating according to a set of rules was an invitation to act as the divine. Instead of producing liberal rationalism, it gave rise to a kind of uber-rationalism – a belief that reason alone was the source of knowledge. Armed with a false certainty as to how things work, it is possible to presume that you can predict how things might work in future. This conceit was expressed rather wonderfully by the French mathematician and physicist Pierre-Simon Laplace, who in 1814 suggested that:

> An intellect which at a certain moment would know all forces that set nature in motion, and all positions of all items of which nature is composed, if this intellect were also vast enough to submit these data to analysis, it would embrace in a single formula the movements of the greatest bodies of the universe and those of the tiniest atom; for such an intellect nothing would be uncertain and the future just like the past would be present before its eyes.

Combine the notion that humankind needs a bit of a nudge – or blueprint – in order to progress, with Laplace's kind of conceit, and you end up almost insisting that someone comes along and tries to reshape humankind on the basis of a blueprint. This is why the French and Russian revolutionaries created institutions – the dictatorial Directory or the Politburo – that concentrated power.

Rousseau argued that the interests of the individual and the whole of society could only be reconciled by what he termed a General Will. Whether he intended it or not, the General Will, which subordinated the citizen-subject, led to the Terror and totalitarianism.

Frenchmen were forced to prostrate themselves before those who governed in the name of the General Will. Citizens who refused to obey the dictates of reason, wrote Rousseau, must be 'forced to be free'. The Committee of Public Safety, like the Venetian Council of Ten, was an unchecked executive and judicial power, with a wide remit. Not for nothing did Isaiah Berlin refer to Rousseau was 'one of the most sinister and formidable enemies of liberty in the whole history of human thought'.

Man, wrote Rousseau, not long before the French Revolution, was everywhere in chains. The Enlightenment, of which he was a leading light, might have come along and cast off the old chains of faith, feudalism and hierarchy. But they went on to shackle humankind to something even more terrible. An absolutist belief in reason led to the guillotine in France. In Russia, it led to the gulag.

Like Rousseau, Marx saw the division of labour as an explanation for humankind's elevation, but as leading to extortion. The expansion of output had happened by siphoning off the surplus from the proletariat. The nudge society needed, he suggested, was not so much the submission to any General Will, but a tyranny of the *proletariat*.

The Anglo-American revolutionaries did none of that fundamentally because they thought differently. First, they rejected the anti-rationalist idea that reason alone is the source of knowledge. But even more importantly, they had an essentially optimistic view of the human condition. Like Hobbes and Locke, they believed that progress was not only possible, but had happened. Human kind had not only been elevated, but by our own agency.

After the upheavals in France and Russia, the new elites in charge wanted the world reborn. Each society was to be reordered according to a shrill, murderous certainty. After the revolutions in first England then America, a Bill of Rights was written to limit the ability of those with power to impose themselves upon society.

While the revolutionaries in France wrote long proclamations about the rights of man, the American revolutionaries simply insisted on those 'inalienable rights to life, liberty and the pursuit of happiness'. While Jefferson might have written the US Declaration of Independence, were not the words in that famous phrase partly Locke's, with his idea of natural rights to 'life and liberty', and, in that insistence on the pursuit of happiness, perhaps, too, an echo of Epicurus?

REASON AND THE LIBERAL ORDER TODAY

The Enlightenment alone was not enough to give us the liberal order, which has proved to be such an essential precondition for the human progress there has been over the past two centuries or so.

Yet there is no shortage of those today who lazily claim that liberal rationalism is all a product of the eighteenth-century Enlightenment. In making such a claim, they overlook that there is much more to liberal rationalism than the Enlightenment – and the Enlightenment gave rise to much more than liberal rationalism.

For a start, many ideas essential to liberal rationalism – from those of Epicurus to Spinoza – emerged long before the eighteenth century. More to the point, if the Enlightenment gave rise to liberal rationalism, it also produced the anti-rationalist ideas that have repeatedly threatened the liberal order, not least during the cold wars and world wars of the twentieth century.

Ever since the Age of Reason, a succession of different '-isms' has arisen in different societies around the world as a sort of secular religion of the state, demanding sacrifice and submission in the service of some higher purpose. The Jacobin's guillotine, the Soviet's gulag and indeed the Nazi's gas chamber were all products of regimes that saw themselves as rational, and acting in accordance with innate ideas – however hideous. Even their new methods of murder were deliberate and by design.

Liberal rationalism rests on something more specific than just 'the Enlightenment'. The most important prerequisite for liberal rationalism is an acceptance that human progress is not only possible and desirable, but that it has happened; what today we call optimism. Liberal rationalism also means rejecting uber-rationalism, that idea that reason alone can be seen as a source of knowledge.

It is striking how many supposed 'liberals' today often seem to believe, in common with the anti-rationalists of the past, that reason alone can be a source of knowledge. As we shall see in the next chapter, many practise a form of bogus empiricism, using reason to determine what verifiable evidence they select in pursuit of their theories or designs.

Many who see themselves as 'liberal' also have an illiberal sense of pessimism, and reject the notion of progress.

Echoing Rousseau, they insist that our elevated material condition is not a kind of advance but a degradation. In his 1974 bestselling book *The Death of Progress*, Bernard James described progress as a 'lethal *idée fixe*'. Despite a bounty of data showing that life has got so much better for so many people, I am constantly amazed at how many who see themselves as liberal simply refuse to accept it. Some, I have discovered, are even made quite angry and downcast by the idea. Ironically, many who see themselves as progressives seem to reject the idea of human progress.

In his bestselling book, *Our Final Century*, Sir Martin Rees cheerfully lists all the things that could wipe out humankind over the next hundred years. From climate change to eco catastrophe, from asteroids to epidemics, there is enough to give every progressive a clear sense that we are living through the end of days. And there are plenty only too happy to believe it all.

As early as the 1970s, the environmental movement warned about the looming catastrophe of overpopulation. In the 1980s, they warned of nuclear war and acid rain. From the 1990s, they warned of global warming. Now it's climate change. In many areas of social science, supposedly liberal opinion is uncomfortable with the concept of primitivism and progress. There is a Rousseau-esque presumption that we have fallen from some sort of pristine pre-industrial past; that the division of labour and mutual exchange has been degrading; that trade is a form of exploitation, not the font of our elevation.

Anti the idea of progress, sceptical of science and technology, liberals have become deeply pessimistic. A certain kind of academic bends over backwards to avoid implying that certain societies with a lower level of technological sophistication (owing to their lower level of specialization and exchange) are less advanced. Cultural relativism means that there is even a reluctance to accept the notion of advance.

Liberalism today has lost sight of the idea of a self-organizing society. Instead, many 'liberals' are advocates for the opposite, of having small elites arrange things for us instead. Writing in the *Financial Times* recently, Janan Ganesh explained how liberals looked on with horror as their 'compatriots voted against the EU'. Indeed. That's because liberals today are on the side of Davos Man, not the *demos*. They favour supranational decision-making over national self-determination. They are on the side of those that presume to make public policy with little reference to the public.

This, not Donald Trump or Nigel Farage, is why liberal rationalism is in trouble. The New Radicals are a consequence of the problem, not its cause.

14

OUR ILLIBERAL ELITE

Reason is in retreat. On both sides of the Atlantic, a crude populism now dominates the public debate. Empiricism, which has been the basis on which informed decisions have been made since the Enlightenment in the eighteenth century, is under siege from false facts and fake news. In place of rationalism, we now have a kind of post-truth politics. Trump's election win is proof of that.

Or at least that is what we are told by our urbane, educated elite, many of whom cannot quite bring themselves to understand why else millions of their compatriots are not voting the way they want. So they have taken to telling us that it's the people who are the problem. The implication is that voters are irrational. Ignorant. Essex Man. Rednecks. Trumpists. Repugnant. And wrong.

According to Jason Brennan of Georgetown University: 'Most voters are ignorant of both basic political facts and the background social scientific theories needed to evaluate the facts. They process what little information they have in highly biased and irrational ways. They decided largely on whim.'

Pesky people, eh? But these kinds of claims are as unconvincing as they are condescending. Reason is indeed in retreat, but not because voters have abandoned it. It is policy-makers and social scientists who are guilty of betraying empiricism. And with respect to Mr Brennan and co., it's those with 'the background in social scientific theories' whose evaluation and expertise has repeatedly shown itself to be the problem. The rise of the New Radicals is a reaction to the elite's arrogance and intellectual dishonesty over many years.

FAKE FACTS

A few weeks before the EU referendum vote, UK Chancellor George Osborne released a Treasury report. If Britain were to vote to leave the EU, it claimed, GDP by 2030 would be 6.2 per cent lower than if we voted to remain. We would be worse off, he suggested, by £4,300 per household, and there would be an additional £36 billion spending deficit. Those were some pretty specific claims. On what basis did the chancellor present such 'facts'?

He used 'detailed economic analysis and rigorous economic modelling', apparently. And if you read the report, there are indeed some extraordinarily complex algebraic formulae used to calculate the precise impact of Brexit on growth, output, trade, foreign investment and much else. Allegedly UK/EU trade would suffer if we left the European Union because, amongst other things:

$$\ln(T_{ijt}) = \alpha_{ij} + \gamma_t + \alpha_1 \ln(Y_{it} * Y_{jt}) + \alpha_2 \ln(POP_{it} * POP_{jt}) +$$
$$\alpha_3 \ln(DIST_{ij}) + \alpha_4 COMLANG_{ij} + \alpha_5 COLONY_{ij} + \alpha_6 BORDER_{ij} + \varepsilon_{ijt}$$
$$= \alpha_{ij} + \gamma_t + \alpha X_{ijt} + \varepsilon_{ijt}$$

Who could possibly argue with that?

But hold on a second. When he was chancellor, George

Osborne and his Treasury officials consistently failed to tell us with any degree of accuracy what the size of the deficit would be the following year – let alone in 2030. In fact, when he first became chancellor in 2010, he forecast that he would have eliminated the deficit by 2015. It turned out that he was some £70 billion out after five years, with the deficit still stubbornly high.

When he was chancellor, Osborne's own Treasury department could not accurately forecast GDP growth six months ahead, let alone fifteen years. His insistence that our GDP would be 6.2 per cent lower in 2030, as opposed to, say, 6 per cent, was ridiculous. And yet, it was on the basis of such 'facts', plucked from a spreadsheet, that Mr Osborne and the political establishment in Britain insisted that we should vote to remain in the EU.

'The curse of our time is fake maths,' wrote Wolfgang Munchau in the *Financial Times*. 'Think of it as fake news for numerically literate intellectuals: it is the abuse of statistics and economic models to peddle one's own political prejudices.' Indeed. The governing classes are marinated in a bogus form of empiricism. They have some nerve accusing the rest of us of un-reason.

The economic future George Osborne pretended to be able to forecast scientifically is, in reality, unknowable. Neither you, me nor George Osborne can possibly know to the last decimal point what impact on the UK economy a Brexit vote in 2016 might have by 2030. We can guess and speculate as to the overall effect, but we cannot credibly claim to know to that level of detail. No algebraic formula is complex enough to take into account every variable.

Economists, runs the old joke, use decimal points to show that they have a sense of humour. But it stops being funny when those who produce these sorts of claims use them as a basis on which to decide what's right for the rest of us. Empiricism means drawing conclusions on the basis of verifiable observations, as opposed to doing so on the basis of theory. There is little verifiable in the observations contained in the Treasury report on Brexit for the simple reason that the future has not yet happened.

Each report was an exercise in guesswork – and ought to be seen as such. Yet they were reported, not least by BBC News, as fact. I recently reviewed the various forecasts that the Office of Budget Responsibility in Britain has made since it was established. OBR estimates about economic growth and public debt are not just more often wrong than right – they are frequently out by a wide margin.

Yet when I pointed this out, I was attacked by an academic at a leading UK university for 'disregarding the data'. Numbers that are nothing more than forecasts – guesswork – are often afforded the status of facts by a certain sort of academic or pundit.

EMPIRICISM AND ENTRAILS

Many centuries ago in ancient Rome, long before the minds of men and women were governed by reason, a priest trained in the art of divination would inspect the entrails of a specially sacrificed sheep. From that inspection, and equipped with knowledge that apparently only they possessed, the elite could then tell everyone else in the city what needed to be done. It must have conferred on them quite some power.

Today's elite do not inspect animal entrails but Excel spreadsheets. Armed with apparently exclusive knowledge and insight, they decide things for the rest of us on everything from climate change to currency union, education to economics – but often by going far beyond where the empirical evidence allows. It turns out that the approach of today's public-policy priesthood is often little more empirical than it was for priests in the past.

It's not just that the data they are looking at is often narrow. The systems they are seeking to model are complex. Most systems that govern the world around us – economic, demographic or ecological – are nonlinear. Which is just a fancy way of saying that they are shaped by so many variables, you cannot predict what the outcome will be if you change one of the inputs. Much of the modelling done by experts assumes that if you change a specific input, you can predict the outcome. It's not just not empirical, it gives empiricism a bad name. It could almost be designed to breed distrust in those that might actually have rather a lot of valuable knowledge of a particular subject.

As David Deutsch has pointed out, much of what passes for empiricism today is what he terms 'inductivism'. That is to say, an observation is made, a general theory is formed, then more observations are made supposedly justifying that theory. It all becomes a bit self-reinforcing.

In so many areas where it is supposed that there is academic rigour – economics, geography, development studies, political science, sociology – this inductivism is used – and mistaken as being the application of empiricism. 'It is so profoundly false in so many ways,' Deutsch writes. 'Perhaps its worst flaw... is the sheer non-sequitur that a general prediction is tantamount to a new theory.'[97] We should not distrust experts. We should distrust inductivism dressed up expertise.

Yet it is on the basis of such non-sequiturs that so much public administration is conducted. A true empiricist approach would, Deutsch argues, be to recognize that the existing theory seeking to explain something was inadequate. From that starting point, possible solutions would be conceived by conjecture. Those conjectured solutions would then be subject to experimental tests and, on the basis of the results, the new theory would either be shown to be an improvement on the old – or otherwise. This has

97 Deutsch, D., *The Fabric of Reality: The Science of Parallel Universes and Its Implications* (1997), p. 60.

been the basis of proper scientific inquiry since the eighteenth century, yet so many social scientists and academics do not seem to adhere to it.

It's reassuring when we hear that government policy is evidence-based, isn't it? But what if that 'evidence' on which it depends has not been independently verified? The majority of academic research is never put to such a test. It is peer-reviewed instead. Peers of whoever wants to publish the paper review it. But does it work? Peer review does not guarantee that there is any proper statistical analysis or rigour. Far from being a hallmark of empiricism, some have suggested that the peer-review process encourages groupthink. Studies have shown that the process has its flaws.[98]

Richard Smith, a former editor of the *British Medical Journal*, describes peer review as a roulette wheel. It helps explain why, in the words of Richard Horton, editor of *The Lancet*, 'much of the scientific literature, perhaps half, may simply be untrue'. If this is a recognized problem in science, imagine how much more of an issue it is likely to be in social science? Remember that next time the government insists that what they demand we do is based on reason.

As that great thinker Karl Popper puts it, knowledge grows by conjecture and its refutation. Replacing one theory with a better one makes the process of acquiring knowledge cumulative – and evolutionary. Too often today our elites work on the assumption that the acquisition of knowledge is anything but evolutionary. That the certainties in science can be found, too, in social science. On these assumptions they build grand conceits, making policy on the basis of flawed theories.

'But who wants politicians who say, "I don't know"?' you might ask. 'Surely the reason why elites have always exaggerated

98 Laframboise, D., 'Blinded with science' (*The Spectator*, 23 October 2016).

the extent of their knowledge is because people want to be led by the knowledgeable?' Not knowing something – and recognizing the limits of our knowledge – are not the same as not being able to find out.

Lots of organizations successfully provide the public with what they want – often a good deal more effectively than anything run by government. Yet they do not start from the position of presuming to know. Take McDonald's, perhaps the most successful restaurant chain ever created. Founded in San Bernardino, California, in 1940, today McDonald's feeds millions of people each week in hundreds of countries. How does McDonald's know what to feed them? Those who run McDonald's know that they don't know. But that doesn't mean no menus.

Instead they use a genuinely empirical approach to determine what to serve which customers in which restaurants. For a start, there's a lot of local variation. A typical McDonald's menu carries 120–140 items, and about 100 will be specific to a region. The individual franchises have a lot of leeway, with only about 40 core items required.

And to get a new item on the menu, McDonald's does not presume to know what will or won't work. Instead they do precisely what David Deutsch might suggest: first, the team at McDonald's Oak Brook headquarters comes up with an idea for a new product – a conjectured solution to the problem of an imperfect menu. Then they subject the new product to lots of tests in a lab, using chefs, food scientists and nutritionists. Then it is exposed to a series of experimental tests involving focus groups.

Tested then tweaked, tweaked then tested, the new product is rolled out first in just a few carefully selected restaurants. Peer review? They test it on the actual customer. In America, chicken items tend to be trialled first in Atlanta, coffee products in the North East, burgers in Texas and salads on the West Coast. At every stage, the assumption is that those with the new idea do not know if it will work or not. There's less room for conceit and cock-up. Things that won't work are exposed as duds early on. There is no room for self-deception on the part of those designing the products.

We live in a world where empiricism is used to decide how fast-food restaurants are run. But when it comes to public policy provision, empiricism is abandoned. Instead we subject young people to the whim of 'experts'.

Empiricism ought to ensure an air of humility. Instead, in its bogus form, it encourages hubris. It fosters a sense among the governing that there is nothing they cannot organize or engineer on behalf of the governed. It's no way to run a chain of fast-food restaurants. It's a bad way to run an education system. It's a pretty disastrous way to try to run a country.

HUBRIS AND SELF-DECEPTION

In the summer of 2011, London was rocked by riots. They seemed to come out of nowhere and, for a few traumatic days, they shocked the nation. In the aftermath, Prime Minister David Cameron launched something called the Troubled Families programme.

The intention was to target 'problem' families responsible for much of the antisocial behaviour and welfare dependency, helping them off benefits and back into work. The programme, it was claimed, could also help cut truancy and offending – and deal with the underlying causes of the riots. Or at least that was the theory. Or, I should say, the prediction.

The programme cost £1.3 billion – yet turned out to be a total flop. Almost half of all families that went through the programme were still living on unemployment benefits eighteen months afterwards – the same as for similar families not on the programme. The programme achieved no noticeable reduction in crime, antisocial behaviour or truancy. Those behind the scheme claimed that their programme was all about 'evidence-led policy-making'. Yet their use of data was deeply flawed. McDonald's does more pre-launch testing before offering a new flavour of McFlurry than David Cameron's government did before embarking on a £1.3 billion government programme.

Under the Troubled Families programme, officials were paying local authorities to provide them with data they insisted was there – an approach that is hardly scientific. Worse, they were then offering local authorities a £4,000 incentive for each local family they found and put through the programme. This, as *Newsnight*'s Chris Cook observed, meant they were 'signing up families, waiting for time to heal a problem or two and then claiming the cash'. [99] It's hardly surprising that those running the programme were seeing such a distorted set of results.

The philosopher Bertrand Russell used to tell an amusing story about a chicken in order to make a serious point about theories and facts. Each day, he said, a farmer came to feed the chicken corn. Based on the evidence, Russell said, if the chicken had been capable of abstract thought, it might well deduce from the evidence that the farmer liked her. When the farmer started to double the amount of corn he gave the chicken each day, the evidence for the chicken's 'friendly farmer' theory literally started to pile up. But then one day the farmer came and, instead of giving the chicken corn, wrung her neck. Not so friendly after all.

The friendly-farmer theory might have been supported by the observable facts but it was fundamentally flawed. And the alternative 'farmer-fattening-up-chicken-to-eat' theory – also supported by the facts – might have better explained what was going on. Those behind the Troubled Families programme simply

99 Kruger, D., Why the troubled families programme must be the last of its kind, *The Spectator*, 23 October 2016.

did not consider that there might be alternative explanations for the data they looked at.

Officials were found to have 'manipulated and misrepresented data'. Was it a straightforward case of wilful conspiracy? I doubt it.

Part of the problem was overconfidence. Officials were so certain that spending public money in this manner could heal society, they never seemed to stop and ask if their assumptions were sound. Experiments that test your hypothesis are, after all, what you do when you are not sure of the truth. They didn't apparently feel the need to challenge their own assumptions.

Local authorities, which stood to earn hundreds of thousands of pounds by playing along with the scheme, did just that. Social workers had a vested interest in a £1.3 billion boondoggle that involved hiring many more social workers.

Just as Bertrand Russell's chicken wanted to believe the farmer was friendly, David Cameron and his officials wanted to believe that the prime minister could somehow fix a broken society. This sort of self-deception permeates almost every level of public administration.

I first got a sense of the way wishful thinking gives rise to the selective use of facts when, as a new MP, I tried to find out why a £16 million new school built in my constituency closed after only a few years.

Opened by the then prime minister, Tony Blair, a few days before the 2005 General Election, it turned out to be a rather expensive election prop given that it shut soon after. So why, I started to inquire, had the school been built in the first place? I did a bit of digging.

I was shown a spreadsheet produced in the council offices which showed that there was going to be a big rise in the number of families with children of school age living in the area. Extrapolating from that, the education experts concluded with a certain linear logic that more young people in that part of Essex had to mean a new secondary school.

But the world is not linear. The raw rise in pupil numbers, it turns out, is not the only thing that decides if there is demand for a new school – and if such a school is viable. Another important factor – not shown in any spreadsheet – is whether the new school envisaged could attract and retain capable teachers, and maintain a high enough standard of education, for parents to want to send their kids there.

The new secondary school failed to do that. It achieved some of the worst results in the country. Parents boycotted sending their children to the new school and even took up home schooling as an alternative. Another factor that threw the future of the new school into doubt was the way that other established schools in the area improved their standards. One significantly expanded its capacity, something that the council planners complained subsequently to me they could not possibly have known about when they took the decision to build a new school. Indeed.

Looking at the council spreadsheet after the new school had been shut, it struck me that even if the forecasts of pupil numbers had been accurate (it was way out), the data on it could only ever explain a few of the factors that determine whether or not a new secondary school has a future. The spreadsheet captured none of this. Yet even if it had somehow managed to capture all such information, if you are really excited about the prospect of a new flagship school project, you might only see the facts that support the outcome you want to see.

Small, self-serving elites don't just mislead the masses. They deceive themselves. Like every priesthood of the past, those who today preside over public administration like to see the world as a place best shaped by deliberate design, with them at the centre of creation and capable of its salvation. It is in that conceit that so many subsequent problems are sown.

THE CONSEQUENCES OF CONCEIT

'It ain't what you don't know that gets you into trouble,' wrote Mark Twain. 'It's what you know for sure that just ain't so.'

Often the delusions of public policy makers are just an honest instance of self-deception. As with the Troubled Families programme, officials found it convenient to see things a certain way, so they did – and the consequences were relatively benign. Blowing billions on additional social workers hardly harmed society, and despite being ineffective, might have done some good in a rather roundabout way.

Sometimes wishful thinking on the part of public policy makers has far graver consequences. Many expert economists, to echo Twain, knew about the benefits of European monetary union. But it wasn't so. Monetary union caused mass unemployment across southern Europe, property booms and busts in Ireland and Spain, systemic banking weaknesses in Germany and Italy, and a massive transfer of wealth from asset-poor to asset-rich.

For forty years, the experts who run the central banks thought they knew best how to manage the money. But it wasn't so either. They presided over a series of financial bubbles, the latest of which almost destroyed the Western banking system. All their models and theories marched far ahead of verifiable facts.

The growth of federal government in America, like the creation of the European Union, reflects at a macro level thousands of micro-conceits on the part of the elite that they know best how to organize the affairs of an entire continent. Yet do the governed on either side of the Atlantic believe that they are run by the rational? Federal government in America has become a byword for incompetence. In Europe, EU institutions cannot even accurately account for how they spend their annual budgets.

Wishful thinking has led to the creation of elaborate schemes to supposedly protect the environment. What we can verify is that such schemes have created an income stream for rent-seekers.

For decades, wishful-thinking Western elites have known all about the benefits of multiculturalism. Yet it appears that in some parts of Britain, Europe and even America, the melting pot isn't melting the way they knew it would. What is increasingly impossible to overlook is the rising degree of social segregation and an invidious form of identity politics.

Honest instances of self-deception are commonplace. But there are also instances of public policy makers deceiving us, if not themselves, because it suits various vested interests.

In the late 1990s, a number of car companies in Europe had a clear technological advantage in the manufacture of diesel engines. So it seems that they set out to ensure that more Europeans bought diesel, as opposed to petrol, cars. Obviously, they could not say that they wanted to rig the market to make a fortune. Instead they invoked bogus empiricism as a pretext for shaping public policy the way they wanted it.

Everyone wants a cleaner environment, right? So, the argument was made by those who lobbied for European car-makers that we had to switch to diesel to cut carbon emissions. Diesel, it's true, emits marginally less CO_2 than petrol. But of course, if you are going to be properly empirical about it, diesel is far dirtier than petrol. It might produce less CO_2 but it annoyingly produces lots of nasty nitrogen dioxide (NO_2). To get around this pesky problem, one or two car companies rigged the evidence, systematically deceiving us with false NO_2 emissions tests. Just like the Troubled Families programme, data was distorted.

For all the sophistry about environmental protections, there was nothing benign or ethical about this fraud. NO_2 is an extremely toxic pollutant. By making hundreds of thousands of Europeans switch to deadly diesel, millions of Europeans were exposed to higher levels of NO_2. According to the European Environment Agency, in 2013 alone an estimated 71,000 Europeans died prematurely as a consequence of NO_2 pollution. Bogus empiricism literally kills people.

It's not just in Europe where big business gets what it wants on the basis of bogus evidence, coupled with concern about the environment. In the United States, there has in recent years been a massive move towards biofuel; that is, fuel that we grow, rather than get out of the ground.

Each year, the world produces 10 billion tonnes of ethanol, mostly from US maize or Brazilian sugar cane. These carbohydrates, rather than hydrocarbons, are used – thanks to large subsidies – to fuel lots of cars. It's a massive industry and subsidized by hand-outs to farmers worth billions of dollars. Starting in the 1990s, huge sums have been spent – at the behest of farmers, lobbyists and various vested interests – fostering an ethanol and biodiesel industry in the United States on the pretext that it protects the planet.

But as with the EU switch to diesel, it turns out that the environmental arguments in favour of the switch are a sham. In order to grow biofuel, massive amounts of fuel get used. So much so that biofuels hardly yield enough energy compared to what it takes to produce them to make it worthwhile. In America and Brazil, great swathes of agricultural land are used to produce fuel, driving up the price of food. As Matt Ridley points out, between 2005 and 2007 almost all of the 51-million-tonne increase in world maize production was swallowed up producing biofuel.

In order to make way for all the palm oil plantations that have sprung up to meet the subsidized demand, forests have been cut down. It's one of the reasons why so much of the orangutan's habitat is being destroyed. And as for cutting carbon dioxide emissions, according to Joseph Fargione of the Nature Conservancy, producing biofuel produces far more CO_2 than biofuel saves by switching away from fossil fuel.

Is it any wonder that more and more voters no longer trust public policy makers?

AN ELITE AUTHORITARIANISM

The risk to the liberal order comes not from the disillusionment of the demos below. It comes instead from a new authoritarianism from on high.

Already, as we saw in Chapter 3, democracy is in peril as power has passed steadily from those we elected to a technocratic elite, presiding over pan-continental federations on either side of the Atlantic. Yet when any angry electorate reacts against this – by electing Donald Trump to the White House in America, or voting for all those other insurgent parties in Britain and Europe – look at the response.

Pundits now openly question democracy on either side of the Atlantic. Supposedly respectable writers like the *Spectator*'s Matthew Parris pen articles explaining why they no longer trust democracy. The kind of arguments that nineteenth-century Tory peers once used to oppose the extension of the franchise – and which for most of the past half-century would have not been taken seriously – can be heard once again.

American commentator Andrew Sullivan argued that Donald Trump in the White House risked the rise of American dictatorship and the end of American democracy. Once Trump won, Sullivan started to suggest that we should dilute democracy to 'cool the people's populist passions'. We ought to allow the experts to override the *demos*. It seems to me that it's the Andrew Sullivans of this world who are the greater risk to democracy.

Trump's election in American has confirmed in the minds of many of the elite the danger of letting the people decide. Jason Brennan, that Georgetown University academic, has even written a book called *Against Democracy*. It argues for an 'aristocracy of the wise'. These are the sorts of ideas that emerged in Italy in the 1920s. We are much closer than we might imagine to the authoritarianism of the elite – and it is this that is the genuine danger to our democracy. If you think I exaggerate, just try to imagine almost any Western government being prepared to allow its citizens a referendum again, after 23 June 2016?

Donald Trump is no American Caesar, about to cross some sort of constitutional Rubicon and seize power in perpetuity. Nigel Farage is no British *signore*; he cannot even get himself elected to the House of Commons. Geert Wilders and Beppe Grillo are no latter-day Sullas. But they might just provide others with the pretext they need to set aside democracy.

The risk is that the New Radicals become little more than a way of registering a protest against this top-down technocracy, rather than a means of stopping it. They may even make things worse – and in doing so, Trump and co. could discredit anyone ever standing on an anti-establishment platform again.

For decades, politics in America, Britain and much of Europe has been run as a cartel, in the interests of insiders. The economy, notionally free-market, has been rigged in the interests of a small, well-connected elite close to the money–power nexus that has arisen in recent decades.

The emergence of this new oligarchy has put the Western world at a crossroads. Either we now go the way of the republics of Rome, Venice and the Netherlands; we allow the oligarchy to take over entirely, and thereby regress. Or we reassert the freedom of the productive against the parasitic. We insist afresh on those things that drive human progress; independence, coupled with interdependence, and a dispersal of power.

If we do not, the West will prove to have been just an aberration. An essentially Anglo-American interlude, which like those other periods of productivity that punctuated human history in the past, lasted a couple of centuries.

What is to be done?

PART IV
OVERTHROW

15

WHAT IS TO BE DONE?

A few weeks ago in central London, I watched a group of protesters holding aloft anarchist signs as they demanded greater government spending. They seemed almost as confused as the fellow who tweeted me his denunciations of globalization the other day – using a mobile device made in Korea and software written in California.

The mood of populist revolt is marred by an angry muddle. While there is a growing sense that power is becoming concentrated, there is a distinct lack of clarity as to the causes. New Radicals on the left offer retro-1960s socialism, raging nonsensically against 'neo-liberalism', as though a surfeit of freedom was the problem. On the right, New Radicals just rage, seemingly oblivious of the way in which global specialization and exchange has elevated living standards. The glibness of so much political punditry hardly helps.

Amid the incoherence are all sorts of opportunities for any sort of loudmouth to emerge, with apparently easy answers. In such an atmosphere, the outspoken will get a cheer in proportion to how much attention they can grab, rather than because they have any meaningful remedies. But we should not see it as the loudmouths' fault.

There is, as we saw in Part I, an emergent oligarchy. Politics is a cartel. Like the economy, it's rigged in the interests of an emerging oligarchy. Many branches of public administration have been overcome by mediocrity. We do need revolutionary change.

But we face a fight on two fronts: the new oligarchy on one side and the worst of the New Radicals on the other. We need to counter the emergence of the new oligarchy with a reform agenda and disperse power to stop the parasites being able to siphon off resources. In doing so, and by not leaving it to angry populists to oppose the emerging oligarchy, our upheaval might just preserve the liberal order. Like some of those earlier upheavals we looked at, our insurgency could be a reassertion of the liberal order.

RECLAIMING REASON

Our revolt must be based on reason, not angry incoherence. We should not reject experts. What we need instead is to ensure that there is genuine expertise in the making of public policy.

The quantum physicist Richard Feynman (1918–88) once described many supposedly scientific studies as 'cargo cult science'. 'In the South Seas,' he explained, 'there is a Cargo Cult of people. During the war they saw airplanes land with lots of good materials, and they want the same thing to happen now. So they've arranged to make things like runways, to put fires along the sides of the runways, to make a wooden hut for a man to sit in, with two wooden pieces on his head like headphones and bars of bamboo sticking out like antennas – he's the controller – and they wait for the airplanes to land. They're doing everything right. The form is perfect. It looks exactly the way it looked before. But it doesn't work. No airplanes land. So I call these things Cargo Cult Science, because they follow all the apparent precepts and forms of scientific investigation, but they're missing something essential, because the planes don't land.'

There is a similar cargo-cult approach in many areas of public policy making. Far from staying true to the Enlightenment, which was a rebellion against authority in regard to knowledge, so much public policy making, with its uber-rationalism and bogus empiricism, is a betrayal of it.

As Feynman pointed out, before the Second World War in America and many Western states, medical science did not routinely used randomized control trials. Doctors preferred instead to act on the assumption that they had some sort of special insight. It was only from the 1950s onwards that, in place of such supposed expertise, randomized trials have been rolled out as the norm.

Many public policy makers today are rather like those early-twentieth-century scientists. They adopt a cargo-cult approach because they presume to know. As experts, they assume that they have a special insight and understanding. But if you are going to claim a special expertise or knowledge, on which basis you are going to try to shape or order society or the economy, might it not be best to at least test your apparent insights?

Everyone would like to reduce social inequality. But if the government programmes claiming to cut inequality are in fact increasing dependence on welfare, ought we not know that? Where are the equivalent of randomized control trials to assess the efficacy of all those billion-dollar welfare programmes? Where are the randomized control trials for all those top-down initiatives?

We would all like to see improvements in education standards. But if new education initiatives are undertaken and expensive new school buildings built, without anyone actually testing the effectiveness of the new approach, how do we know if they work?

'Sure,' I hear you say, 'we could all do with a bit of an empirical approach before making public policy.' But it's a lot more than just a bit more empiricism.

'Empiricism,' writes David Deutsch, 'never did achieve its aim of liberating' us from authority.[100] Empiricism might have helped us escape the clutches of those pre-eighteenth-century sources of authority but, unfortunately, it opened the way to a new set of misconceptions about knowledge needing authority. To quote David Deutsch again: 'The misconception that knowledge needs authority to be genuine or reliable dates back to antiquity, and it still prevails.'[101]

To reclaim reason, we need to not only ditch the notion that reason alone is the source of knowledge. We should recognize that there are no authoritative sources of knowledge. No absolutely reliable means of justifying ideas as being true. This is called 'fallibilism'. Think of it as a kind of uber-empiricism.

'Science,' said Feynman, 'is the belief in the ignorance of experts.' Good science, and good social scientists, too, should recognize this. Yet so often our illiberal elite are instead imbued with a false sense of certainty on everything from economic systems to the environment and education. From fallibilism should spring humility. We should – as the Enlightenment ought to have taught us – appreciate that not all that is worth knowing is yet known.

In our insurgency against the new oligarchy and the illiberal elite, we should not hold aloft blueprints, ready to remake the world. What we need is something far more subversive instead: optimism.

100 Deutsch, D., *The Beginning of Infinity: Explanations that Transform the World* (2011), p. 8.
101 Ibid., p. 9.

OPTIMISM

Revolutionaries always get to the stage when they wonder, 'What is to be done?' From the Gracchi brothers in Rome to Lenin in Russia, at that stage they invariably produce some blueprint for change: redistribution of land, or the means of production. Reordering of institutions in pursuit of some abstract idea of what might work – some sort of '-ism'. It's almost always been a disaster.

Revolutionaries, as much as any priesthood, often like to believe in some sort of ultimate revealed truth. Our revolt should be the antithesis of all that. It should be built on the even more radical insight that there is no ultimate revelation. No perfect knowledge and therefore no perfect blueprint.

There is something deeply pessimistic about the idea of an ultimate revealed truth. Like our illiberal elites who presume a wisdom unsubstantiated by experience, revolutionary blueprints for change imply that all there is to know is now known. This is it.

Being an optimist does not just mean being cheery about the future. Optimists in a less colloquial sense recognize that what they know in the future might be more than they know now – and that by acquiring better knowledge, problems can be overcome in future.

If you are an optimist in this sense, you ought to be immune to the idea of blueprints and grand plans because you recognize that they might soon be outdated.

Progress comes from emergent order. The conditions that allow human progress and innovation – independence, interdependence and dispersed power – are so vital precisely because they enable self-organization and emergent order.

When we ask, 'What is to be done?' our answer must not be to impose grand plans, but to set in place systems, for everything from banks and money to public services and political parties, so that decisions can be taken without top-down direction. Since we do not know all there is to know, we must not seek out solutions based on the idea that there are any perfect answers to be imposed by fiat. What we need instead is change that ensures a process of continual variation and error correction.

Public policy-making failures are inevitable. Even if, at any one moment in time, those who set interest rates or determine the national curriculum get it right, conditions change. Demand for credit shifts. The kinds of skills young people need are not constant. What is suitable one year, will be less so the next.

Rather than seeking to set interest rates perfectly, we need a way of ensuring that a small clique of central bankers are not able to impose the consequences of their mistakes and misapprehension on the rest of us. Instead of pretending that there is a perfect national curriculum for the country, we need to allow the curriculum to evolve to meet the needs of millions of individual children. Politics must abandon the pretence that any one set of politicians has any perfect answers. We need instead a system that ensures misguided dogmas and pet projects do not damage the rest of us.

16

TAKING DOWN
THE BANKSTERS

- Break the money-power nexus that allows government to live beyond its means, as the elite enrich themselves at our expense.
- Radical change to bank law to stop them conjuring credit out of nothing, privatizing profits yet socializing losses.
- Make those who own banks liable for their customers' cash and require all banks to adopt open programme interfaces.
- End the state monopoly of money, so allowing currency competition.
- Rescue capitalism by redefining capital.

A strangler fig begins its life as just another tiny green sapling growing in the crown of a tall tree. Living alongside lichen, moss and all manner of other treetop flora, it tries to eke out a living high above the forest floor. It's hard to imagine that something so small and nondescript could be such a deadly threat to the giant on which it is perched. And to start with, it isn't. It struggles to draw whatever nutrients it is able to from its surroundings.

Then it sends down a single, spindly root far below to the forest floor. And the moment that the root makes it to the soil, the host tree is doomed. Able to draw nutrients up from the soil, it suddenly switches into something much more deadly. No longer just another scrawny freeloader hitching a ride on a host tree, it overwhelms its host. Once parasitic elites, like that strangler fig, are able to find a way of drawing off wealth from a new source, they, too, are able to engulf the rest of the society on which they sit.

In the late Roman republic, the elite established a way of siphoning off wealth from outside Italy by the acquisition of an empire. First the root went into the rich soil of Sicily, then Pergamum and Spain. The elite flourished, becoming an oligarchy that was able to choke the body politic of the rest of the republic. In Venice, the parasitic elite planted tendrils in the East. After they sacked Constantinople, they took over the extensive Byzantine estates in Crete and eventually Cyprus. For the Dutch, the sudden influx of wealth came from the East Indies. Even in England, which we often regard as a free-trading nation, the wannabe oligarchs of the eighteenth century made a good go of putting down roots to extort what they could from Ireland, the West Indies and India.

The oligarchy emerging in our midst today enriches itself not by transferring wealth from overseas colonies, but from the future. It's not provincials that today's parasites make pay, but posterity. They siphon resources not using galleys or sailing ships, but bonds, banks and the manipulation of money.

If we are serious about ending the emergent oligarchy, we need first to stop them sucking up the surplus.

SIPHONING OFF THE SURPLUS USING BONDS

Every time a government bond is sold, it is an exchange; the government that issues the bond gets cash to spend today and, in return, the bondholder gets a guarantee that they will get a slice of future tax revenues. In other words, the bondholder buys a claim on the future. A bond is therefore a form of redistribution; tomorrow's productive are made to pay for our today.

Billions of pounds' worth of bonds are issued every month, and each time an enormous amount of wealth is taken from tomorrow so that it might be spent today. For every ten dollars or pounds that the governments of America or Britain spent last year, one of them was using money that had been borrowed from the future by issuing a bond. In Japan, 38 per cent of government spending last year came from bond debt. Long after that revenue has been spent, that money will have to be repaid by productive people and businesses in America, Britain and Japan who may not even yet exist.

Roman citizens living in Italy in the early days of empire did not pay many taxes. Yet the state spent a great deal on armies and civil engineering. It was the provinces that paid the difference. Again, today it's tomorrow that we make pay. If citizens in the UK this year were to pay for the public services they enjoy, as opposed to passing on the bill to the grandkids, we would need to generate an amount of additional tax revenue consummate to increasing income tax by 8 pence in the pound, and hiking up VAT by 5.5 per cent. In the US, federal tax revenues would need to rise 35 per cent.

Yet Western governments use bonds to live far beyond our means – and pass the cost onto tomorrow. The French government last ran a balanced budget in the early 1970s. Britain has only balanced the books in six of the past forty-three years. Successive American governments have been billing tomorrow for decades, too.

The so-called global financial crisis was really a Western debt crisis, caused by the massive accumulation of debt. According to the Congressional Budget Office (CBO), US public debt totals almost $14 trillion. It is expected to increase under Trump, reaching $23 trillion by 2026, and could be more than double that by 2046. Japan's debt is also put at $14 trillion, with the Eurozone's $12 trillion. Add in unfunded spending commitments alongside on-balance-sheet debts, and it is even higher. According to American academic and politician Laurence Kotlikoff, if you include all the off-balance-sheet stuff, US debt stands closer to $100 trillion. That is a great deal of wealth that we will be spending before anyone has actually produced it.

When the Roman oligarchy extorted distant provinces, they did so aided by the *publicani*, giant tax-collecting conglomerates. When our elite extort our tomorrow, they are assisted by the banks. Like the *publicani*, banks today buy up bonds, giving governments a ready flow of cash to spend now. In return they get the right to tax revenues tomorrow. Far from creating wealth, many banks today, like the parasitic Roman *publicani*, help a small elite hoover it up.

Like those in Rome with a stake in the *publicani*, or the Dutch regent rich, or the Venetian nobles, there is a vested bondholder interest emerging in the West today. By 1650, almost half of the Venetian state's tax take went to bondholders. In Holland, too, by the eighteenth century over half of tax revenues went on debt repayment. Already in Britain, we have reached the stage where bondholders receive a larger slice of tax revenue – £47 billion each year – than we spend on defence. In Japan, meanwhile, 43 per cent of the tax take goes on bondholders.

This year, bondholders will receive a quarter of a trillion dollars in interest payments from American taxpayers. By 2026, the CBO estimates annual interest payments will total some $700 billion. It's a lot of wealth being redistributed. By 2080, they estimate that interest payments on public debt will amount to 12 per cent of GDP.

US households are already working for bondholders. Each US

taxpayer is liable for over $150,000 of debt, and the amount they are liable for has increased faster than average earnings for over a decade.[102] By 2020, between 15 and 20 per cent of tax revenues will be spent on servicing public debt. By 2030, an estimated 36 per cent of tax revenues will go to the bondholders. By 2040, 58 per cent. By 2050, 85 per cent.

A money–power nexus has emerged with a vested interest in plundering posterity. These twenty-first-century parasitic *publicani* are in some states, like Greece, already more powerful than the elected governments. They get to decide who pays what rates of tax and receives what level of public services. England fought a civil war, and America a revolution, to establish the principle that there should be 'no taxation without representation'. Yet over the past generation, the money–power nexus has undermined this basic principle that has underpinned the West's success.

Thanks to bonds and banksters, governments have been able to increase spending without having to increase taxation – and without much regard to any sort of representation. Until recently, when politicians debated how much to spend on public services, the discussion was always tempered by the notion that taxes would have to rise to pay for it all. Due to the ability and willingness of governments to spend by borrowing, rather than taxing, increases in public spending are not matched by any kind of corresponding rise in taxes. In fact, in the US we have seen successive administrations cut taxes and increase public spending.

Bonds and borrowing have, in effect, rendered redundant the conventional constraint upon unaccountable government. Governments no longer need permission from the people – or their representatives – before spending, because they no longer need to raise taxes to spend. If Western finance ministers wanted

102 *Forbes Magazine*, 'Guess How Much You Owe?' April 24, 2015.

to increase taxation, they would need to ask permission from a parliament or congress of some kind. There would be some sort of political downside, even if they won the argument and the vote. But by issuing bonds, they do not need the permission of any parliament. If only Charles I had thought of issuing 'ship bonds', rather than a new tax – 'ship money' – he might have kept his head.

Perhaps we should insist on some sort of legislative oversight for the issuance of bonds? It's an idea – and indeed in certain US states and cities, a referendum is held to approve the issuance of local government bonds. But even if we were to find a way of doing something similar on a national level, tomorrow's voters who will have to pay the bill on those bonds are not around. There is no constituency of the future sitting in today's Parliament or Congress to vote down such demands.

No. Instead we need to destroy the ability of banks and big government to pass on such large debts to tomorrow – preferably before tomorrow arrives. And to do that, we need to get to the root of the money–power nexus by preventing banks from being able to extend debt and credit indefinitely.

SWITCH OFF THE MAGIC MONEY MACHINE

In 2008, just before the bubble burst, British banks had balance sheets five times larger than the total GDP of the UK economy. That sounds impressive, right? If you are some City hotshot then you might be forgiven for thinking that those sorts of statistics mean you are much more valuable than those mere mortals from the suburbs.

But what does the runaway size of banks' balance sheets really mean? It means that they have a magic money machine that allows them to conjure credit out of nothing, and build up eye-watering amounts of debt. As we saw in Chapter 5, banks are able to do this because, legally, when you pay money into your bank account, they – not you – own it. That allows them to issue credit against it – multiple times.

On this simple legal fact is built the whole pyramid scheme of fractional reserve banking. It's a magic money machine – for banks and for government, too. Banks are able to extend credit out of nothing, profiting from the interest. So much so, in fact, that in 2007, on the eve of the banking crisis, for every £1 deposited in a British bank, there were £44 of credit claims. As the great economist Irving Fisher explained, 'Our national circulating medium is now at the mercy of loan transactions of banks; and our thousands of checking banks are, in effect, so many irresponsible private mints.'

Why do governments allow banks to have this magic money machine? Because they gain from the consequences of it, too. Governments are able to exchange all those bonds for cash because fractional reserve banking ensures there are takers for all those IOUs. Rome lived by siphoning off the surplus from the provinces. America today does not only live beyond her means by borrowing from tomorrow – she borrows from abroad, too. Able to issue US dollar-denominated debt, she has been able to finance yawning trade deficits.

Switch off the magic money machine, and there would be fewer takers for US bonds and dollar-denominated debt. Which is precisely the point, and why we must switch it off. Big banks have become part of a large, cosy, stodgy cartel exactly because they are in cahoots with big government. The 2007 banking crisis was caused by banks overextending their balance sheets. They gave credit that they had conjured from nothing to debtors who could not pay. Once the pyramid of IOUs started to unravel, the credit evaporated but the debts it left were very real.

Yet those that oversaw the banking sector comprehensively failed to see it coming. In Britain, Europe and America, the regulators – who had spent the previous decade insisting on all manner of elaborate compliance in banking – simply failed to ask the right questions. They had, like all bogus empiricists, assumed that the process they were peering at was linear. They simply could not foresee the sort of eventualities – like a halt to inter-bank lending – that brought the system down.

Do we really think that giving such institutions – and in some cases the same individuals – yet more regulatory responsibility is the answer? That's really all that the Dodd–Frank Act and other legislative responses have done since the banking bubble burst. We need more substantial change that gets to the root of the problem, and that means appointing a different kind of regulator: the banks' customers.

How? By re-establishing in law the fact that when they, the customers, deposit money in a bank, it remains their money. Ever since the Bank Charter Act of 1844, the bank has owned the money and you, as the customer, only own a claim to it. Because the bank owns the money, it is able to lend against it multiple times. This is the only legal fact that separates fractional reserve banking from elaborate fraud. Once the law is amended to ensure that you, the customer, own the money, the bank may not lawfully lend it out – generating all that candy-floss credit – without your permission. If it did, the bank would be guilty of fraud.

'The horror!' many will screech. 'Carswell wants to end fractional reserve banking! It will be the ruin of Western capitalism as we know it!' Actually, Western capitalism is on course to do a pretty good job of ruining itself right now. And I am not suggesting that we end fractional reserve banking any more than the regulators ban it when they insist on regulations. No, what I am suggesting is that we rein in its worst excesses – just as the tried-yet-failed regulators want to do, but using the customer as the ultimate arbiter of risk.

Under my proposal,[103] it would still be possible to lend against your deposits, but only if you – the customer – specified that you were happy to have the bank lend multiple lines of credit against your money. Put your money in an ordinary deposit account, and the money by law would remain yours. The bank could not extend endless credit against it. They would keep it safe for you and – as some full reserve bank entrepreneurs are looking to do in London now – they would match what you held with highly liquid reserves. The rate of interest you got from your savings would be low – but it would be safe.

Tick the box that says you want to put your money in a loan account, however, and what you pay in would be the bank's to extend credit against. The risk would be higher – but so, too, would be the rate of interest on the account (which of itself might be a novel experience for many savers). In the old days, there used to be a vertical separation in banking – the old Glass–Steagall separation – between retail and investment banking. Under my proposal, instead of that kind of vertical split between types of banks, the division would be horizontal within them.

'But some customers might keep some of their savings in deposit accounts and some in loan accounts,' you point out. Exactly. Like with traditional building societies in Britain, there would be different accounts, with customers free to decide how much of their savings to have in each. And by shifting money from loan accounts to deposit accounts – or vice versa – the customer would be determining the bank's capital reserves.

If a bank was regarded as well run, with sensible management, customers would be willing to place a high share of their savings in the loan accounts – thereby allowing the bank to extend

103 I presented a bill in the House of Commons to achieve this legal change in November 2010 as the Financial Services (Regulation of Deposits and Lending) Bill.

more credit and expand their balance sheet. But if the bank had a reputation for carelessness and the management was seen as irresponsible, the customer would move money out of the loan accounts into the more secure deposit accounts. This would restrict the ability of the bank to extend credit, *de facto* forcing up the bank's capital ratio.

At the moment, top-down regulators insist on the same capital ratios for all banks, regardless of who runs them and how sensible they are. Banks are able to expand their balance sheets according to how much risk the top-down regulator allows. Under my proposal, it would be the actual customers that determine the extent to which the balance sheet could balloon.

At the moment, banks are able to indulge in a form of financial alchemy. They can convert ordinary deposits into massive speculations – and the only thing that prevents them from doing so recklessly are top-down regulators. Under my proposal, the customer would constrain them, too.

Switching off the banks' magic money machine would be unpopular with officialdom. How else are they supposed to offload all those bonds in return for cash? But that is precisely why it is essential that we do it. If fractional reserve banking is properly constrained, banks would no longer be able to keep on underwriting government overspend. If governments wanted to keep spending as much as they do, we would have to approve of it and pay higher taxes. Alternatively, they would have to live within their means. Either way, we would no longer be able to pass the bill onto tomorrow.

Oh, and another happy consequence would be that we would end asset price inflation – which is the largest driver of social inequality in the West today. Without government and banks messing about with the money system, assets would no longer keep increasing in value relative to wages. In other words, society would be fairer, too.

MAKING BANKERS RESPONSIBLE

If you own a bank, people pay money in so that it might be kept safe. Those who own banks ought therefore to be liable for the security of their customers' deposits, no? That's certainly the way it used to be. Until 1934 in America, if you owned a bank and for whatever reason you were unable to pay back the depositors their money, you as a shareholder were liable and stood to lose much more than just the value of your shareholding to pay them back.

During the Wall Street Crash in 1929, hundreds of American banks collapsed. According to popular myth, this left many American's unable to recover their deposits – and facing ruin. In reality, it was not those with deposits in the failed banks who bore the brunt of the bank failures. No, those who faced real ruin were those who owned the banks. After the initial shock of the markets and banks crashing, many of those who were unable to retrieve their deposits from the banks successfully sued the shareholders of the banks to recover the money.

Something similar had happened in Britain a generation or so earlier. When the City of Glasgow Bank went bust in 1878, it ruined most of the bank's 1,200 shareholders who had to pony up to pay back the depositors their money. But in the aftermath of these bank failures on either side of the Atlantic, the banks lobbied the politicians to intervene. Even though the City of Glasgow Bank had, like those banks in America, recklessly extended credit. Despite the fact that the directors of the bank had then committed fraud to conceal the scale to which they were overextended – making matters vastly worse – the rules were rewritten to make the taxpayer liable for such losses.

The idea of government-backed bank deposits sounds reassuring, doesn't it? But from this little comfort came big consequences. Once the state – rather than those who actually owned the bank – was liable for the banks' losses, the banks were on to a pretty good thing. No wonder more capital was attracted to banking.

It became an extraordinarily privileged business. Not only could they conjure up out of nothingness the thing that they sold – credit – but those who owned shares in them could keep private any profits that they made, while counting on the state to rescue them if their own overextended balance sheets incurred large losses. We need to change the law on limited liability so that those who own banks have some liability for their customers' deposits. It is, for heaven's sake, one of the reasons why customers put their money in banks in the first place.

'But hold on,' you might think. 'We need limited liability laws. They underpin capitalism and capital risk.' It's true that to some extent limited liability law encourages entrepreneurship by providing investors with the assurance that the most they could ever lose in a business is what they invested. In return for that legal protection, those whom the shareholders appoint to represent them – the directors – have an obligation to ensure that the business's liabilities do not recklessly exceed its assets.

But, of course, when it comes to banking, the balance sheet is, if you like, back to front. A bank treats a deposit as a liability – which it is, if you think about it, since it is an obligation by the bank to pay that customer back what they have paid in. At the same time, a bank's assets are, thanks to fractional reserve banking, conjured from nothing. Which explains why RBS *et al* could rapidly build up a balance sheet that claims to be in excess of our total GDP. Given the topsy-turvy nature of a bank's balance sheet, not to mention its size, how can the normal approach to limited liability apply? It should not.

None of this really seemed to matter much when there were no bank failures. Banks kept building their balance sheets, exchanging deposits for government bonds. Governments kept enjoying the proceeds of all those bonds they issued, without ever having to make good on the promise to be the ultimate guarantor of bank deposits. All felt okay.

And then, as we know, there were a series of bank failures starting in 2007. Governments had to underwrite bondholders with bailouts.

Of course, if those who own shares in a bank stand only to lose the value of their shares, they will have less of an interest in the size of the balance sheet than those running the bank create – or the risk inherent in it. And why would they? If you only stand to gain from profits generated by extending credit, rather than losses incurred when the candy-floss credit pyramid goes pop, why would you care? Those who owned shares in RBS and all the others didn't.

While many banks built up reckless balance sheets using their magic money machine, not everyone was so reckless. Goldman Sachs, for example, stood out for being rather conservative. Why? Perhaps, as Mervyn King and others have suggested, it owed something to the fact that Goldman was, until recently, a partnership. Banks that are partnerships are owned by the partners, and the partners stand to lose directly if the bank incurs losses.

Other banks – such as Berenberg – which are still partnerships, have been notably more careful, avoiding risky credit and maintaining higher reserve ratios and cash balances. Perhaps what we need is not only to make those who own banks liable for their depositors' money, but make the management liable for some of the losses, too. Those who work at senior management level in banks need to be liable for the first few millions of losses, and those who own shares in banks should be liable for the next few hundred million. Only after those who run and own banks have taken the hit, should the rest of us be expected to pay.

Discussing this idea with a senior bank executive recently, they recoiled in horror at the idea. 'Who is going to want to own shares in our bank if they have such open-ended liabilities?' he asked. People who take an interest in the running of the bank, rather than rentier investors looking only at the next dividend, perhaps?

If we change the law to make those who own banks liable for the loss of depositors' money, those who own bank shares might stop thinking and acting as rentier investors – and take more of an interest in their customers. They would, for a start, recognize bank customers as customers, and not simply a source of dividends.

'But won't these sorts of draconian changes mean the end of banking?' you might ask. If banks are not able to inflate their balance sheets the way they were, and if those who own banks are liable for the credit banks create, what will happen to all those poor bankers? Perhaps a different way of looking at it is that banks have had the most extraordinary sorts of privileges conferred upon them over the past century or so. They have grown big and bloated as a consequence. Now is the time to remove those privileges.

Perhaps we might one day look back at bankers as we do today at all those other small, sectional privilege-interests of the past? What weavers and guild workers, coalminers and dockworkers once did seemed central to the prosperity of everyone else. No more. Thanks to big data technology, lenders will be able to provide customers with financial services without the need for big buildings or expensive bonuses. Automation in financial services – 'fin tech' – is going to allow us to have banking services – facilitating payment, raising capital, issuing debt – without necessarily needing a bank at all.

If banks were required to adopt open banking application programme interfaces – that's tech-speak for systems that speak to each other – we might see a fin tech revolution that would allow us to bank without banks – or the big, bonus-dependent bankers attached.

THE END OF MONOPOLY MONEY

Down the ages, governments have given themselves the monopoly to issue currencies – and then debased the coinage or currency to suit themselves. Deliberately debasing a currency is an easy way for a government to siphon off resources from the rest of us. Putting more money into circulation makes what cash the population holds worth less.

Between AD 1 and AD 200, the Roman emperors debased the silver *denarius* by cutting the silver content. What it took the Romans two centuries to do, our governments have achieved in two generations. Since 1971, inflation has diminished the value of the pound by 93 per cent. Once Richard Nixon broke the link between the US dollar and gold, there was little to constrain the amount of money that the state put into circulation – apart from the state itself, hardly a guarantee of probity.

I do not propose that we return to the gold standard – although I believe it is significant that the Chinese government has a deliberate policy of building up its gold reserves and turning some of those enormous US dollar holdings that it has into what Keynes, perhaps prematurely, called a 'barbarous relic'. What we need instead is a system of self-organizing currency – not another grand plan or gold standard.

Digital technology means that we are moving to a world where currency competition becomes a possibility. Instead of having to buy and sell things using the Mark Carney Pound or the Donald Trump Dollar, we can use a range of different currencies, including private currencies and crypto-currencies. Bitcoin might have caused a lot of excitement but I suspect it is really the system that underpins it – blockchain technology – that could transform the way we manage money.

Up until now, currency has been issued by someone, some-place centrally. When kings and queens issued coins, they were deliberately designed to be difficult to forge. Why? Because the currency was issued centrally, and ensuring no one could forge it was integral to ensuring that only the centre could circulate it. Once we moved to a world in which money was recorded as an electronic transaction on a computer, banks and governments devised centralized systems to keep track of who had what.

But blockchain technology is revolutionary because instead of a central ledger keeping track of who has what amount of money, the blockchain system is a dispersed record-keeping system, run by volunteers on many computers across the world. It's not on any one file someplace. It's in thousands, perhaps tens or hundreds of thousands, of locations.

The decentralized ledger system time-stamps and stores exchanges of value, preventing any one person altering the ledger. This makes it harder to debase the currency – as kings and governments tend to do – by issuing ever more of it. Bitcoin, I suspect, could be to decentralized currencies what the ZX Spectrum was to personal computers; an early prototype that popularized an idea, without actually allowing anyone to do much.

But perhaps it is only a matter of time before a central bank somewhere starts issuing a state-backed blockchain currency, which cannot be debased or devalued but that can be used in ways that bitcoin perhaps never will be? Already, the Bank of England is looking at the application of blockchain technology to create a decentralized system of financial transactions. According to Ben Bernanke, former chairman of the US Federal Reserve, blockchain technology could 'promote a faster, more secure and more efficient payment system'.

Double-entry bookkeeping transformed the way people did business in medieval Europe. I suspect that blockchain technology – a kind of decentralized system of bookkeeping – will, as Mr Bernanke suggests, transform the way we run our currencies. It marks the beginning of the end for state-run monopoly money. We should encourage it by making multiple currencies legal tender[104] and supporting the creation of payment systems managed through blockchain technology.

In hyper-inflation Zimbabwe, people started using the US dollar. No one decreed it or ordered it, but it just sort of happened. We need to encourage a move away from monopoly money, too – and we are starting to see the first, tentative steps towards this already with the advent of digital currencies like Bitcoin.

In Kenya and Uganda, the M-Pesa payment system, which uses mobile phones, allows millions of Africans to have access to financial services without using banks. How long before the M-Pesa unit of currency on the mobile system is decoupled from the local shilling? In a world where the market capitalization of Apple is greater than many economically developed states, it is not inconceivable that Apple, or Google or Facebook, could start to issue their own credit or *de facto* currency. Perhaps even blockchain currencies that cannot be debased by the board.

Having a 100-per-cent fiat currency, combined with unrestrained fractional reserve banking, has put a lot more money and credit into circulation. And as we have seen earlier, it's banks, as much as officialdom, that decide how much of the stuff there is – and who gets it. Central bankers are able to generate as much money as they want, and with so-called quantitative easing, that's pretty much what they do. Central bankers conjure money out of nothing – and give it to banks. Who are – conveniently – able to then buy up more of those government bonds.

Quantitative easing has created a great glut of cheap credit, pushing up the value of assets, such as London flats and FTSE 100 shares, while depressing interest payments to ordinary savers. This has led to a massive transfer of wealth from regular people

104 I introduced the Currency and Bank Notes Bill in the House of Commons to make multiple currencies legal tender in September 2011.

to the uber-rich. At the heart of a supposedly capitalist system, capital is now allocated not by the pricing mechanism but by central bank bureaucrats.

If capitalism is to survive, we must redefine capital. We need currency competition, ending the state monopoly over money. Doing so, while ending the ability of banks to magic credit from thin air and of governments to live off tomorrow, would arrest the further expansion of the emerging oligarchy. If we are serious about ending this oligarchy, we need to be prepared to take bold steps to cut the parasites off from the source of their wealth – not just vote for those who rage against the injustice of it all.

To date, none of the New Radical movements has developed a critique of the problem that might allow them to deal with it. On the contrary, some of the early signs are that Donald Trump wants to move in precisely the opposite direction. Rather than tearing apart the money–power nexus, he seems to advocate measures that would strengthen it.

Anti-oligarchs ought to try to stop bonds being used as a vehicle to plunder posterity so as to enrich the elite today. Yet Trump's economic advisor, Anthony Scaramucci, has indicated that, far from restraint, Trump is set to embark on a massive fiscal stimulus – lowering taxes, raising spending and passing the bill on to the grandkids. Again. It's been the common denominator for almost every US president's economic policy since the early 1970s. Trump has rightly recognized that capitalism has been corrupted. But what is his answer?

If he does indeed embark on the sort of trillion-dollar Keynesian spending splurge his team seems to suggest, he will not be restoring American capitalism, but replacing it with corporatism. A Japanese-style fiscal stimulus in America is likely to be as ineffective as it has been in Japan. Why? Because as we saw in Chapters 4 and 5, the cause of the problem is the credit cholesterol in the system, that massive credit bubble that preceded the slowdown. It is that which has caused a chronic misallocation of capital. No amount of fiscal spending will fix that, without first switching off the magic money machine.

Adopting a Japanese approach to fiscal stimulus will mean taking on Japanese levels of debt – and redirecting who gets a share of the proceeds of plundering posterity. For parasitic elites, perhaps that is the attraction of such schemes. It's not just Trump thinking in these terms. Labour's Corbynistas are advocating a policy that is strikingly similar. They talk about moving away from easy-money policies for banks – QE – and switching to Keynesian spending on capital projects instead – so-called 'people's QE'. Moving from one to the other means that the circle of those who benefit from the proceeds of plunder will widen.

Far from fewer bonds, if the Trumpists and Corbynistas get their way, we won't just be siphoning off the surplus from tomorrow's producers. We will be expropriating it *en masse*. Like the Romans, Trump and Corbyn offer the twenty-first-century version of bread and circuses; public spending that someone else pays for, and low interest rates.

Rather than making bankers responsible, Donald Trump is appointing more of them to oversee monetary policy. He's putting the parasitic *publicani* in charge of the public purse. Instead of taking steps to tackle rentier investors, he looks set to water down legal requirements in America that insist fund managers invest in the interests of those whose savings they hold. A New Radical leader wanting to take on the cronyism at the heart of capitalism ought to be doing precisely the opposite, reinforcing the fiduciary responsibilities to shareholders as owners, not just investors.

Until we switch off the magic money tree, we will continue to see expansion in the size of the state. For all Trump's talk about smaller government, he seems determined to undo some of the provisions in the Dodd–Frank Act in America, which, however imperfect, is today the only real restraint on bankers conjuring candy-floss credit again.

New Radicals ought to be in the business of encouraging greater globalization; more specialization and exchange. Instead, the New Radicals on the right seek tariff protection. On the left, Corbyn and co. see free trade as a dirty term. Instead of undermining capitalism, we ought to clean it up.

17

CLEANING UP CAPITALISM

- Rein in the ability of corporate executives to enrich themselves at the expense of shareholders and customers.
- Radical reform of corporate law to give back control to those who own the business.
- Remove the system of special privileges built by big corporations and lobbyists to rig the market.
- A new global system of international trade arrangements, based on mutual recognition of one another's standards, starting with a new Anglo–American free-trade agreement.
- A new kind of corporate contract to meet the needs of the digital 'sharing economy'.

'Don't be so daft, Carswell,' you might say. 'This stuff about bonds and banks is all very well, but it's not what those who supported your previous party were really after. No one is taking to the streets marching against Quantitative Easing. Your wonky policy proposals are way too obtuse. What we need', you insist, 'is a simple, straightforward answer: redistribution.'

WHY NOT JUST REDISTRIBUTE WEALTH?

If a small elite is hoovering up riches by rigging the economy and manipulating the money system, surely the answer is to take some of it back? Share out the riches of the rich. Simple.

That, more or less, is the response from people like Thomas Piketty. Having argued that capital is being accumulated by a small elite at a faster rate than the economy expands, Piketty, like most of those on the New Radical left, advocates a new set of taxes to take capital from the few and spend it in the name of the many. It's not just the left. New alt-right members of Team Trump in America have suggested capping the amount of wealth any one individual can acquire. (It is not clear if the sort of wealth threshold they have in mind would be below or above Mr Trump's net worth.)

Faced with oligarchs amassing wealth, it may seem obvious that anti-oligarchs should seek to reapportion that wealth. But the problem is that, if they do so, they are simply replacing one sort of redistributive exchange with another. Economics then becomes a series of competing claims, with one vested interest insisting on redistribution against the claims of another. And that doesn't solve the problem. When it has been tried, it has catastrophically failed.

It is more or less what Tiberius Gracchus attempted over two millennia ago. Farm workers, you may recall, had lost their jobs due to an influx of cheap labour from overseas and giant corporate farms, the *latifundia*. Massive inequalities of wealth arose as a tiny few enriched themselves by laying claim to the tax proceeds of the provinces. So, Gracchus responded by insisting on a form of redistribution. The plunder of Pergamum began as an initiative of the Gracchi brothers, looking to use it to fund their social reforms. Tiberius Gracchus wanted to use the proceeds of plunder to pay for land redistribution. His brother, Gaius, who succeeded him after his murder, used the proceeds of provincial plunder to pay for the corn dole he instigated.

But what did piling one form of redistribution on top of another actually achieve? No matter what Tiberius Gracchus intended, the proceeds of plundering Pergamum ended up enriching the patrician faction in the Senate much more than the poor plebeians in the Forum. Instead of elevating the condition of the Roman poor, the Gracchi's policies instead cemented it in place for the next four centuries. Making the Roman plebeians co-recipients of the proceeds of plunder did not resolve the agrarian crisis. Rather, the corn dole made it impossible for small-hold farmers in Italy to earn a living through the free market.

Gracchus's redistribution ended up not dispersing power, but centralizing it. Instead of restoring the status of freemen-farmers, it made more citizens into supplicants. Plundering the provinces proved to be the final nail in the coffin of Rome as an agrarian republic of free, small-hold farmers. Far from ending oligarchy, it gave Roman emperors a personal stranglehold over Roman life and politics. Like the Gracchi, the New Radicals today risk not stopping parasitic elites, but ending up as their useful idiots.

Parasitic oligarchies are always sustained by redistribution. Anti-oligarchs that advocate redistribution play straight into their hands. After watching the banking bubble burst and then the massive bailouts that followed, Robert Peston penned a book about the inadequacies of crony capitalism. What was his answer? Something he called the 'new capitalism'.

Peston has been vague about the detail but he implies that we should embellish precisely the sort of supranational systems and structures that helped land us in this mess in the first place. 'New capitalism' seems to involve the sort of people who live in Brussels and Washington – who presided over the financial crisis – having even more of a say. The economy is to be organized and arranged by some sort of top-down design. Which would mean more power to Davos Man. How original.

The solution to problems caused by redistributive exchange is never more redistributive exchange. However much one kind of redistribution might counter the injustices of some other, together they each undermine free, mutual exchange – the engine of progress. With one kind of redistribution piled on another, we always regress. Two thousand years on from the Gracchi, it's amazing how few seem to grasp this.

The New Radical left's approach is based on a misdiagnosis of the problem. Again and again, they shout about 'neo-liberalism'. But oligarchy is not emerging because of a surfeit of the free market. On the contrary: it has arisen because our supposedly free-market capitalist system has been rigged. The problem is not neo-liberalism, but 'neo-privileges'. What we need to do is not further restrict the free market, but sweep away the corporatist constraints that vested interests have imposed upon it.

We do not need a 'new capitalism'. We need to renew capitalism: to free it from the bogus, crony kind that we have today. And we should start by taking on big business.

STRIPPING AWAY CORPORATE PRIVILEGE

If we want to ensure our future prosperity, we must not get into the business of more redistributive exchange. We must make it easier for mutual, free exchange. Which means stripping away the restraints that inhibit it. Like Venice after the *Serrata*, a small elite thrives in large part thanks to privilege: grants, tax breaks and legal protections given by the state to a select few at the expense of everyone else. Privilege now needs to be rooted out.

Being an incorporated company is a privilege. Indeed, at one time, it was considered so special to be a limited liability company that to become one required an act of Parliament. It's absolutely right that business ventures should be able to incorporate, with all the legal rights and assurances that they bring. Yet with those rights come responsibilities – which big corporations no longer fulfil.

The idea of a corporation has been corrupted. As we saw in Chapter 4, shareholders have come to be seen as investors, rather than owners. Directors of the board as colleagues of the management, rather than legal fiduciaries upholding the interests of the owners. Corporations have come to be seen simply as a set of legal contracts, rather than as a privileged class of institution created to ensure capital and labour could collaborate.

Many corporate executives no longer serve either shareholders or the long-term interests of the firm. As described in Chapter 3, corporate chiefs often help themselves to greater and greater shares of the revenue, even as the value of the company they run falls. Corporate boards award pay packages worth millions to the senior management, instead of giving proceeds back to the owners of the business. Corporate chiefs may talk the language of enterprise but they aren't risking their own capital. In fact, all too often, they stand to profit by means of extracting wealth from those who are risking their capital – the shareholders.

The conflict of interest between executives and shareholders goes beyond basic pay. I know of arrangements in the City made between executives working in two different banks who agree to charge one another inflated – and entirely unnecessary – fees when working on different bond-issuance deals. On the back of these fees, the executives can claim a much larger bonus – ripping off the shareholders of both banks. Worst of all, the directors at one of the banks involved preferred to look the other way, rather than fulfil their fiduciary duty to the shareholders. It's the sort of ploy one might have expected from the Dutch East India Company (VOC) – whose name became a byword for corruption in the eighteenth century – not the City in the twenty-first.

By 1622, when the VOC's charter was up for renewal, ordinary shareholders had had enough of parasitic bosses enriching themselves at the expense of the company they owned. So, activist shareholders successfully lobbied to ensure that they were paid a proper dividend. They managed to ensure that shareholders were given new rights to appoint people to the board.

We need some similar changes, too, in order to break open boardroom cartels. At the moment, boards – like the clique that ran the VOC – are effectively self-selecting. *De facto*, sitting board members decide who gets to sit on the board – and they choose people just like them. A mini-industry has grown up in London based on finding the right sort of people to slot in as directors; people who look the part, act the part and think in clichés. Hardly the sort of people to hold the management to account. Those who can – shareholders – have been disenfranchised.

Shareholder democracy, long subverted, needs to be restored. It needs to be the shareholders who shortlist and select members of the board. Appointments should be made as part of a competitive process, with directors chosen by means of an election between multiple candidates. As the Conservative MP Jesse Norman has suggested, shareholders must also be able to nominate entirely independent non-executive directors.

As well as determining who sits on the board, shareholders need a direct say on certain issues. Shareholder votes on pay should no longer be advisory, but binding. And those committees that put forward recommendations for executive pay should always have a clear majority of non-executive members. The current practice that allows executives to exercise proxy votes on behalf of shareholders should be outlawed.

At the same time, we need to vigorously enforce the trust law of ownership in financial institutions. Rather than simply being bought a good lunch once a quarter, directors of investment trusts and pension funds should be made clearly legally accountable for the proper exercise of their votes as shareholders.

Companies exist in order to bring people, capital and

technology together. Just as charter companies were created for specific ventures in seventeenth-century Holland and England, and *commenda* businesses were created for individual trading voyages in twelfth-century Venice, perhaps we need a new, more *ad hoc* arrangement to bring together the different ingredients that make a successful business today. The digital economy has given rise to the so-called 'sharing economy'. It's not only those looking for somewhere to stay in Paris for a weekend who can use the new technology to get precisely what they are looking for. Digital means that business ventures that once would have had to invest in large capital equipment can lease it instead.

Commerce is going to happen not through permanent, standing arrangements and structures, but on a project-by-project basis. People will work for projects, not for firms. The boundary between a permanent employee and a contractor will blur. What we may need is a new kind of corporate legal framework; one that is *ad hoc* and ephemeral. A contract that confers the legal privileges of incorporation on capital and people that come together on a temporary, *ad hoc* basis. Think of it as a sort of Venice-style *commenda* contract, formed for a specific project or venture, though not for the needs of medieval merchants in the Mediterranean, but the sharing economy in the twenty-first century instead.

At the same time, blockchain technology will, I suspect, enable the emergence of self-organizing companies. Far-fetched, you think? Okay. Once London has a fleet of driverless taxis linked to Uber, what's to say an algorithm won't manage the contracts that service and maintain the fleet – and pay the proceeds to a bank account on the other side of the planet? Who has liability then? How do you define ownership then? The person who created the algorithm, or the entity that signs a lease for a new driverless car every time an old one needs replacing?

How do you create corporate laws to govern that sort of self-organizing enterprise? The very idea of what constitutes a company may be about to change. All the more reason to allow a kind of '*commenda* dot com' contract, with all the flexibility that that would entail.

REGULATORY PARASITISM

A constituent came to see me in a wheelchair the other week. He was not disabled but he happened to have helped invent a new kind of motorized wheelchair and was keen to demonstrate its versatility. I was impressed. He also wanted to know if his new kind of motorized wheelchair was approved for use in the UK. 'Who says you need permission?' I asked somewhat naively. 'If something is not banned, you can use it, right?'

Wrong, it turns out. There is a set of standards and regulations, you see. Self-propelling wheelchairs are classified and assessed. If your version of a self-propelling wheelchair does not fit the standard prescribed, it might not actually be banned – but it's a non-starter. You might be able to get one or two intrepid individuals to buy one, but few distributors are prepared to take the risk unless all the boxes have been ticked. They might not be approved to use green lanes, you see. Or conform with the rules for the use of 'Invalid Carriages on Highways Regulations, 1988, section 8, paragraph (3)'. Or something.

Who makes these regulations? Not, for the most part, elected legislators but bureaucrats. Government departments make secondary legislation. Advisory bodies suggest protocols and procedures that must be adhered to. An alphabet soup of agencies oversees a blizzard of regulations. It's not only national regulators that are churning out red tape, but supranational bureaucracies, too. In 1992, the European Community created the single market. Ostensibly about free trade, it turned out to be something very different – and handed enormous power to the modern-day mandarins. Far from allowing people to sell in one EU member state what they made in another, the single market created a common set of standards – and insisted that no one could produce or sell unless they complied with it. Instead of freeing trade, the single market restricts it. It's a permission-based system: without the permission of EU regulators, commerce is forbidden.

Listening to my enterprising constituent complain about the rules and regulations, I was reminded of what Étienne Balázs wrote about Ming China, where there were rules and regulations for many things. By the end of the fifteenth century, it was made illegal to build any ship with more than two masts. Heaven forbid that anyone might have tried to design a new wheelchair.

Just as in China in the Middle Ages, excessive rules and regulations are stifling enterprise and innovation in the West today. In area after area, from motorized wheelchairs to medical equipment, from financial services to food, there are rules and regulations. Specifications must be met. Standards complied with. The result is that product design is often determined less by entrepreneurs than by bureaucrats. No one can bring a new product to market unless it complies with our mandarins' ideas of what it should look like. According to my constituent, the real problem with his design in the eyes of officials is that it only has two wheels.

It also means that big is getting beautiful in business once again. Whereas in the 1970s and 1980s when big business was giving way to smaller, nimbler upstarts, today that process has been thrown into reverse. That has happened partly because only large corporations have the clout and standing to operate in the restricted sectors. Regulatory restraint, like tariffs, are always about suppliers trying to tilt things in their favour – at the expense of the consumer.

With the proliferation of top-down regulation, the biggest profits are now to be made in those areas of economic activity where privileges – in the form of permissions, compliance requirements or insider knowledge – prevail. Which is why, far from opposing regulation, a whole host of vested interests rather like the rise of this permission-based system. Big business, in particular, approves.

The biggest players are the only ones with the resources to shape the system of privileges to their own advantage. An entire industry of lobbyists and lawyers has grown up around the corporate interest in influencing officials and rigging the rules. A revolving door between corporate boardrooms and government agencies ensures that regulators always have the best interests of their past, or future, employers at heart. Economists call this phenomenon 'regulatory capture'.

The gains from exploiting corporate privilege are huge. The reason corporations spend so much on lobbying and compliance is because it is often more profitable than catering to market demand. Winning over officials becomes more lucrative than satisfying consumers. The result is the creation of a corporate cartel. Companies that ought to be rivals actually find they have more to gain by colluding in parasitism, for mutual gain.

To return to my analogy from nature: when a strangler fig germinates in the branches of a tree, very occasionally it finds that another fig has got there first. If so, the different strangler figs often merge into one as they overwhelm their host. Their branches fuse together to form a single organism. Vested interests that look to envelop the rest of society with their privileges often act in concert, too. Corporations form associations to lobby regulators as a collective. The aim is to shut out competition by raising barriers to new entrants. Disruptive innovation by small upstarts becomes forbidden.

The extent to which the rules of international commerce have been rigged is evidenced by the concentration of profit. According to a survey by the McKinsey Global Institute, 10 per cent of the world's public firms generate 80 per cent of the profits. Indeed, capital is especially concentrated in certain areas made profitable through the granting of privileges.

But there are even more pernicious consequences to regulatory capture than inequality. As the strangler fig grows in strength, it envelops the entire trunk of its host. The tree begins to rot, hollowing out from the inside. Engulfed by vested interests, our economy is starting to hollow out, too. Corporate privilege is steadily eroding the West's capacity to produce, invent and compete.

Far from freeing up trade, the single market, in particular, achieves the opposite. It has killed off innovation and intensive economic growth in Europe. Indeed, it is doing to Europe in the twenty-first century what medieval guild constraints did to Venice: ensuring that we become progressively less competitive. Since 1991, the EU economy has grown by just 49 per cent. This compares to GDP growth of 83 per cent for the United States and 114 per cent for Australia. Meanwhile India has expanded by 382 per cent and China by 877 per cent.

Three decades ago, the twelve countries that then constituted what became the EU registered 25 per cent of global patents. Today, that has fallen to a pitiful 4 per cent. Less intensive economic growth and innovation – ever a consequence of more top-down design.

INTERDEPENDENCE AND INDEPENDENCE

So, what's the answer? There is a need for regulation. We need to ensure that those who produce and sell things do so to certain standards. When you buy a car or food or a children's toy, you need to know that it has passed some basic standards to give you assurance.

But that does not mean we should agree to be governed by only a single set of standards, set by supranational rule-makers like the EU. 'Not so fast, Carswell,' you interject. Throughout this book, you have said there needs to be interdependence between different states in order to prosper. Yet you Eurosceptics are always banging on about independence. You're trying to get rid of precisely the kind of international co-operation we need!'

Why do we think that independence and interdependence are mutually exclusive? You do not need to stop being a self-governing state in order to trade and exchange with other states. On the contrary, both are essential to intensive economic growth – and, as we have seen, they have been throughout history. Venice was not part of the Holy Roman Empire nor Byzantium, yet she traded freely with both. The Dutch and the Americans were independent after their respective revolts, yet they were part of a wider network of global trade and exchange.

Superficially, the argument that interdependence requires orchestration is appealing. But it is as bogus as the idea that the sun will only rise the next day if you hand over the harvest to the temple priests. We simply do not need to empower our twenty-first-century supranational priesthood to do more business with the neighbours. Trade does not happen because of official fiat, but because someone in one state wants to buy something produced by someone in another. Specialization and exchange do not occur as a favour to anyone, but because it is in the mutual interests of everyone involved to do so.

Look carefully at the systems of supranational rule-making that have emerged in the past few decades. It is clear that those behind this system have taken the need for some sort of regulation, and some kind of interdependence across borders, as a pretext for something very different. Ruling elites have treated interdependence as a means to their end. They have cited it to justify their orchestration of our affairs. It has become a pretext for organizing things by design.

The European Union, an essentially political project, was created on the pretext of facilitating economic interdependence, initially through the integration of the coal and steel industries. Interdependence was then cited as the reason for creating the

Euro. It's also the pretext for all those global treaties on climate change. And it's in the name of enhanced interdependence that EU member states have handed over ever more powers to unelected officials in Brussels. It is in the name of supranational co-ordination that a whole new series of privileges and rules have been imposed, covering everything from capital ratios to carbon quotas.

But nowhere is this pretext more apparent than in international trade. The EU claims to have over forty trade deals in place with around fifty countries, but despite calling them Free-Trade Agreements they turn out to be precisely the opposite. They stipulate that trade may only happen if it conforms with bureaucratic requirements. Indeed, many of these supposedly 'free-trade' deals foist quotas on often poorer countries, preventing them from selling their exports to the EU.

Again and again, we are told how – following long, complex negotiations – 'free-trade' deals like TTIP or the Canadian–EU trade agreement might be possible. But hold on. If these agreements were about giving permission for the goods and services sold in one country to be sold in another, and vice versa, what would there be left to negotiate? It is because these deals are corporatist agreements, with all manner of privileges hidden in each sub-clause, that they take so long. The EU's so-called free-trade agreements effectively extend to international trade the kind of prescriptive, top-down, permission-based approach on which the European single market has been created. In terms of prosperity and job creation, it's not a template with a great record of success.

It's not only the EU. The United States has fourteen 'free' trade agreements with twenty different countries and is a long-standing member of the World Trade Organization. But like the EU's trade deals, they are full of rules and quotas and restrictions. Many of these deals permit trade, they do not free it.

Yet maintaining the fiction that these agreements are what free trade looks like comes at a cost. Not just for real free trade – which not only increases overall prosperity, but spreads wealth rather than concentrating it in a tiny corporate cartel – but, increasingly, for the elites themselves. Supranational regulation is provoking a popular backlash. The fallacy that interdependence requires a supranational elite and the sacrifice of independence – which the ruling classes themselves have perpetuated – is the root cause of the 'liberal' crisis. Elites are discovering the ire of the *demos*, as it wakes up to the subversion of democracy.

So, what's the alternative to supranationalism? Elites would have you believe it's protectionism. Many New Radicals, from Donald Trump to Bernie Sanders, seem to agree. But they're mistaken. All protectionism does, compared to the system of supranational regulation, is replace one set of trade barriers – regulations – with another – tariffs. That merely substitutes one set of favoured vested interests for another. It ensures the market is rigged to give different people special privileges. It concentrates wealth in an alternative group of big corporations. It still makes the majority worse off for the sake of a privileged few. It doesn't fundamentally change the system at all. By pursuing protectionism, New Radicals are set to squander the opportunity for change.

Permissions-based trade and protectionist trade are really two sides of the same coin. The real alternative to both is genuine free trade – achieved through mutual standards recognition. Imagine that you go on holiday to America. You eat food that has been approved by US regulators. You might drive a car that has met US federal standards. Fancy a bit of shopping at the local mall? You will buy clothes that have been manufactured to a US specification. If, heaven forbid, you fell ill, you would be treated with medicines that had been approved by the federal pharmaceutical regulator, the FDA.

You would not, I imagine, refuse any of those products because they had been approved by a US, rather than a UK or EU, regulator. So why is it that when you return to the UK, you are prevented from consuming any of those items unless they have also been approved by a UK or EU regulator?

If we had real free trade, you would be able to. A free-trade agreement between several countries would mean that whatever it was legal to buy and sell in one could be legally bought and sold in the others, too. Each country would continue to go about regulating its own affairs. But if citizens wanted to buy something that had been approved for use by another country's regulator, they would be free to do so. Rather than one uniform set of standards, there would be multiple.

Multiple standards are not so unusual; indeed, they are already the norm in education. Today in Britain, sixth-formers sit an exam when they are eighteen. In many cases the exam is an A-level. But some can sit the International Baccalaureate instead. Some sit AS-levels, too. Others do none of those things but sit something called a Pre-U exam instead. Each of those exams is, in their different way, an assessment of what the pupil has learnt.

Mutual standard recognition between comparable Western regulatory regimes would produce something similar. Just as someone is free to sit the International Baccalaureate exams, administered by a body in Switzerland, so we would be free to buy chocolate or cheese approved by a Swiss regulator. Indeed, restricting that freedom makes very little sense. The government does not ban you from buying and bringing back home US-regulated products if you visit the States. So why do they presume to ban you from buying them once you're back in the UK?

'Might this not mean a regulatory race to the bottom?' No. Regulators would still have a legal duty to keep people safe, but you might get a regulatory regime that was a little more circumspect and considered. If the UK regulator knew that another rule-maker was having to make the same assessments that they were having to make, it would be more careful to ensure that the rules they imposed were proportionate. The onus would be on regulating what needed regulating, rather than making rules as an end in itself.

Regulators might stick to regulating the outcomes – the functionality of the finished product – rather than interfering as they increasingly do with the process of its production. Moreover, because more than one agency would determine the standards in any one area, the system would be less open to lobbying by vested interests looking to rig the rules to their advantage. If one regulatory agency was captured by a particular vested interest – as many have been – they could not skew the market a certain way as easily as they do so today.

'Might not a system of different regulatory regimes lead to chaos and complexity?' Quite the opposite. It's the current attempts to impose uniform standards in the European single market, and to govern transatlantic trade through TTIP, that create complexity and confusion – not to mention a blizzard of red tape. Trying to harmonize different standards will always be more complicated than permitting both.

On 23 June 2016, Britain voted to leave the European Union. We should seize the opportunity that leaving the single market represents. Instead of being part of a system of uniform, standard regulation, we should embrace the alternative of mutual standard recognition. We should use it to ensure unrestricted free trade not only with Europe, but with the rest of the world.

A trade deal between the UK and the US, based on mutual standard recognition, would have profound implications – and not only for Anglo–American trade. Once Britain and America have signed such a compact, it would be possible for other states to join on the same terms – an agreement to recognize each other's standards, with occasional caveats.

Indeed, it could transform the international trade system, with a widening circle of states opting into a system of inter-dependence, rather than relying on the (stalled) system of trade deals by top-down design. The top-down system favours those that supply products, at the expense of consumers. Mutual standard recognition will allow us to have regulation, without constricting the consumer; it would reconcile independence – nations making their own rules – with interdependence – the need to allow individual buyers and sellers to exchange freely.

WHAT SHOULD WE DO ABOUT
WINNERS TAKING EVERYTHING?

Regulatory restraint is a major reason why capital has become concentrated in a corporate cartel. But it's not the only reason. The digital revolution has played a part, too. Digital is creating a number of near monopolies. We are starting to see the emergence of a small collection of hyper-firms – Google, Apple, Uber and Amazon, for example. They are becoming ubiquitous and often, in a sense, unrivalled.

Digital technology has allowed these companies to overturn many of our assumptions about marginal costs and economies of scale. It enables the best to have not just the major market share, but monopoly market share. The New Radicals' response to these digital behemoths is the same as their approach to the concentration of capital in other sectors: rules and redistribution. They have demanded more regulation from Uber. More tax revenues from Google and Apple. They put all their faith in concentrating power in the oligarchical institutions. Once again, their proposed solution is self-defeating.

Rather than counter the concentration of wealth that digital has created, we should take on the privileges that have helped make it possible. That entails removing the restraints that prevent alternatives arising: not just regulatory barriers to entry for new competitors, but also rules on patents and intellectual property.

Patents were invented for a reason. In exchange for an innovator sharing their knowledge with everyone else, they were granted a temporary monopoly to use the know-how. But, today, patents and intellectual property rules instead act as a means of restraining rivals. Big firms use them as a barrier to entry.

Because obtaining a patent is a costly business, start-ups are less able to afford them. The system, with its high legal fees, favours large firms. At the same time, uncertainty as to the validity of patents (see the effect of the new Patent Trial and Appeal Board in the US) means patents do not necessarily guarantee clear rights. Instead they confer an advantage in court, during a future legal battle. Consequently, patents end up restraining smaller firms, but less so the large. Big firms often seem to ignore intellectual property rights. Look at the battle between Microsoft and Apple, and then more recently between Apple and Samsung.

In seventeenth-century England, just prior to the country's economic take-off, hundreds of monopolies were swept away. Perhaps we need to think of abolishing the last kind of legal monopolies – patents – too. If the hyper-firms no longer had a barricade of patents around their product, they would soon face competition. Capital would no longer become quite so concentrated.

'I'm an economic nationalist,' explained a member of Team Trump recently. But before you respond, ask yourself if Team Trump might not actually have rather a lot in common with New Radicals on the left. Both rage against neo-liberalism, seeing economics as a zero-sum game. 'The globalists gutted the American working class,' explained Trump advisor Steven Bannon, 'and created a middle class in Asia.'

There is little sense in those fourteen words that both Asians and Americans might have gained by increased interdependence.

Or that, instead of 'the globalists' forcing folk to buy and sell stuff from each other, it happened because free people wanted to do so. There are ominous hints that the New Radical administration in the White House will want to embark on a trillion-dollar spending programme, pouring money into everything from infrastructure and defence to biotech and energy innovation. They are not looking to clean up capitalism. If the New Radicals in the White House really do spend trillions in this way, they will crush it.

To be sure, output will rise – it could hardly fail to under such a spending plan. Employment will soar and wages may increase too. For a while. But so will debt and redistribution. Tomorrow will be plundered to raise living standards today – and eventually today will become tomorrow. All that spending – that 1930s New Deal-style spending – will mean the creation of a command-and-control American economy. And inevitably more top-down design – ending up with less intensive growth and elevation. That won't renew America. It will bring to an end the two centuries of exceptionalism that made her great to begin with.

The idea of a self-organizing economic system is under attack from New Radicals on the left and right, and has been subverted by the supranational elite for decades. If we don't clean up capitalism, its critics will prevail.

18

NEW RIGHTS

- A new legal right allowing citizens to declare themselves independent of the state, allowing them to commission public services for themselves using public money.
- A right to know who is living on the public payroll.
- Enshrining the right to free speech and press freedom.
- Cleaning up the cronyism entrenched in public broadcasting.

With revolutions often come new rights. After the English revolution of 1688 came the Bill of Rights of 1689. Once they had adopted their Constitution, the American's tacked on ten constitutional amendments – their Bill of Rights – in 1791. Following the French and then the Russian revolutions, all manner of new rights for humankind, citizens and workers were proclaimed.

But of course, as we now know, while the Anglo-American rights did restrain the state effectively – albeit imperfectly – the post-revolutionary rights declared in France and Russia were not very effective in keeping individuals away from the guillotine or the gulag. Why did the post-revolutionary rights in England and America prove much more effective than those in France and Russia?

To me, the most striking thing about reading the US Bill of Rights is its brevity and simplicity. Like the US Constitution, to which it is in effect an appendix, it is succinct and to the point – as indeed was the English Bill of Rights, from which it borrows. It's little more than a list of things that government cannot do.

The First Amendment to the Constitution insists that no law can be made prohibiting the free exercise of religion, or freedom of speech or the press. The Fourth Amendment forbids warrants being issued without probable cause. Amendments Five and Six enshrine the right to trial by jury. The Tenth makes it clear that powers not expressly put in the hands of the federal government do not belong to it.

Contrast the specific simplicity in the US Bill of Rights to the sort of rights set out, at great length, in the French Declaration of the Rights of Man and of the Citizen. Or with the Declaration of the Rights of the Working and Exploited People, written by Lenin in 1918.[105] It's not just the verbosity of these documents, nor even their presumptuousness. The trouble is that these 'rights' are not really restraining the powerful. They are almost an insistence that officialdom acts.

Our revolution needs to confer on us new rights but not lofty, abstract rights that invite authority to act on our behalf. We need instead rights that limit the elite's presumption to know what is best for us.

---

105 Section 4 of Lenin's Declaration of Rights insisted: 'For the purpose of abolishing the parasitic sections of society, universal labour conscription is hereby instituted.' In other words, people were forced to work in the name of ending extortion. It would be funny if millions had not then died as a consequence.

WRONG RIGHTS

'But we already have rights,' many will insist. 'There is the European Convention on Human Rights. Something you Eurosceptics are seeking to abolish. And then there's the EU Charter of Fundamental Rights – something you are committed to leaving.'

Part of the problem is that these rights are weak where they need to be strong. If you read the European Convention, there is little specific about it. Unlike the list of Anglo-American rights, everything is qualified and open to interpretation. Article Ten, for example, is often cited as a safeguard on press freedom but is so equivocal that it allows for the opposite – statutory regulation of the press, something that has not happened in England since the 1690s.

The very ambivalence of these rights is an open invitation to judicial activism, and thus places power in the hands of judges. The judicial oligarchy, like every other, tends to unconsciously approve of the idea of doing things by top-down design. So, unsurprisingly, these rights end up as an insistence that authority acts, with a plan and a blueprint. Such a rights regime leaves little space for the alternative idea that we have a right to be free from such blueprints and grandiose schemes.

Like those proclaimed in France in the late eighteenth century or Russia in the early twentieth, the rights enshrined in the European Convention and Charter of Fundamental Rights are lofty and abstract. They empower those that seek to order society, not those who say 'leave alone'. They are anything but liberal. Worse, the sort of rights enshrined in these documents are often actually a claim over others. Far from setting out what the state may not do, they are an insistence on what it should do – with someone else's money. The EU Charter of Fundamental Rights, for example, insists that everyone has a right to certain public services.

What is most invidious about these so-called rights is the assumption behind them that it is up to an elite to provide things for us by top-down design. Such 'rights' are not only antithetical to the idea of a self-organizing society, they enshrine the presumption that it is for an elite to organize us in the first place.

To make matters even worse, many New Radicals, on both the left and right, are starting to advocate yet another bogus right: to a 'Basic Income'. Digital technology and automation, they tell us, will mean millions of jobs disappearing. And there is something in this. It's not only drivers who will lose their jobs to driverless cars, nor supermarket checkout staff who are being replaced by automated checkouts. Automation – and, in time, artificial intelligence – is going to have a significant impact on areas like law and medicine, too. Tens of thousands of jobs in financial services are likely to disappear in the next few years, and not only in retail banking, but investment banking and fund management, too.

The disruption caused by modern technology is giving a new lease of life to some rather old ideas about redistribution. According to those that advocate a Basic Income, each adult in the country should be paid an equal monthly amount. For the rich, it would be a tax break. For the poor, a welfare benefit to compensate them for the jobs that digital (or China or Mexico – pick your culprit) took away.

Ignore the fact that the maths behind this idea does not add up (if everybody is being paid a Basic Income each month, someone else will have to pay for it). Overlook the evidence that the jobs market is already coping rather well with automation.[106] Set aside the political consequences of creating a society in which large numbers of people are encouraged to live at the expense of others. For all the talk about automation and coping with the

---

106 According to Office of National Statistics data between 2011 and 2016 the number of jobs in Britain grew by 2.5 million, with 3.6 million created and 1.1 million destroyed, most of the new jobs being high quality jobs at low risk of automation.

implications of artificial intelligence, the idea of a Basic Income is not new at all. It's more or less precisely what they started doing in Rome two thousand years ago, when they instigated the corn dole.

Far from progressive, those that advocate a Basic Income are trying to implement a policy first enforced by Gaius Gracchus over 2,000 years ago. That, too, was a Basic Income. That, too, was paid to every citizen as a right – when, in reality, it was a claim over the produce of others. It is almost the very definition of parasitism.

Digital will – and is – causing enormous disruption. New innovations will see the concentration of enormous fortunes for a few. But the response should not be to retreat from mutual exchange towards redistributive exchange. We should not seek salvation by piling one set of privileges on another. We need rights that secure for us the conditions that enable human progress; rights that reinforce free exchange – not only of goods and ideas, but opinions; rights that disperse power – not concentrate it in the hands of judges or commissioners. Our rights must safeguard the idea of a self-organizing society, not expose it to the designs of parasites.

A RIGHT TO DECLARE OUR INDEPENDENCE

Many of our existing rights as citizens place a duty and an onus on the governing to act on our behalf. These 'rights' encourage us to become ever more dependent on what the state can do for us. What we need instead is the right to declare ourselves independent of the state. Citizens should have the right to opt out from having those who govern corralling us with their grand designs. We need to give people legal rights to request and receive control over 'their' share of public spending for certain public services where it is viable to make personal provision.

Last Christmas, my dog was sent a Christmas card by the local vet. After a quick sniff, the card was of no interest to our family pet. Of course, the card was really just a clever way of the vet reminding me, the owner, to renew the small annual amount I pay them to insure my dog and provide any care needed. It's good marketing from a healthcare provider who has to keep customers sweet to stay in business.

If only my constituents were treated that way by those that provide them with medical care. Many of them cannot get an appointment with the doctor when they need one. On the couple of occasions I have had to call the vet, they answered the phone right away. The one time that the dog was unwell, they even offered to pop around to the house on a Saturday. Yet when my constituents need to see a GP, they cannot get to see one on a Saturday full stop.

They often cannot even get through on the phone to make an appointment. When they do get through, they are frequently told that they will have to wait a week or two to be seen. For many of my constituents, there is, in effect, no longer a system of primary healthcare on which they can depend. Which is why so many end up going straight to the accident-and-emergency department at the local hospital for what are regularly relatively minor ailments.

But please do not blame my constituents, who have spent their lives paying into the system, for clogging it up. Far from being sent Christmas cards by healthcare providers, they are reduced to acting as supplicants. It's degrading, outrageous and wrong. What sort of society are we in where dogs have better access to primary healthcare than humans?[107] Many GP surgeries cannot even send their patients an appointment card, let alone a Christmas card. Put it like that and you see how shockingly awful things are.

107 According to a report on Sky News on 30 December 2016, some of the country's leading vets claimed that pets get better medical care than their owners, with more innovation in clinical treatment, too.

Of course, different governments have been promising to improve things since before I ever stood for election. Plans are made. Legislation is passed. The local NHS is restructured. But still folk never seem to be able to access healthcare the way they ought to be able to. We need a different approach. Rather than wait for someone to fix it all by top-down design, we need to give citizens rights to get what they need themselves – unless we want to keep on living in a world in which canines get better access to healthcare than their owners.

The fundamental problem is that Western welfare states were created half a century ago on the understanding that we would all pool our resources, through the tax system, and the state would then see to it that we are all provided for. But it doesn't work the way we were promised. Many of my constituents spent their working lives paying into the collective pot, on the understanding that when they retired they would be provided for in old age.

Western pay-as-you-go pension schemes, of course, don't set aside the money that is paid in each year. The money my constituents paid in through the 1960s, 1970s, 1980s, 1990s and then the Noughties, was not squirrelled away. The state spent it. Pensioners today are provided for not from the proceeds of their taxes, but by taking off today's taxpayers. And they in turn will be provided for by the next generation. Hopefully. Who will then be funded by the one after. Or not.

You see, pay-as-you-go pensions are really a Ponzi scheme. An ever larger number of people are drawn into it, believing that what they have paid in will mean that they get something back. But eventually there is going to come a generation that has paid into it and then discovers that there is nothing in the pot.

Again, successive governments have been aware of the problem. They have understood that the unfunded liabilities implicit in the scheme are eye-watering. Yet they – just like Charles Ponzi, the original perpetrator of this sort of scam – have carried on taking the contributions of those duped into thinking that there will be something for them at the end of it.

We need new rights that change the premise of the Western welfare system. Rather than paying in with some hazy idea that you – and everyone else – will get something back, we need to ensure that every individual has much more clarity. Instead of pooling resources to provide for people, we need new rights that allow us to start personalizing.

In the US in 2011, the government bought an average of $24,268 of public services for every adult American. In the UK, it was $20,208, Japan $15,586 and in France, $23,635. That's an awful lot of money for services being commissioned on our account. Citizens should be given the right to self-commission their share if they are a parent wanting a school place for their child, or a patient needing healthcare for their family.

Pooling resources has left the citizen short-changed. It has created state monoliths that are better at spending money in the interests of those that work for the public services than those actual members of the public they are supposed to serve. Too often the pooled payment pot has been spent not on the things we, as citizens, need, but on projects that interest or enrich officialdom.

Rather than creating elaborate schemes to redirect public resources better, we need to give citizens simple legal rights to self-commission certain services themselves. That's not to say that parents would get cash in lieu of a school place for their child. But if they requested control of their share of local authority funds, the school would only get the money if it could attract the child to the school.

Patients would not be given money to spend but they could ask for their share of the local primary care budget to be paid into a personalized health account – with GPs having to satisfy their customers to get the money. The money would follow the patient, rather than the patients the money. Who knows, once they have fixed their appointment-making system, they could even get around to sending out Christmas cards! And instead of handing your lifetime pension payments over to officialdom, how about having a personalized pension pot, like they already do in Chile?

One of the reasons why the idea of a Basic Income is so objectionable is that it breaks the link between what each of us contributes and what we receive. To use the jargon, it makes welfare systems less contributory. We should be looking to modernize welfare provision in the twenty-first century by moving in precisely the opposite direction; making it personal. Instead of flat payments drawn from pooled resources, regardless of what you pay in, we should create a hyper-personalized system, with personalized accounts and plans. Australia has led the way with the idea of superannuated pension payments. But new rights should allow us to opt out across whole swathes of public service provision.

Rather than everything being provided for by top-down design, we should be able to make more choices to suit ourselves and our circumstances. Welfare is supposed to provide a security net for the needy. In reality, it ends up being used by corporate interests to keep their payroll costs down. In-work benefits, paid for out of the pooled system of welfare provision, were created in Britain and elsewhere to support the low-paid. Instead, they have encouraged low pay. Public money is in effect used to pay employees what their employer ought to provide. Like those giant Roman farming corporations, these latter-day *latifundiae* rely on the state to supply them with a constant flow of cheap, exploitable labour.

Unfair perhaps to characterize it as slave labour, but it is hardly free either. The effect has been to trap people into low-wage, menial jobs. Any change of job or circumstances runs the risk that the individual might lose the tax credits that they depend upon to make ends meet. Subsidizing low-pay jobs has meant more low-pay jobs. This helps explain poor productivity performance in many Western states. As the elites make more profit, workers are paid less and the taxpayer has been left to pick up the bill.

Personalized welfare would ensure that support could be directed at those who need it, not used as a subsidy to allow big companies to spend less on their workforce in the knowledge that the public will pick up the bill. Big business would no longer be subsidized for paying below-market wages. A Basic Income, by contrast, would guarantee that for millions of employees, businesses did not feel the need to pay them as much.

And just in case you thought that personalizing public services would be all too hideously complicated, bear in mind what digital technology now allows us to do. Already Estonia has put almost all of its public services online. Blockchain-enabled networks could allow us to provide personalized public services through dedicated accounts. Blockchain is a way of taking out the middle man, and not just when managing money. With decentralized ledgers, what once could only be organized by central direction can be orchestrated as effectively without. This makes it perfectly feasible to allow individuals control over their own personal budgets, with personalized spending allowances.

'Won't that mean having to issue everyone with ID numbers and infringe on their privacy?' No. Blockchain technology means avoiding the dangers of a centralized database. Rather than all the data relating to your personalized health plan or your child's individual learning account resting in the hands of a central authority or official, you could use blockchain ledgers to manage your money and allocate it to approved providers. You could do all that securely and with the extraordinary degree of anonymity that blockchain currently provides Bitcoin-users.

Granting people legal rights to oversee their share of primary healthcare, education or retirement money would put individual members of the public in control of public services. They would be shaped not according to the blueprint of an incoming minister, but by the actions of millions of citizens. The very idea of self-commissioning public services would, no doubt, enrage all sorts of vested interests. But I suspect that public expectations mean that the electorate will be open to the idea.

The internet is creating a world in which self-selection – from Netflix to where we work – is increasingly a cultural norm. The idea that we must passively accept the education or healthcare choices made available to us by officialdom, rather than selecting what we want, is increasingly antiquated. Behind the political insurgency in many Western states sits a new set of expectations. Digital gives people control. They're used to getting what they want, when they want it. Yet top-down state provision hasn't kept up. Third-rate, unresponsive public administration is one of the main reasons why the public is so disenchanted. New rights are needed to meet this new set of public expectations.

A RIGHT TO SEE WHO'S ON THE PAYROLL

As well as giving citizens a legal right to control their share of public money, we should give them the right to see who is receiving public money. As legislatures have lost control of public finances, and as the state has managed to increase public spending without a corresponding rise in taxes, a number of vested interests have emerged with a stake in high public spending.

In Venice, there was a long list of people in the *Libro d'Oro*, 'the golden book', living at public expense. In the Dutch republic, a system of sinecures arose, such that even when in the mid-eighteenth century excessive public spending was correctly diagnosed as a cause of Dutch decline, nothing was done about it. As in England under the Whig oligarchy, a twenty-first-century version of the 'old corruption' has emerged: quangocrats on over £250,000 per year, big contractors able to take on lucrative public finance projects, opera houses and art projects indulged with public money, subsidies for universities able to hoover up fees in the form of government-backed loans.

In fact, as in Rome, it's not only the elite who are enjoying the proceeds of plunder. Today bread and circuses are provided for millions of citizens, as well as for the patrician class. Millions of people on the public payroll have a vested interest in more money for the public sector – and public spending going on headcount, rather than necessary improvements in public services.

The circle of those with an interest in the proceeds of state largesse is wide, and widening. In America today, almost half of all households receive benefits from at least one government spending programme.[108] That figure has increased from less than 30 per cent in 1983. The percentage of households who have received food stamps has risen from 8.3 per cent in 1983 to 16.5 per cent in 2012. The share of American households receiving some sort of means-tested benefit is up from 18.8 per cent in 1983 to 35.4 per cent today.[109]

There is only one way to address this problem. All public spending needs to be made public. If any individual, organization or business receives, say, over £500 payment per month from any public source, it should be made public. If we can see whose name is in the golden book, we might change attitudes to the system of state sinecures that has grown up in the name of tackling inequality, and all the other pretexts used to allow people to live at someone else's expense. Let us see a list of those, like the heads of the BBC or those who run the local NHS, with their six-figure salaries.

'That's an outrageous idea,' some will say. 'How dare you intrude on people's privacy.' But it's public money. The public has a right to know. In Sweden, everyone's tax records are a matter

108 Watkins, D. and Brook, Y., *Equal Is Unfair* (2016). p. 183, table 7.1
109 Ibid.

of public record. You can go online and look them up. If the amount someone pays to the state is public, surely knowing how much the state pays them is all the more pressing? It's the public's money they are getting, so why shouldn't the public know about it?

Perhaps if we could see who was in receipt of what payments, we might change our attitudes to welfare? To be sure, there might be some extreme instances where exceptions ought to be made. But as a default rule, if you receive any public money, in whatever form, worth more than a certain amount a month, the public ought to be able to know about it.

When government pays for something, the costs are usually shouldered by many, while the beneficiaries are fewer. This means that there is often a strong incentive for a few to act as a vested interest, lobbying for spending – but there's much less of an incentive on the part of those paying for it to resist. Taxpayer-funded vested interests are the inevitable consequence. Only by open-sourcing who is getting what will we able to rein in the system of state sinecures that has emerged.

'It would be ridiculously difficult,' some will argue. 'Public organizations already have enough difficulty complying with Freedom of Information rules.' This is where digital rides to the rescue. My local council now automatically publishes a list each month of every item of spending over £500. It's cheap to do and almost automatic once set up. It's simply a case of open-sourcing some internal accounting systems. The cost is negligible.

'But what about commercial confidentiality?' others will argue. 'Businesses would not like it.' Just think that through. Why might we be afraid of a business, contracted to provide services paid for with public money, revealing how much it is getting? Because another business might come along and offer to do the job for less? When commercial confidentiality is invoked, what it means is that the two parties behind the payments want them kept secret and are nervous of others seeing the numbers. Why? Because it would become apparent that the deal is duff.

Far from being a bad thing, forcing public-sector organizations to reveal who they pay to do what would help ensure better value for money.

THE NEW INTOLERANCE

The idea of granting people the right to opt out of state provision of public services will anger some readers. 'How dare he think that!' numerous broad-minded 'liberals' might murmur. The notion that we should have a legal right to see who is getting any amount of public money over £500 a month might enrage them. 'It's intolerable,' many who regard themselves as tolerant will say.

Enragement. Anger. Intolerance. Such sentiments have become the common currency of public policy debate in Britain and America. Political discourse has been coarsened. In America, the 'alt-right' is on the rise – often angry and intemperate. The far left is shrill and certain, and not only on social media. One lot seem to want to signal their virtue, the other lot their vice. It's often hard to tell them apart.

The student union of City University in London – an institution renowned for its journalism courses – recently voted to ban certain newspapers from campus since they found their coverage of current affairs objectionable. Across Britain and America, university students have started to 'no-platform' speakers with views that they oppose. As they grow more intolerant, universities have started to declare their campuses 'safe spaces' from where their students can be saved from having to come across an opinion that conflicts with their own.

I could have done with a safe space a few days after the last election when I was set upon by an angry mob of mostly student protesters for the sin of having been elected as a UKIP Member of Parliament. But what I fear far more than any mob is the new insistence on moral superiority. It is no longer enough to disagree with your opponents. Increasingly politics in liberal democracies is all about seeking to discredit the other side. To disparage not only their argument, but their motives. To delegitimize them, not just their point of view.

My suggestion, for example, that we could have personalized health accounts will, I am certain, be falsely presented by some as evidence of wanting to 'abolish the NHS'. (It isn't.) By positioning me as an opponent of the NHS (I'm not), some will then imply that my motives are suspect (they aren't) and any ideas I might have on how to make it work better must therefore be deemed as beyond the pale. End of debate.

The idea that two individuals might study the same set of facts, yet come to different conclusions, no longer seems acceptable. Instead, it is seen as necessary to downgrade to a lower moral level any individual who happens to think differently. What accounts for this new nastiness?

If you believe the Fourth Estate – established broadcasters and the press – it's all the fault of the Fifth Estate – bloggers, social media and the new non-mainstream outlets. The coarsening of public debate is a consequence of this digital democratization, they say. Now that everyone has a voice on Facebook and Twitter, the elite are not on hand to filter out the wrong sort of views. We are now witnessing the rise of 'post-truth' politics, they say.

Not even George Orwell could have foreseen this 'world in which the population, the punters, the voters would create their own manipulative, dishonest media', explained London-based political pundit James O'Brien. Got that? The *demos* have deluded themselves, apparently. According to O'Brien and co., 'the population' are 'dishonest' because now that they own their own means of distributing news and opinion, they have a habit of expressing their own views. All those smartphones and Facebook accounts have made them 'manipulative', now that they no longer subscribe to James's opinions.

James O'Brien is, of course, a BBC presenter on one of their flagship news programmes, *Newsnight* – which has for years reported the views of people like Mr O'Brien as the news. Since when was it Orwellian for people to be able to articulate and form their own opinions, rather than rely on the BBC's O'Brien *et al* to tell them what to think?

There is, indeed, an online insurgency. But it would be wise to ask what it is that the rebels are rebelling against. It's not just that people with the ability to articulate their own opinions have the temerity to do so. This 'alt-opinion'-forming is a rejection of the old media elite foisting their views on the rest of us disguised as news. For years, a slow, seething resentment has been brewing. If the explosion of 'alt-opinion' by the Fifth Estate is at times ugly, we ought to at least recognize that it is a reaction against the obnoxious, if subtler, form of intolerance of the Fourth Estate.

In the run-up to the US presidential election, many more people on Facebook engaged with stories posted by avowedly partisan blog sites than with items posted by mainstream news outlets such as the *New York Times*, NBC News, the *Washington Post* and other worthies. This was reported – by the mainstream media – as 'fake news' v. 'true news'. And the greater popularity of the former over the latter was taken as yet more evidence of the sort of 'post-truth' politics that allowed Donald Trump to defeat Hillary Clinton.

But hold on. Since when was something 'fake' unless posted by the likes of the *Washington Post* or the *New York Times*? Does something only become 'post-truth' if the mainstream media doesn't agree with it? Categorizing every story posted by every non-mainstream source as 'fake' in this way implies it is false, fictional, made-up. But that clearly wasn't the case. Who is being a bit 'post-truth'?

To me, the way that the mainstream media reported this 'fake news' story epitomizes the problem. I'm not sure that intolerance started with the internet. If there is a new intolerance, perhaps we ought to recognize that part of it is a response to the old intolerance of a mainstream media that for years has told us what to think, rather than report on what people think.

'But the BBC and MSNBC and other established broadcasters are balanced,' some will insist. 'They are objective, unlike Fox News and all those other outlets.' The BBC certainly has a requirement to maintain at least some outward form of objectivity. Equal airtime is (usually) given to different party spokespeople. For the most part, one assertion will be matched in most programmes with some kind of counterpoint. But the mainstream media – on both sides of the Atlantic – tend to tell only stories that confirm their own views.

For years, our priesthood of pundits have reported their 'narrative' as the news, selecting facts accordingly to support it. Is it any surprise that those who prefer an alternative narrative then come along online and start being similarly selective with facts, or worse? Fake news is inductivist reporting; a kind of bogus empiricism and it has become an established norm amongst mainstream media and not just the alt-media.

In the run-up to the EU referendum campaign, the BBC would endlessly introduce pro-EU guests as neutral observers and experts – but anti-EU speakers as 'right wing' and partisan. We were constantly invited by the BBC and other broadcasters to see the referendum as a choice between pro-business, economic pragmatism and anti-immigrationism.

What underlines their bias is an assumption – perhaps unsurprisingly if you are in the business of broadcasting – that things ought to be done to the rest of us by a few. That society, like a giant programming schedule, should be set according to someone's design. Being part of a corporation gives many who work at the BBC a *déformation professionnelle* that is inherently corporatist.

Don't believe me? Then consider the way that the BBC has reported Brexit since the referendum result. They have endlessly talked about post-Brexit trade arrangements as if trade was somehow synonymous with trade deals – that the former only happens when the latter are put in place by policy makers.

The BBC and other broadcast outlets have continually conflated the issue of Britain having access to the EU single market with the question of where Britain should continue to be obliged to conform to every single-market rule and regulation. It's almost as if they imagine that markets are made from on high, rather than being a consequence of autonomous action from below.

Because the mainstream broadcast media tend to see the world as a more planned place than it actually is, they tend to report more favourably about plans than they should. For years before the UK referendum, the BBC and others had an implicit sympathy towards those who sought to organize the affairs of tens of millions of Europeans by grand design. That grand plan – from the Exchange Rate Mechanism in the 1980s and the Euro in the 1990s to the EU itself in the Noughties – was reported as rational. Opponents of taking part in such grand schemes were depicted as anti-reason.

This does not only happen when it's Europe being debated. On everything from climate change to the banking crisis to immigration, the mainstream broadcast media constantly implies that things are best done according to some sort of plan.

This is why, a decade after the financial crisis began, I cannot ever recall any BBC output that ever even questioned why central bankers should control the economy or set interest rates. It's why, in the age of Netflix and self-selection, we never seem to see programmes commissioned by the BBC that examine the idea of self-commissioning public services.

Worst of all, the broadcast media has reinforced the thudding fallacy that sustains supranationalism: that interdependence can only be achieved by a loss of independence. They have acted as handmaidens in the imposition of a new world order in which small supranational elites take more power, all in the name of expediency and empiricism.

Driving the new intolerance is the faux altruism of the elite that insists all who doubt their grand designs are not only wrong, but morally suspect. The rise of alt-opinion online is a pushback against that.

A FREE EXCHANGE OF OPINION

What should we do to tackle the new intolerance? Some want more top-down control. In Britain, we are now drifting dangerously toward *de facto* state regulation of the press – something we last saw in the 1690s. After the US presidential election, pressure grew on Facebook and others to edit their algorithms to keep out the 'fake news'. Or perhaps one should say, to do the job of the old media elite in keeping out opinions that the elite did not approve of. Rather than doing what I do, and using the block button, people are bullying Twitter into taking down accounts that are simply a bit too strident.

The answer to the new intolerance is not top-down regulation, or an insistence that opinion be distributed by design. What we need instead is to ensure that opinion is exchanged more freely. How?

First, we need a new legal right, rather like the US First Amendment, to enshrine unambiguously our right to free speech. The European Convention on Human Rights has proved simply too vague. It has failed to prevent the *de facto* regulation of the press in Britain and elsewhere in Europe. It has done nothing to safeguard free speech on publicly funded university campuses.

In an age where all of us can broadcast and publish each day, we need our freedom of expression enshrined in law. As in America, this would make it much harder to sue individuals for libel or slander if they are simply expressing their honestly held – however daft or ridiculous – point of view. Such a right means allowing people the right to say silly things, to offend, insult and annoy – religious groups as well as US Republicans. But it is not a right to incitement. It is perfectly possible to have a right to free speech, which would strengthen press freedom, without allowing individuals to do and say things that would stir up hatreds and antagonism.

Having enshrined the freedom of the media – press or broadcast, corporate or personal – we should strip away the privileges of the Fourth Estate – the old media elite – and ensure that they are on an equal footing to the new Fifth Estate. In Britain, the BBC, run by a small, self-regarding clique, is granted over £3 billion a year in public money, paid for by every household with a television on pain of going to prison. Like Netflix, the BBC ought instead to become a subscription service, funded by people free to choose to pay for its services – or not. The BBC licence fee is indefensible – so we should stop paying it.

On 16 December 1773, a vigilante group, the Sons of Liberty, stormed aboard ships belonging to the East India Company in Boston harbour – and threw the tea they were carrying into the water. In doing so, they were not so much protesting against British rule as against a particular manifestation of it: the insistence that they could only buy tea via the East India Company, which had a monopoly on the trade.

We, too, are forced to do business with a large, self-serving corporation, the BBC. Unless the governing classes, so long beholden to this media oligarchy, are prepared to allow people a choice as to whether to pay for the BBC licence fee, it is only a matter of time before an orchestrated campaign of non-payment begins. No doubt the Brahmins of broadcasting at the BBC will regard this non-payment campaign when it comes as a form of insurrection by the latter-day Dalits, the untouchables, the lower orders – those who James O'Brien calls 'the population'. So be it.

The BBC licence fee is not the only form of entrenched privilege enjoyed by the old media elite. The cosy arrangements that use public subsidy and favour to sustain ITV and Channel 4 need investigating, too. Rules that ensure the Fourth Estate get special access to political and financial inside information ought to be reviewed. Why should those who write for Guido Fawkes not have a parliamentary press pass, while those who write for the *Independent* do?

There needs to be an investigation into who commissions whom to make what programmes. Why do the same small set of big-name broadcasters get to make so many programmes? It seems as if a small clique of well-connected insiders is able to monopolize programme production. The commissioning clique that runs the BBC needs replacing with a proper process of open competition.

If you have the privilege of holding a public broadcasting licence then, in the spirit of the Northcote–Trevelyan reforms that ended cronyism in the civil service, you ought to at least explain to the public who you get to make what programmes and for what purpose. With the power to broadcast to millions must come responsibility. Subjective opinions are fine but there is a duty to ensure that they are presented as such by broadcasters, the way they are in most other media.

If we stop being told what to think by people who see the world in terms of top-down design, we might at last start to have a political discourse that is not based on the conceit of top-down designers. It might finally be possible to articulate alternative points of view about everything from environmental policy to the European Union, without running the risk of causing outrage from the mainstream media. Or invoking that nasty narcissism, masquerading as altruism, which smeared anyone prepared to offer even a slightly different opinion as to how we might handle, say, the Mediterranean migration crisis. Or which seeks to discredit and delegitimize anyone who does not instantly agree with the groupthink.

What we are witnessing across the Western world, according to those whose job it is to provide us with analysis, is a battle between two groups. In Britain, America and much of Europe, they say, are two opposites: on one side sit the inward-looking, angry nativists, and on the other, outward-looking liberals. If it is presented to you like that, it's hard not to side with the latter. But perhaps what we are witnessing is something slightly different.

It's an awakening, not by an angry, reactionary, rejectionist proletariat, but by a *demos* that sees through the delusions of an intensely illiberal 'liberal' elite which insists that it knows the answers. After the Brexit vote, I lost count of the number of times I heard politicians and pundits describe it as a 'wake-up call'. But then they carried on regurgitating the same sort of glutinous groupthink we have all heard before. The elite still seek to respond to the insurgency in terms of a blueprint – coming up with a better plan.

No. It is the idea of blueprints that is the problem. The insurgency is happening because it is no longer plausible for the elite to presume to know what is best for the rest. The insurgency is against not only those who presume to know what is best for us, but against the notion that anyone should presume to know.

Our insurgency is about rediscovering the idea of a self-organizing society, in which power is dispersed and the productive are able to trump the parasitic.

19

WHO SHOULD YOU VOTE FOR TO MAKE THIS HAPPEN?

O ften in politics, we are invited to believe that one party or their leader has all the answers. Remember how Tony Blair and New Labour were once the great hope, winning consecutive landslides by promising to make things better? Then there was Barack Obama, who was going to heal America, before Donald Trump came along saying he would make it great again.

THE 'BIG MAN' MYTH

This is the 'Big Man' myth of politics (it almost always is a man) and it is a fallacy. Unfortunately, almost all parties are in the business of selling us this falsehood. Parties are little more than machines dedicated to promoting their leader, cult-like, as the answer to everything. If only you would vote to elevate this person to high office, they seem to say, all would be made well.

But, of course, the world does not work like that. No one leader, no matter how articulate or wise, can reshape the world for the better from the Oval Office or Number 10. When, inevitably, such high hopes are unmet, it further feeds into the sense of disappointment with politics. But the problem with politics is not the inadequacies of individual Big Men, however multiple their failings. It's the bogus notion that it takes a Big Man to fix things for us in the first place.

With all parties promoting the idea that a Big Man can reshape things for the better, politics inevitably becomes a contest to mould things by design. The blueprints might differ but they are all built on the same conceit. This, not the *demos*, is the reason for our post-reason politics.

The great insight to arise out of the eighteenth-century Enlightenment was that order can emerge where nobody is in charge. Yet today our political process more or less guarantees that whoever is elected to hold office is blind to this insight. We are left instead with leaders, in every party, assuming – as Matt Ridley puts it – that the world is a much more planned place that it is.

Are the New Radical movements any sort of answer to this? Not really. They, too, are selling us a myth that a new, omniscient Big Man will emerge to be the answer to everything. They, too, want us to believe that one person – Trump or Farage, Grillo or Wilders – is going to lead us to the promised land. But the one they each promote is no more 'the one' than those against whom they rail.

Political parties, whether insurgent or establishment, epitomize the idea of top-down control. They are themselves run by small cliques and so incline towards policy solutions that put small cliques in control. There is no one person or party we can elect to give us the change we need – and there never will be.

Change will come instead when we stop thinking in terms of changing politicians and focus instead on changing the way that we do politics – or rather, the way that politics is done to us.

Each of the solutions I have so far proposed to rein back the emerging oligarchy is the antithesis of top-down design. They are instead about establishing self-organizing systems. Rather than rely on central bank bureaucrats, I have suggested a system to allow bank reserve ratios to be determined by the actions of bank customers; I have proposed currencies controlled by competition, not officials; corporations regulated by those who own them and those who buy from them; and public services controlled by individual members of the public.

With such self-organizing systems, it would no longer be up to the right education minister, or the right sort of central banker, to come up with the right answer. Outcomes would be decided by the actions of many, rather than a few. We need to establish self-organizing systems in politics so that instead of small cliques at the top of parties determining the shape of politics, many more people get a say.

POLITICS WITHOUT PRIVILEGE

Political parties in most Western states have formed a cartel. They have rigged the system, either by drawing up boundaries or creating an electoral system that minimizes competition between them, so keeping out any upstarts. As so often where competition is reduced, the established players grow lazy and ineffective.

The established parties are remarkably bad at what they do. They are awful at representing local people, and at aggregating votes and opinion. They take millions of pounds or dollars and are hopelessly bad at using it to campaign with. In Clacton, I have twice taken on and defeated the established parties by doing for myself, often on a laptop, what political parties spend millions failing to do well.

Digital has allowed me – and potentially anyone – to communicate with tens of thousands of voters directly. Easily available information and data about the electorate enabled me to put together a data platform that I believe is more accurate than anything the big parties possess. I was able to mobilize an effective ground campaign, using digital and modern, alongside old-fashioned grassroots meetings in village halls. The big parties I stood against were so short of volunteers, they had to bus in large numbers of activists from outside, possibly breaking rules on campaign spending limits as they did so.

The team I assembled through local fish-and-chip suppers outnumbered them – and all without the need to bend any election laws. Clacton was not a one-off, an aberration. What I did in a single seat, Vote Leave then achieved at a national level. They created a 'pop-up' party using the internet in a matter of months. Over the course of the ten-week campaign, their pop-up party delivered about seventy million leaflets using volunteers. They built a new, online data platform – VICS – that mobilized a nationwide team, while showing their activists which voters to target in which streets.

The big corporate parties pour millions into hiring over-opinionated 'experts' who only come across the electorate when they collect their dry cleaning. Enormous sums are spent on almost entirely useless political advertising, with ads dreamt up by overpaid mediocrities working for big ad companies.

Vote Leave instead created a targeted digital ad campaign, which served up about one billion targeted digital adverts in the weeks before the vote, mainly through Facebook.[110] Their self-produced ads were empirically tested, rather than being the product of self-styled 'experts' second guessing what the electorate thought.

Vote Leave's experience convinces me that at every single stage – mobilizing supporters for a ground campaign, identifying key

---

110 For insights into how Vote Leave used data, read Dominic Cummings' blog posts at dominiccummings.wordpress.com

voters and messages, and even fundraising – it is now possible to do politics without a party. Just as the Fifth Estate of bloggers and social media are displacing the Fourth Estate of established press and broadcasters, we need to encourage new 'pop-up' campaigns and parties to come along and break the old cartel.

That means stripping away the entrenched privileges that keep the cartel in place. I was encouraged by some to take this large dollop of public cash and pay it into party coffers.[111] The Labour Party does that with the approximately £6 million it gets each year. It's a state subsidy for political parties. Short Money – like the BBC licence fee – must go. As must all the other sorts of subsidy – the free election literature, the free leaflet delivery, the free broadcasts – that help keep the established parties in business.

Nowhere in the US Constitution is there any reference to either the Republicans or Democrats. In Britain, our constitution was created in a struggle between the crown and Parliament, freemen and women and a courtly elite – not Labour against Tory. Yet political parties have been allowed to game the system, making themselves central to it.

In many Western states, established parties operate what are in effect a series of no-compete agreements with each other. The boundaries of congressional districts are drawn to ensure that they will always be the possession of one party – with the *quid pro quo* being that neighbouring districts are drawn up to be fiefdoms of the other side. In Britain, in the same year that working men were given the vote, a monopolistic electoral system of one MP per seat was introduced where previously constituents had generally had a choice of two or three MPs.

So we need electoral reform, not to do away with constituencies (as proposed by reformers on the left) but to strengthen them.

111 I handed most of the Short Money entitlement back to the taxpayer.

Instead of one MP per constituency, we need to ensure choice and competition in even the sleepiest electoral backwater by having two member seats. We need to halve the number of constituencies and have two MPs per seat. Not only would that mean choice and competition in even the safest seat, it would make the composition of the House of Commons significantly more proportional – but not so much so that a governing majority in Parliament would be impossible.

In America, it should no longer be for congressmen and women to choose their electorates through gerrymandering. If those elected to the national legislature came from constituencies in which there was a degree of real choice and competition – in other words, a realistic prospect of losing your seat at the next election – you would answer properly to the people, rather than to the party machine that is currently the key to election success.

Perhaps the most important reform we could introduce to break the stranglehold of the parties on politics is a proper right of recall. In Britain, a bastardized version of recall was introduced by the former Lib Dem leader, Nick Clegg. Unfortunately, it is a recall mechanism with no actual recall vote involved and it is up to a committee of grandees in Westminster to trigger the process. It's worse than useless. In place of this nonsense measure, we need to ensure that if one in five local voters sign up for it, there is a local referendum on whether to recall the sitting MP. That might change the topic of conversation in the Commons tearooms.

Rules on election spending in Britain also need rewriting. They have been drafted not to keep big money out of politics, but to ensure that the bosses of the big parties get to spend it. Caps on what local constituency candidates can spend are kept low, while parties nationally are allowed, in effect, an unlimited level of spending on a national campaign.

But as we have seen in Britain, the big parties pour their national spend into local constituencies when it suits them. The effect of the cap is simply to ensure that local candidates are dependent on the national party, which can swamp any local, capped efforts in a seat. What we need is to curb what parties can spend nationally but raise the threshold on what individual candidates can spend in their own campaigns locally.

In Britain, we have a parliamentary, not a presidential, system. Spending should be through candidates standing to get into Parliament, not party machines promoting the virtues of any presidential figure.

A RADICAL REALIGNMENT?

The success of New Radical parties reflects a realignment that is underway. In many Western states, the traditional blue-collar base is becoming detached from traditional parties on the left.

From the US Democrats, to UK's Labour, to the French Socialists, everywhere the left seems to be in trouble as their vote slips away from them. How well the New Radicals have performed, to a large extent, has boiled down to how effective they have been in scooping those votes up.

Traditional leftist parties are in trouble fundamentally because they are an alliance – between their blue-collar base and leftist elites. And that alliance is starting to break down.

The success of many centre-left parties rested on an assumption about fairness. But the blue-collar base that voted for such parties, and the leftist elites who tend to run and influence such parties, have, it turns out, very different notions about fairness.

To the sort of people who run the UK Labour Party in Westminster, or the US Democrats in Washington, fairness tended to mean equality. But to that blue-collar base, fairness means something subtly different. It means getting back from the system what you put into it. It means not jumping the queue for housing or benefits. It means, in other words, something that could give you plenty of cause for complaint when you consider how many welfare systems are actually run in many Western states.

Back in that post-war period when blue-collar voters loyally turned out for centre-left parties, those who ran such parties presumed that they could direct economic and social affairs. Indeed, that assumption was a big part of their appeal. But today, perhaps that proposition is just not quite so plausible anymore. For a nation that watches Netflix, and where self-selection is a cultural norm, is the idea of an elite directing things for the rest of us attractive?

The opportunity for new insurgent parties to transform politics is there, not least if they begin to offer new rights to the sort of personalised public services outlined in Chapter 18. But will they take it? Will they be the ones to kill off the old cartel? I joined UKIP in the hope that we would be.

POLITICS WITHOUT PARTIES

The trouble is that the New Radical parties suffer from the same conceits as any other. The start-up parties, like UKIP or the Five Star Movement, have an unfortunate habit of becoming mini-me versions of the larger ones.

They, too, are run by small cliques. They are dominated by domineering leaders, who – just like all the others – are supposed to be the answer to everything. And if you are in the business of offering one person as the answer to everything, you are inevitably going to be all about top-down design. I cheered at first when Jeremy Corbyn was elected Labour leader in the belief he might help – in more ways than one. But these New Radicals on the left stick blindly to the idea of redistribution. They are unable to see how free exchange has elevated the human condition, or the way in which it is redistribution that ultimately sustains oligarchy. Unless you champion free exchange, you can have no answers to the emerging oligarchy. Morally you become its accomplice.

What about a new party? We have already seen some efforts to establish new party platforms for an anti-politics insurgency. In Britain, something called Team Jury spent a lot of money getting nowhere at the 2005 General Election. We will, I'm sure, see others try something similar.

Just as some of the most fervent anti-EU campaigners damaged the campaign to leave the EU, I fear that some of the wannabe insurgent leaders may give such anti-politics initiatives a bad name. Insurgent leaders have a long history of being oligarchy's best advertisement. Having new parties or movements that are the product and plaything of plutocrats does not just look bad. It makes it almost impossible – given the tendency such people often have to presume to know best – to aggregate the insight and knowledge needed to run campaigns and candidates that can win.

The answer to the problem of party politics is not to create another party. It's to do politics without one. No cliques or pluto-crats. No insiders pretending to be outsiders. What is a political party? Ultimately it is a means of aggregating votes, by bringing together money, a message, volunteers and campaign skills. Why do we need a party to do that? The days when you had to be part of a big party in order to do the things that parties do are over. It is significant that some of the more successful political contenders recently – Trump, Saunders, Macron – all ran almost independently of their party.

Digital means that the tools you need to do politics are on the outside – there to be used by outsiders. If only they know what they are doing. Already on my laptop I have a voter identification system as good as anything any established party has. Vote Leave has put online, free for anyone to download, all the data sources needed to build a voter identification system. Meanwhile, Facebook and other social media mean that anyone with something worth saying, and a proper appreciation of how to use these tools, can communicate easily and cheaply with almost every household in the country.

A generation ago, an ambitious candidate wanting to run for Congress went first to Washington to seek support from party bosses. Today, they'll try to appeal to a super PAC. It is only a matter of time before they'll try Crowdpac. Crowdpac, the initiative started by former David Cameron staffer Steve Hilton, allows individual candidates to raise funds not from big donors but with lots of little contributions online. And from those contributions can come the funds needed to win – and freedom from the vested interests of lobbyists and the vanity of plutocrats.

In other words, politics can become self-organizing. Rather like the way I do it in Clacton – and how I intend to keep on doing it. As I have already described, Blockchain technology allows us to have alternative currencies, like Bitcoin, run without any central oversight. This sort of distributed ledger technology is in its infancy but it may well be the start of something very big indeed. Distributed record-keeping technology allows the creation of self-organizing systems that may be run without any central oversight. Collectivism free from the central direction of a small clique – the elusive dream of every freedom movement in history.

Already innovators are talking about building blockchain companies, enabling transactions to take place without any intermediary coordinating or organizing them. How long before someone tries to build a blockchain party? Or rather a blockchain platform that allows those essential features of a party – aggregating voters, messages and money – to be downloaded through a decentralized platform? Instead of a small clique – the Cameronians or the Corbynistas, the Trumpists or Farageists – trying to sell us the latest incarnation of the Big Man myth, a party could emerge that was not in the hands of any faction.

A self-organizing, online party would allow members to pay for membership, choose candidates and support policies without the mediation of any party hierarchy. It may seem fanciful, as Bitcoin would have sounded only a few years ago, but bypassing the party machine would truly empower the people.

If parties are no longer run by small cliques touting us the newest Big Man myth, they might stop believing that Big Men are best able to organize human social and economic affairs by grand design. Perhaps then we can be free to get on with that spontaneous process of innovation and ingenuity that has driven human progress – and that Big Men have only ever hindered.

THE ONLY *-ISM* THAT COUNTS

The rise of the New Radicals is seen by many as evidence that the great unwashed are anti-reason. But it is this notion – not any apparent demagogues – that is the true threat to democracy. It is already becoming a pretext for the authoritarianism of the elite.

It is not the *demos* in our democracy that is the problem. It is the elite. The European Enlightenment was so important not so much for the acquisition of any new piece of knowledge, but for the rediscovery of an ancient insight into the nature of knowledge – that knowledge is cumulative. What we might know today is an improvement on what we knew before, and by implication what we might one day know will be better than what we know now.

This underpinned the realization that the world is created by self-organization, without intent or purpose. It led to the insights of Adam Smith and others that morality and economic order are emergent phenomena. It led to the Darwinian discoveries. It underlay the realization that scientific inquiry must be a clash, or contest, of hypotheses advanced to be disproved.

Yet our elite today have trampled on this great insight. They act as if knowledge is some sort of revelation. They presume a certainty of knowledge and wisdom. Like the seventeenth-century

French philosopher René Descartes, they think as though the world and all that is in it is a mere machine, operating according to the laws of motion and mechanics. As if all human economic and social systems were a giant, complex piece of clockwork, which once understood can be re-engineered.

And on that Cartesian conceit – reason as rationalism, untempered by true empiricism, let alone fallibilism – they build models, for the economy or education provision or the climate, which presume to explain every outcome and variable.

The European Union is their unprecedented political experiment, and multiculturalism an unprecedented social experiment. Global fiat money is their unprecedented economic experiment. Limiting CO_2 emissions, a vast scientific experiment. Descartes believed that the giant clockwork system was the creation of God. Our elite have compounded their arrogance by acting as if they were God, that they might be the architects of the machine-like systems that govern our affairs.

But they aren't. The European project was meant to deliver peace and harmony across a continent. Instead, it has reduced tens of millions of Europeans to a life of debt, unemployment and lost opportunity. Multiculturalism has evolved into safe spaces and identity politics that, far from ending stigmatization based on background, has established an inverse moral hierarchy of race, religion, gender and sexuality. Fiat money was meant to make the monetary system more secure. Instead, it has facilitated financial crises and transferred wealth from average earners to the super-rich. And far from controlling the sea levels, the elite cannot even control our borders.

The grand designs of our elite are as self-serving as the creeds of all those other parasitic elites in history. The elite are in crisis precisely because they presume to know more than they do. They lack fallibilism. And in their arrogance, they see those who do not subscribe to their grand follies as purveyors of un-reason.

Digital means disintermediation; from news reporting to investing, book-keeping to booking a taxi, digital takes out the middle man. In a world of networks and hyper-connectiveness, collective action very much happens, but without top-down direction and the pretext for parisitism that that has always provided. It is no longer a question of whether we might like to see the world as self-organizing. It unquestionably is.

All of the proposals outlined in this book are about allowing for self-organizing systems: bank reforms that switch off the magic money machine from which the emerging oligarchy enriches itself, blockchain parties that cannot be controlled by a clique, new rights that enshrine our independence, reforms to capitalism and corporations. But on their own they are not enough to determine if we succeed.

What will determine if we successfully overthrow the emerging oligarchy is how we think. To overthrow the oligarchy, we need to stop believing; in them and their grand designs. It is not nihilism to stop believing in our priesthood of parasites. It's reason. Instead of belief, we need to know; that knowledge is cumulative, order is emergent, progress comes from self-organizing systems.

Instead of another -*ism* or ideology, we need a philosophy. One that reflects the essential truth about the world and all that is in it: there are no extraneous agents engaged in the design, generation, maintenance or moral regulation of the world, or of human affairs. We are our own agency. The engine of our own progress sits within ourselves, our ability to specialize and exchange – once free from the restraint of parasitic interests.

That great insight is ultimately the only thing that stands between us and oligarchy. It is all that has ever stood between us and oligarchy. It's an insight that has coincided with the great periods of progress in human history – but it has been no coincidence. When that insight has lain dormant, the parasites have always overwhelmed the productive. But if that insight is allowed to live in the minds of men and women, the productive stand a chance against the parasitic.

It's an insight as relevant today as it has been at any time since it was first articulated in Greece two and a half thousand years ago.

SELECT BIBLIOGRAPHY

Why Nations Fail: The Origins of Power, Prosperity and Poverty, by Daron Acemoğlu and James A. Robinson.

Bankers' New Clothes: What's Wrong with Banking and What to Do About It, by Anat Admati.

This Is Your Brain on Parasites: How Tiny Creatures Manipulate Our Behavior and Shape Society, by Kathleen McAuliffe.

History of the Roman Republic, by Klaus Bringmann.

Before the Industrial Revolution: European Society & Economy 2000–2700, by Carlo M. Cipolla.

The Economic Decline of Empires, by Carlo M. Cipolla (1970).

Paper Promises: Money, Debt and the New World Order, by Philip Coggan.

A Republic No More: Big Government and the Rise of American Political Corruption, by Jay Cost.

Roman Republic, by Michael Crawford.

Fabric of Reality, by David Deutsch.

The Beginning of Infinity: Explanations that Transform, by David Deutsch.

Corruption of Capitalism, by Richard Duncan.

Liberalism: The Life of An Idea, by Edmund Fawcett.

Political Order and Political Decay: From the Industrial Revolution to the Globalisation of Democracy, by Francis Fukuyama.

The Great Degeneration: How Institutions Decay and Economies Die, by Niall Ferguson.

Premodern Financial Systems, by Raymond Goldsmith.

The Swerve, by Stephen Greenblatt.

Dutch Republic, by Jonathan Israel.

The Establishment, and How They Get Away With It, by Owen Jones.

The End of Alchemy: Money, Banking, and the Future of the Global Economy, by Mervyn King.

Early Islam and the Birth of Capitalism, by Benedikt Koehler.

Wealth and Poverty of Nations, by David S. Landes.

Venice: A Maritime Republic, by Frederic C. Lane.

De Rerum Natura, by Lucretius.

Contours of the World Economy 2–2030 AD, by Angus Maddison.

Company: A Short History of a Revolutionary Idea, by John Micklethwait.

Fourth Revolution: The Global Race to Reinvent the State, by John Micklethwait.

The New Few or A Very British Oligarchy, by Ferdinand Mount.

History of Venice, by John Julius Norwich.

And Man Created God, by Selina O'Grady.

Capital in the Twenty-first Century, by Thomas Piketty.

The Better Angels of Our Nature: The Decline of Violence in History and Its Causes, by Steven Pinker.

Evolution of Everything, by Matt Ridley.

Rational Optimist: How Prosperity Evolves, by Matt Ridley.

Embarrassment of Riches: An Interpretation of Dutch Culture in the Golden Age, by Simon Schama.

Inventing the Individual: The Origins of Western Liberalism, by Larry Siedentop.

Roman Market Economy, by Peter Temin.

Expert Political Judgement, by Philip Tetlock.

The First Modern Economy: Success, Failure, and Perseverance of the Dutch Economy, 1500–1815, by Jan de Vries and Ad van der Woude.

Battling the Gods, by Tim Whitmarsh.

Epicureanism at the Origins of Modernity, by Catherine Wilson.

The World of Yesterday: Memoirs of a European, by Stefan Zweig.

INDEX